KAUAI

WELCOME TO KAUAI

Hawaii's ultimate tropical paradise, Kauai has amazing natural wonders to explore, from the velvety green, accordion-folded cliffs of Napali Coast to the multicolor vistas of Waimea Canyon. Sun seekers choose favorites from more than 50 miles of beaches, while hikers and kayakers have abundant options in unspoiled beauty. Best of all, laid-back Kauai is one of the state's least-crowded islands, with low-key resorts and mellow former plantation villages. Places like the North Shore's Hanalei Bay, with its turquoise water, are perfect for simply relaxing.

TOP REASONS TO GO

★ **Beaches:** Pristine strips of sand and palm-fringed shores make vacation dreams real.

★ **Napali Coast:** Its towering cliffs astonish all who see them from land, sea, or air.

★ **Outdoor Fun:** Kauai offers great surfing and snorkeling, plus top-notch golf and hiking.

★ **Charming Towns:** Artsy Hanapepe, colorful Hanalei, historic Koloa, and more.

★ **Kayaking:** Paddling on a river is a tranquil way to discover the island's allure.

★ **Scenic Drives:** The North Shore's Highway 560, the West Side's Waimea Canyon Drive.

Fodor's KAUAI

Publisher: Amanda D'Acierno, *Senior Vice President*

Design: Tina Malaney, *Associate Art Director*; Erica Cuoco, *Production Designer*

Photography: Jennifer Arnow, *Senior Photo Editor*; Mary Robnett, *Photo Researcher*

Maps: Rebecca Baer, *Senior Map Editor*; Mark Stroud and Henry Colomb (Moon Street Cartography), David Lindroth, *Cartographers*

Production: Angela L. McLean, *Senior Production Manager*

Sales: Jacqueline Lebow, *Sales Director*

Marketing & Publicity: Heather Dalton, *Marketing Director*; Katherine Punia, *Publicity Director*

Business & Operations: Susan Livingston, *Senior Vice President, Strategic Business Planning*; Sue Daulton, *Vice President, Operations*

Fodors.com: Megan Bell, *Executive Director, Revenue & Business Development*; Yasmin Marinaro, *Senior Director, Marketing & Partnerships*

Copyright © 2017 by Fodor's Travel, a division of Penguin Random House LLC

Writers: Joan Conrow, Charles E. Roessler

Editors: Eric B. Wechter, Douglas Stallings

Production Editor: Carrie Parker

6th Edition

ISBN 978-1-101-87990-0

ISSN 1934-550X

All details in this book are based on information supplied to us at press time. Always confirm information when it matters, especially if you're making a detour to visit a specific place. Fodor's expressly disclaims any liability, loss, or risk, personal or otherwise, that is incurred as a consequence of the use of any of the contents of this book.

SPECIAL SALES

This book is available at special discounts for bulk purchases for sales promotions or premiums. For more information, e-mail specialmarkets@penguinrandomhouse.com.

PRINTED IN THE UNITED STATES OF AMERICA

10 9 8 7 6 5 4 3 2 1

CONTENTS

CONTENTS

ABOUT THIS GUIDE

Fodor's Recommendations

Everything in this guide is worth doing—we don't cover what isn't—but exceptional sights, hotels, and restaurants are recognized with additional accolades. Fodor'sChoice★ indicates our top recommendations. Care to nominate a new place? Visit Fodors.com/contact-us.

Trip Costs

We list prices wherever possible to help you budget well. Hotel and restaurant price categories from $ to $$$$ are noted alongside each recommendation. For hotels, we include the lowest cost of a standard double room in high season. For restaurants, we cite the average price of a main course at dinner or, if dinner isn't served, at lunch. For attractions, we always list adult admission fees; discounts are usually available for children, students, and senior citizens.

Hotels

Our local writers vet every hotel to recommend the best overnights in each price category, from budget to expensive. Unless otherwise specified, you can expect private bath, phone, and TV in your room. For expanded hotel reviews visit Fodors.com.

Top Picks	Hotels & Restaurants
★ Fodor'sChoice	⛨ Hotel
	↵ Number of rooms
Listings	
⊠ Address	⦿ Meal plans
⊠ Branch address	✕ Restaurant
☎ Telephone	⛱ Reservations
🖶 Fax	🜲 Dress code
⊕ Website	▭ No credit cards
✉ E-mail	Ⓢ Price
🎫 Admission fee	
⊙ Open/closed times	**Other**
Ⓜ Subway	⇨ See also
↔ Directions or Map coordinates	☞ Take note
	🏌 Golf facilities

Restaurants

Unless we state otherwise, restaurants are open for lunch and dinner daily. We mention dress code only when there's a specific requirement and reservations only when they're essential or not accepted.

Credit Cards

The hotels and restaurants in this guide typically accept credit cards. If not, we'll say so.

EUGENE FODOR

Hungarian-born Eugene Fodor (1905–91) began his travel career as an interpreter on a French cruise ship. The experience inspired him to write *On the Continent* (1936), the first guidebook to receive annual updates and discuss a country's way of life as well as its sights. Fodor later joined the U.S. Army and worked for the OSS in World War II. After the war, he kept up his intelligence work while expanding his guidebook series. During the Cold War, many guides were written by fellow agents who understood the value of insider information. Today's guides continue Fodor's legacy by providing travelers with timely coverage, insider tips, and cultural context.

EXPERIENCE KAUAI

WHAT'S WHERE

1 **North Shore.** Dreamy beaches, green mountains, breathtaking scenery, and abundant rain, waterfalls, and rainbows characterize the North Shore, which includes the communities of Kilauea, Princeville, and Hanalei.

2 **East Side.** This is Kauai's commercial and residential hub, dominated by the island's largest town, Kapaa. The airport, harbor, and government offices are found in the county seat of Lihue.

3 **South Shore.** Peaceful landscapes, sunny weather, and beaches that rank among the best in the world make the South Shore the resort capital of Kauai. The Poipu resort area is here, along with the main towns of Koloa, Lawai, and Kalaheo.

4 **West Side.** Dry, sunny, and sleepy, the West Side includes the historic towns of Hanapepe, Waimea, and Kekaha. This area is ideal for outdoor adventurers because it's the entryway to the Waimea Canyon and Kokee State Park, and the departure point for most Napali Coast boat trips.

■ **TIP→** On Kauai, the directions "mauka" (toward the mountains) and "makai" (toward the ocean) are often used. Locals tend to refer to highways by name rather than by number.

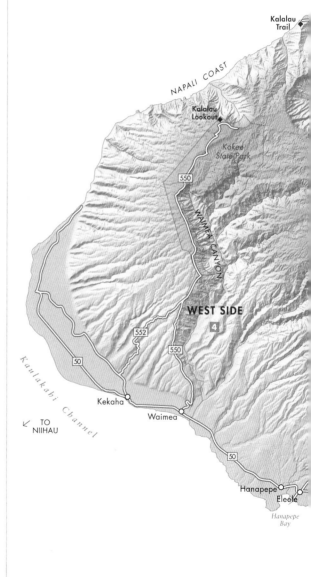

1

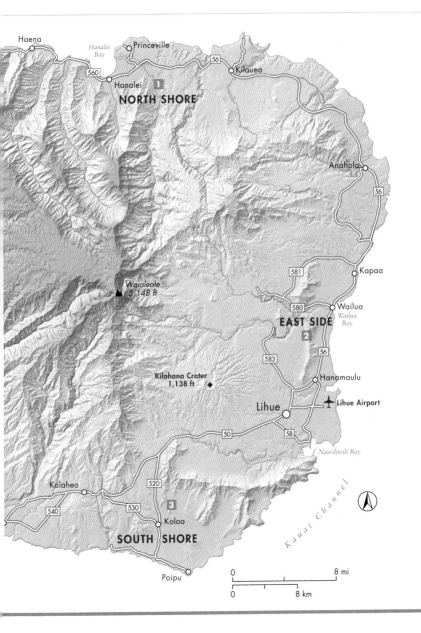

Haena

Hanalei Bay   Princeville

560   Hanalei   **1**

NORTH SHORE

56   Kilauea

Anahola

56

581   Kapaa

580   Wailua
EAST SIDE   *Wailua Bay*

2

583   56

Kilohana Crater
1,138 ft ◆   Hanamaulu

Lihue   ✈ Lihue Airport

50   58

Nawiliwili Bay

Waialeale
5,148 ft ▲

Kalaheo

520

540   530   **3**

Koloa

SOUTH SHORE

Kauai Channel

Poipu

| 0 | | 8 mi |
| 0 | | 8 km |

KAUAI PLANNER

When You Arrive

All commercial and cargo flights use the Lihue Airport, 2 miles east of the town of Lihue. It has just two baggage-claim areas, each with a visitor information center.

A rental car is the best way to get to your hotel, though taxis and some hotel shuttles are available. From the airport it will take you about 15 to 25 minutes to drive to Wailua or Kapaa, 30 to 40 minutes to reach Poipu, and 45 minutes to an hour to get to Princeville or Hanalei.

Visitor Information

Information Hawaii Beach Safety. ⊕ *www. hawaiibeachsafety.org.* **Hawaii Department of Land and Natural Resources.** ⊕ *hawaiistateparks.org.* **Kauai Vacation Explorer.** ⊕ *www.kauaiexplorer.com.* **Kauai Visitors Bureau.** ⊠ *4334 Rice St., Suite 101, Lihue* ☎ *808/245–3971, 800/262–1400* ⊕ *www.kauaidiscovery.com.* **Poipu Beach Resort Association.** ☎ *808/742–7444, 888/744–0888* ⊕ *www.poipubeach.org.*

Getting Here and Around

Unless you plan to stay strictly at a resort or do all of your sightseeing as part of guided tours, you'll need a rental car. There is bus service on the island, but the bumpy buses tend to run limited hours.

You most likely won't need a four-wheel-drive vehicle anywhere on the island, so save yourself the money. And although convertibles look like fun, the frequent, intermittent rain showers and intense tropical sun make hardtops a better (and cheaper) choice.

If possible, avoid the "rush" hours when the local workers go to and from their jobs. Kauai has some of the highest gas prices in the Islands. ⇨ *See "Travel Smart Kauai" for more information on renting a car and driving.*

Island Driving Times

It might not seem as if driving from the North Shore to the West Side, say, would take much time, as Kauai is smaller than Oahu, Maui, and certainly the Big Island. But it will take longer than you'd expect, and Kauai roads are subject to some heavy traffic, especially going through Kapaa and Lihue. Here are average driving times that will help you plan your excursions accordingly.

Haena to Hanalei	5 miles/15 mins
Hanalei to Princeville	4 miles/10 mins
Princeville to Kilauea	5 miles/10 mins
Kilauea to Anahola	8 miles/12 mins
Anahola to Kapaa	5 miles/10 mins
Kapaa to Lihue	10 miles/20 mins
Lihue to Poipu	13 miles/25 mins
Poipu to Kalaheo	8 miles/15 mins
Kalaheo to Hanapepe	4 miles/8 mins
Hanapepe to Waimea	7 miles/10 mins

Money-Saving Tips

There are ways to travel to paradise even on a budget. Pick up free publications at the airport and at racks all over the island; many of them are filled with money-saving coupons. Access to beaches and most hiking trails on the island is free to the public. Grocery stores and Walmart generally stock postcards and souvenirs; they can be less expensive here than at hotel gift shops. For inexpensive fresh fruit and produce, check out farmers' markets and farm stands along the road—they'll often let you try before you buy.

Choose high-end restaurants for lunch rather than dinner (check hours). Lunch is often less expensive. Early evening happy hour deals are a great way to save money while sampling the chef's specialties. If you're staying in a condo, eat in or pack a picnic when you can.

Dining and Lodging on Kauai

Hawaii is a melting pot of cultures, and nowhere is this more apparent than in its cuisine. From luau and "plate lunch" to sushi and steak, there's no shortage of interesting flavors and presentations.

Whether you're looking for a quick snack or a multicourse meal, we'll help you find the best eating experiences the island has to offer.

There are several top-notch resorts on Kauai, as well as a wide variety of condos, vacation rentals, and bed-and-breakfasts to choose from. Selecting vacation lodging is a tough decision, but fret not—our expert writers and editors have done most of the legwork.

Looking for a tropical forest retreat, a big resort, or a private vacation rental? We'll give you all the details you need to book a place that suits your style. Quick tips: Reserve your room far in advance. Be sure to ask about discounts and special packages (hotel websites often have Internet-only deals).

Seeing Napali

Let's put this in perspective: even if you had only one day on Kauai, we'd still recommend heading to Napali Coast on Kauai's northwest side. Once you're there, you'll soon realize why no road traverses this series of folding-fan cliffs. That leaves three ways to experience the coastline—by air, by water, or on foot. We recommend all three, in this order: air, water, foot. Each one gets progressively more sensory.

Napali Coast runs 15 miles from Kee Beach, one of Kauai's more popular snorkeling spots, on the island's North Shore to Polihale State Park, the longest stretch of beach in the state, on the West Side of the island.

If you can't squeeze in all three methods—air, water, and foot—or you can't afford all three, we recommend the helicopter tour for those strapped for time and the hiking for those with a low budget. The boat tours are great for family fun.

Whatever way you choose to visit Napali, you might want to keep this awe-inspiring fact in mind: at one time, thousands of Hawaiians lived self-sufficiently in these valleys.

HAWAII TODAY

Hawaiian culture and tradition here have experienced a renaissance over the last few decades. There's a real effort to revive traditions and to respect history as the Islands go through major changes. New developments often have a Hawaiian cultural expert on staff to ensure cultural sensitivity and to educate newcomers.

Nonetheless, development remains a huge issue for all Islanders—land prices are still skyrocketing, putting many areas out of reach for locals. Traffic is becoming a problem on roads that were not designed to accommodate all the new drivers, and the Islands' limited natural resources are being seriously tapped. The government, although sluggish to respond at first, is trying to make development in Hawaii as sustainable as possible.

Sustainability

Although sustainability is an effective buzzword and authentic direction for the Islands' dining establishments, 90% of Hawaii's food and energy is imported.

Most of the land was used for monocropping of pineapple or sugarcane, both of which have all but vanished. Sugarcane is now produced only on Maui, while pineapple production has dropped precipitously. Dole, once the largest pineapple company in Hawaii, closed its plants in 1991, and after 90 years, Del Monte stopped pineapple production in 2008. The next year, Maui Land and Pineapple Company also ceased its Maui Gold pineapple operation, although in early 2010 a group of executives took over one-third of the land and created a new company. The low costs of labor and transportation from Latin American and Southeast Asian pineapple producers are factors contributing to the industry's demise in Hawaii. But the Islands have perfected a sugar pineapple that is way less acidic than the usual ones. Although the imports have proved daunting, they have also set the stage for great agricultural change to be explored.

Back-to-Basics Agriculture

Emulating how the Hawaiian ancestors lived and returning to their simple ways of growing and sharing a variety of foods have become statewide initiatives. Hawaii has the natural conditions and talent to produce far more diversity in agriculture than it currently does.

The seed of this movement thrives through various farmers' markets and partnerships between restaurants and local farmers. Localized efforts such as the Hawaii Farm Bureau Federation are collectively aiding the organic and sustainable agricultural renaissance. From home-cooked meals to casual plate lunches to fine-dining cuisine, these sustainable trailblazers enrich the culinary tapestry of Hawaii and uplift the Islands' overall quality of life.

Tourism and the Economy

The $10 billion tourism industry represents a third of Hawaii's state income. Naturally, this dependency caused economic hardship when the financial meltdown of recent years affected tourists' ability to visit and spend. But the tourism industry has bounced back strong once again.

One way the industry has changed has been to adopt more eco-conscious practices, as many Hawaii residents feel that development shouldn't happen without regard for impact to local communities and their natural environment.

Belief that an industry based on the Hawaiians' *aloha* should protect, promote, and empower local culture and provide more entrepreneurial opportunities for local people has become more important to tourism businesses. More companies are incorporating authentic Hawaiiana in their programs and aim not only to provide a commercially viable tour but also to ensure that the visitor leaves feeling connected to his or her host.

The concept of *kuleana*, a word for both privilege and responsibility, is upheld. Having the privilege to live in such a sublime place comes with the responsibility to protect it.

Sovereignty

Political issues of sovereignty continue to divide Native Hawaiians, who have formed myriad organizations, each operating with a separate agenda and lacking one collectively defined goal. Ranging from achieving complete independence to solidifying a nation within a nation, existing sovereignty models remain fractured and their future unresolved.

The introduction of the Native Hawaiian Government Reorganization Act of 2009 attempts to set up a legal framework in which Native Hawaiians can attain federal recognition and coexist as a self-governed entity. Also known as the Akaka Bill after former Senator Daniel Akaka of Hawaii, this bill has been presented before Congress and is still pending.

Rise of Hawaiian Pride

After the overthrow of the monarchy in 1893, a process of Americanization began. Traditions were duly silenced in the name of citizenship. Teaching the Hawaiian language was banned from schools, and children were distanced from their local customs.

But Hawaiians are resilient people, and with the rise of the civil rights movement they began to reflect on their own national identity, bringing an astonishing renaissance of the Hawaiian culture to fruition.

The people rediscovered language, hula, chanting, and even the traditional Polynesian arts of canoe building and wayfinding (navigation by the stars without use of instruments). This cultural resurrection is now firmly established in today's Hawaiian culture, with a palpable pride that exudes from Hawaiians young and old.

The election of President Barack Obama increased Hawaiian pride. The president's strong connection and commitment to Hawaiian values of diversity, spirituality, family, and conservation have restored confidence that Hawaii can inspire a more peaceful, tolerant, and environmentally conscious world.

The Arts

The Hawaiian Islands have inspired artistic expression from the time they were first inhabited. From ancient hula to digital filmmaking, the arts are alive and well. Honolulu is the artistic hub of the state. The Honolulu Museum of Art has an impressive permanent collection and hosts major exhibitions throughout the year. It comprises four locations including the spectacular Shangri La, the former home of heiress Doris Duke, filled with Islamic treasures. The Hawaii Theater in Honolulu—a restored art deco palace—stages theatrical productions, concerts, and films. The Maui Arts & Cultural Center (MACC) has a 1,200-seat theater for concerts, theatrical productions, and film, as well as an amphitheater and art gallery. Numerous art galleries thrive on the Islands.

KAUAI
TOP ATTRACTIONS

Napali

(A) Some things defy words, and the Napali Coast is one of them. Besides, *beautiful, verdant, spectacular,* and *amazing* lose their meaning after repeated usage, so forget trying to think of words to describe it, but don't forget to experience Kauai's remote northwest coastline any which way—by air, water, or trail, preferably all three.

Waimea Canyon Drive

(B) From its start in the west Kauai town of Waimea to the road's end some 20 miles uphill later, at Puu O Kila Lookout, you'll pass through several microclimates—from hot, desertlike conditions at sea level to the cool, deciduous forest of Kokee—and navigate through the traditional Hawaiian system of land division called *ahupuaa.*

Hanalei Bay

(C) Families. Honeymooners. Retirees. Surfers. Sunbathers. Hanalei Bay attracts all kinds, for good reason—placid water in summer; epic surf in winter; the wide, 2-mile-long crescent beach year-round; and the green mountain backdrop striated with waterfalls—also year-round but definitely in full force in winter. And did we mention the atmosphere? Decidedly laid-back.

Spas, Spas, Spas

(D) Kauai is characterized by its rural nature (read: quiet and peaceful), which lends itself nicely to the spa scene on the island. The vast majority of spas could be called rural, too, as they invite the outside in—or would that be the inside out? For a resort spa, ANARA Spa is not only decadent but set in a garden. A Hideaway Spa sits in a grove of old-style plantation homes, and Angeline's traditional Hawaiian spa, Muolaulani, is in her home. The

Halelea Spa at the St. Regis boasts 12 treatment rooms with a variety of massage offerings, including fruit and flower treatments.

Highway 560

(E) This 10-mile stretch of road starting at the Hanalei Scenic Overlook in Princeville rivals all in Hawaii and in 2003 was listed on the National Register of Historic Places, one of only about 100 roads nationwide to meet the criteria. Indeed, the road itself is said to follow an ancient Hawaiian walking trail that skirts the ocean. Today, Route 560 includes 13 historic bridges and culverts, most of which are one-lane wide. Be patient.

River Kayaking

(F) The best part about kayaking Kauai's rivers is that you don't have to be experienced. There are no rapids to run, no waterfalls to jump and, therefore, no excuses for not enjoying the scenic sights from the water. On the East Side, try the Wailua River; if you're on the North Shore, don't miss the Hanalei River. But if you have some experience and are in reasonably good shape, you may choose to create a few lifetime memories and kayak Napali Coast.

Sunshine Markets

(G) Bananas. Mangos. Papayas. Lemons. Limes. Lychees. The best and freshest fruits, vegetables, flowers—and goat cheese—are found at various farmers' markets around the island. Just don't get there too late in the day—much of the best stuff goes early. Aside from the county-affiliated venues, a number of community-based markets have sprouted on church grounds, small parks, and other nontraditional venues. To find one near you, just ask the concierge or any local person—chances are they frequent one nearby. If you want to slide in as a local, wear flip-flops and a T-shirt and maintain a cool attitude.

WHEN TO GO

Long days of sunshine and fairly mild year-round temperatures make Hawaii an all-season destination. Most resort areas are at sea level, with average afternoon temperatures of 75°F–80°F during the coldest months of December and January; during the hottest months of August and September the temperature often reaches 90°F. Only at high elevations does the temperature drop into the colder realms, and only at mountain summits does it reach freezing.

Kauai is beautiful in every season, but if you must have good beach weather, you should plan to visit between June and October. The rainy season runs from November through February, with the windward or east and north areas of the island receiving most of the rainfall. Nights can be chilly from November through March. Rain is possible throughout the year, of course, but it rarely rains everywhere on the island at once. If it's raining where you are, the best thing to do is head to another side of the island, usually south or west.

If you're a beach lover, keep in mind that big surf can make many North Shore beaches unswimmable during winter months, while the South Shore gets its large swells in summer. If you want to see the humpback whales, February is the best month, though they arrive as early as October and a few may still be around in early April. In winter, Napali Coast boat tours can be rerouted due to high seas, the Kalalau Trail can become very wet and muddy or, at times, impassable, and sea kayaking is not an option. If you have your heart set on visiting Kauai's famed coast, you may want to visit in the drier, warmer months (May–September).

Hawaiian Holidays

If you happen to be in the Islands on March 26 or June 11, you'll notice light traffic and busy beaches—these are state holidays not celebrated anywhere else. March 26 recognizes the birthday of Prince Jonah Kuhio Kalanianaole, a member of the royal line who served as a delegate to Congress and spearheaded the effort to set aside homelands for Hawaiian people. June 11 honors the first island-wide monarch, Kamehameha I; locals drape his statues with lei and stage elaborate parades. May 1 isn't an official holiday, but it's the day when schools and civic groups celebrate the quintessential Island gift, the flower lei. Statehood Day is celebrated on the third Friday in August (admission to the Union was August 21, 1959). Check the daily *Garden Island* paper for other events.

TOP 5 KAUAI BEACHES

With more than 50 miles of sandy shores—more than any other Hawaiian island—Kauai is a beach bum's dream. It's easy to give in to "Hawaii time" and spend your trip relaxing on the sand. Here are some of our top places to park your beach towel.

Haena Beach Park (Tunnels Beach)

Even if all you do is sit on the beach, you'll leave here happy. The scenic beauty is unsurpassed, with verdant mountains serving as a backdrop to the turquoise ocean. Snorkeling here is the best on the island during the calm summer months. When the winter's waves arrive, surfers line up on the outside break.

Hanalei Bay Beach Park

When you dream of Hawaii, this is what comes to mind: a vast bay rimmed by a wide beach and waterfalls draping distant mountains. Everyone finds something to do here—surf, kayak, swim, sail, sunbathe, walk, and celebrity-watch. Like most North Shore beaches in Hawaii, Hanalei switches from calm waters in summer to big waves in winter.

Mahaulepu Beach

You'll have to drive through private property to reach this gem, though the beach—like all in Hawaii—is public. The 2-mile stretch is unlike anything else you'll find on Kauai. The land is rugged, with limestone cliffs, caves, and sand dunes. Although swimming here isn't always recommended, it's a great spot to wander around or take a hike along the Mahaulepu Heritage Trail, a beautiful coastal path.

Poipu Beach Park

The *keiki* (children's) swimming hole makes Poipu a great family beach, but it's also popular with snorkelers and moderate-to-experienced surfers. And although Poipu is considered a tourist destination, Kauai residents come out on the weekends, adding a local flavor. Watch for the endangered Hawaiian monk seals; they like it here, too.

Polihale State Park

If you're looking for remote, if you're looking for guaranteed sun, if you're thinking of camping on the beach (permit required), drive down the bumpy 5-mile-long road to the westernmost point of Kauai. Be sure to stay for the sunset. Unless you're an experienced water person, we advise staying out of the water due to a steep onshore break. You can walk for miles along this beach, the longest in Hawaii.

TOP 5 KAUAI OUTDOOR ADVENTURES

Kauai's spectacular scenery makes getting outdoors a must-do activity for most people.

There are endless options here for spending time outside enjoying waterfalls, rivers, coastlines, and canyons, but here are a few of our favorites.

Tour Napali Coast by Boat

Every one of the Hawaiian Islands possesses something spectacularly unique to it, and this stretch of folding cliffs is it for Kauai. To see it, though, you'll want to hop aboard a boat. You may opt for a leisurely ride aboard a catamaran or a more adventurous inflatable raft. Some tours offer the opportunity to stop for snorkeling or a walk through an ancient fishing village.

Kayak the Wailua River

The source of the Wailua River, the largest river in all Hawaii, is the center of the island—a place known as Mt. Waiale-ale—reputedly the wettest spot on earth. And yet it's no Mighty Mississippi. There are no rapids to run. And that makes it a great waterway on which to learn to kayak. Guided tours will take you to a remote waterfall. Bring the whole family on this one.

Hike the Kalalau Trail

The Sierra Club allegedly rates this famous, cliff-side trail a difficulty level of 9 out of 10. But don't let that stop you. You don't have to hike the entire 11 miles. A mile hike will reward you with scenic mountain cliffs and ocean views—in winter, you might see breaching whales—and sights of soaring seabirds and tropical plant life dotting the trailsides. Wear sturdy shoes, pack your camera, and be prepared to ooh and aah.

Enjoy a Helicopter Ride

If you drive from Kee Beach to Polihale, you may think you've seen all of Kauai, but we're here to tell you there's more scenic beauty awaiting you. Lots more. Save up for this one. It's not cheap, but a helicopter ride over the Garden Island will make you think you're watching a movie with 3-D glasses. For breathtaking photos with no glass reflection, or if you just want a thrill, consider a doorless helicopter tour.

Zipline over the Trees

It may not feel natural to take a running leap over the ledge of a valley, but it sure is fun. Guides clip your harness to wires and slow you down for landings, leaving you free to enjoy ocean and mountain views as you "fly" over treetops and across valleys. Most outfitters offer a shorter "express" version of their signature tours, though we recommend the full tour so you have time to catch your breath—you're sure to lose it screaming.

TOP 5 KAUAI SCENIC SPOTS

Verdant valleys, epic cliffs, plunging waterfalls, and majestic canyons are just a few of the features you'll find on Kauai. You might almost get used to the stunning green mountains that jut out of the land as you drive from place to place—almost. There are countless places to safely stop and take in the view; here are some of our favorites. Just don't forget a camera.

Hanalei Valley Overlook

On the way to Hanalei (about 1,000 yards west of the Princeville Shopping Center), this pull-off provides views of the Hanalei River winding its way through wet *loi* (taro patches) framed by jagged green mountains. If you're staying on the North Shore, don't just stop here once. The colors will change over the course of a day, or with the weather.

Kee Beach

At the end of the road on the North Shore, Kee Beach is as close as you can get to the fabled cliffs of Bali Hai. Surrounded by palm and almond trees, this stretch of white-sand beach is a great spot for viewing sunsets. The Kalalau Trail begins here; if you're up for a somewhat vigorous uphill hike, the first quarter-mile or so of the trail takes you to views of both Kee and the misty cliffs of Napali. Warning: depending on time of year, parking and amenities are at a premium.

Kilauea Lighthouse

Albatrosses, great frigate birds, and nene are just a few species among the thousands of seabirds that nest along the cliffs surrounding the Kilauea Lighthouse. This is the northernmost point on Kauai—in fact, it's the northernmost point in the main Hawaiian Islands. You'll get sweeping views of the North Shore here. If you hang around for a little while in winter, you're almost sure to see a whale pass by.

Spinner dolphins are often below to further amuse you.

Opaekaa Falls

It would be tough to visit Kauai without seeing a waterfall; after rain it seems like every mountain is laced with white streaks of water. Opaekaa is one of our favorites because it's always running, rain or shine. Water from the mighty Wailua River falls more than 100 feet in a lush green setting. The lookout to the left before you reach the parking lot for the waterfall overlook takes in the scenic Wailua River Valley all the way down to the ocean.

Waimea Canyon

The oft-used term *breathtaking* does not do justice to your first glimpse of Waimea Canyon (sometimes called the Grand Canyon of the Pacific). Narrow waterfalls tumble thousands of feet to streams that cut through the rust-color volcanic soil. There are plenty of spots along Route 550 to stop and stare at the canyon's awesome beauty—we recommend using the designated lookouts; they have parking and restrooms. Impressive vistas don't stop at the rim of the canyon. Continue on to the end of the road to Kalalau Lookout for a view through the clouds of otherworldly Kalalau Valley; it's one of Kauai's most identifiable icons.

KIDS AND FAMILIES

With dozens of adventures, discoveries, and fun-filled beach days, Hawaii is a blast with kids. Even better, the things to do here do not appeal only to small fry. The entire family, parents included, will enjoy surfing, discovering a waterfall in the rain forest, and snorkeling with sea turtles. And there are plenty of organized activities for kids that will free parents' time for a few romantic beach strolls.

Choosing a Place to Stay

Resorts: All the big resorts make kids' programs a priority, and it shows. When you are booking your room, ask about "kids eat free" deals and the number of kids' pools at the resort. Also check out the size of the groups in the children's programs, and find out whether the cost of the programs includes lunch, equipment, and activities.

On the North Shore the best bet is the St. Regis Princeville Resort, where kids can spend the day (without their parents) exploring local sea life with a marine biologist. The Kauai Marriott Resort is a good choice on the East Side, and on the South Shore both the Grand Hyatt Kauai and Sheraton Kauai Resort have kids' programs.

Condos: Condo rentals are a fantastic value for families vacationing in Hawaii. You can cook your own food, which is cheaper than eating out and sometimes easier (especially if you have a finicky eater in your group), and you'll get twice the space of a hotel room for about a quarter of the price. If you decide to go the condo route, be sure to ask about the size of the complex's pool (some try to pawn a tiny soaking tub off as a pool) and whether barbecues are available. One of the best parts of staying in your own place

is having a sunset family barbecue by the pool or overlooking the ocean.

On the North Shore, there are numerous condo resort choices in Princeville, including Hanalei Bay Resort with eight tennis courts and two pools. On the South Shore, Outrigger Kiahuna Plantation is a family favorite, with an excellent location that includes a swimmable beach adjacent to a grassy field great for picnics.

Transit Vacation Rentals (TVRs): The new kids on the block are rentals in homelike dwellings that are licensed for such activity. These rentals, and others that are "under the table," have in essence created another resort area along the North Shore—think private home with exclusive beach access. Make sure your renter is operating legally before plunking down your plastic.

Ocean Activities

Hawaii is all about getting your kids outside—away from TV and video games. And who could resist the turquoise water, the promise of spotting dolphins or whales, and the fun of body boarding or surfing?

On the Beach: Most people like being in the water, but toddlers and school-age kids tend to be especially enamored of it. The swimming pool at your condo or hotel is always an option, but don't be afraid to hit the beach with a little one in tow. There are several beaches in Hawaii that are nearly as safe as a pool—completely protected bays with pleasant white-sand beaches. As always, use your judgment, and heed all posted signs and lifeguard warnings.

Generally calm beaches to try include Anini Beach and Hanalei Bay Beach Park on the North Shore, Lydgate State Park and Kalapaki Beach on the East Side,

Poipu Beach Park on the South Shore, and Salt Pond Beach Park on the West Side.

On the Waves: Surf lessons are a great idea for older kids, especially if Mom and Dad want a little quiet time. Beginner lessons are always on safe and easy waves and last anywhere from two to four hours.

The Blue Seas Surfing School is best for beginners, and you can book your kids a 1½-hour lesson for $75.

The Underwater World: If your kids are ready to try snorkeling, Hawaii is a great place to introduce them to the underwater world. Even without the mask and snorkel, they'll be able to see colorful fish darting this way and that, and they may also spot turtles and dolphins at many of the island beaches.

Get your kids used to the basics at Lydgate State Park on the island's East Side, where there's no threat of a current. On its guided snorkel tours, SeaFun Kauai will show kids of all ages how to identify marine life and gives great beginner instruction.

Land Activities

In addition to beach experiences, Hawaii has rain forests, botanical gardens, numerous aquariums (Oahu and Maui take the cake), and even petting zoos and hands-on children's museums that will keep your kids entertained and out of the sun for a day.

On the North Shore, kids will love Na Aina Kai, a garden with a 16-foot-tall Jack and the Beanstalk bronze sculpture, gecko maze, tree house, kid-size train, and tropical jungle, and on the East Side is Smith's Tropical Paradise, a 30-acre botanical garden.

Horseback riding is a popular family activity, and most of the tours on Kauai move slowly, so no riding experience is required. Kids as young as two can ride at Esprit de Corps.

When it rains on Kauai, kids don't have to stay indoors. ATV tours are the activity of choice. Try Kauai ATV Tours, which has two-passenger "Mud Bugs" to accommodate families with kids ages five and older.

After Dark

At night, younger kids get a kick out of luau, and many of the shows incorporate young audience members, adding to the fun. The older kids might find it all a bit lame, but there are a handful of new shows in the Islands that are more modern, incorporating acrobatics, lively music, and fire dancers. If you're planning on hitting a luau with a teen in tow, we highly recommend going the modern route—try Luau Kalamaku in Lihue. The best luau for young kids on Kauai is Smith's Tropical Paradise, in Wailua. A tram tour takes families through the botanical garden before dinner, and the show starts with some high-tech pyrotechnics. Also, guests actually leave their dinner tables to walk to the amphitheater, which means young ones don't have to sit still the entire evening.

THE HAWAIIAN ISLANDS

Oahu. The state's capital, Honolulu, is on Oahu; this is the center of Hawaii's economy and by far the most populated island in the chain—its roughly 1 million residents add up to more than 70% of the state's population. At 597 square miles, Oahu is the third largest island in the chain; the majority of residents live in or around Honolulu, so the rest of the island still fits neatly into the tropical, untouched vision of Hawaii. Situated southeast of Kauai and northwest of Maui, Oahu is a central location for island-hopping. Pearl Harbor, iconic Waikiki Beach, and surfing contests on the legendary North Shore are all here.

Maui. The second largest island in the chain, Maui is northwest of the Big Island and close enough to be visible from its beaches on a clear day. The island's 729 square miles are home to about 150,000 people but host more than 2 million tourists every year. With its restaurants and lively nightlife, Maui is the only island that competes with Oahu in terms of entertainment; its charm lies in the fact that although entertainment is available, Maui's towns still feel like island villages compared to the heaving modern city of Honolulu.

The Big Island. The Big Island has the second-largest population of the Islands (almost 190,000) but feels sparsely settled due to its size. It's 4,038 square miles and growing—all the other Islands could fit onto the Big Island and there would still be room left over. The southernmost island in the chain (slightly southeast of Maui), the Big Island is home to Kilauea, the most active volcano on the planet; it percolates within Volcanoes National Park, which draws nearly 3 million visitors every year.

Kauai. The northernmost island in the chain (northwest of Oahu), Kauai is, at approximately 622 square miles, the fourth-largest of all the Islands and the least populated of the larger Islands, with about 70,000 residents. Known as the Garden Isle, this island is home to lush botanical gardens as well as the stunning Napali Coast and Waimea Canyon. The island is a favorite with honeymooners and others wanting to get away from it all—lush and peaceful, it's the perfect escape from the modern world.

Molokai. North of Lanai and Maui, and east of Oahu, Molokai is Hawaii's fifth-largest island, encompassing 260 square miles. On a clear night, the lights of Honolulu are visible from Molokai's western shore. Molokai is sparsely populated, with about 7,300 residents, the majority of whom are Native Hawaiians. Most of the island's 79,000 annual visitors travel from Maui or Oahu to spend the day exploring its beaches, cliffs, and former leper colony on Kalaupapa Peninsula.

Lanai. Lying just off Maui's western coast, Lanai looks nothing like its sister Islands, with pine trees and deserts in place of palm trees and beaches. Still, the tiny 140-square-mile island is home to about 3,200 residents and draws an average of 75,000 visitors each year to two resorts (one in the mountains and one at the shore), both operated by Four Seasons, and the small, 11-room Hotel Lanai.

Hawaii's Geology

The Hawaiian Islands comprise more than just the islands inhabited and visited by humans. A total of 19 islands and atolls constitute the State of Hawaii, with a total landmass of 6,423.4 square miles.

The Islands are actually exposed peaks of a submersed mountain range called the

Hawaiian Ridge–Emperor Seamounts chain. The range was formed as the Pacific plate moves very slowly (around 32 miles every million years, or about as fast as your fingernails grow) over a hot spot in the Earth's mantle. Because the plate moves northwestwardly, the Islands in the northwest portion of the archipelago are older, which is also why they're smaller—they have been eroding longer and have actually sunk back into the sea floor.

The Big Island is the youngest, and thus the largest, island in the chain. It is built from five different volcanoes, including Mauna Loa, which is the largest mountain on the planet (when measured from the bottom of the sea floor). Mauna Loa and Kilauea are the only Hawaiian volcanoes still erupting with any sort of frequency. Mauna Loa last erupted in 1984; Kilauea has been continuously erupting since 1983.

Mauna Kea (Big Island), Hualalai (Big Island), and Haleakala (Maui) are all in what's called the post-shield-building stage of volcanic development—eruptions decrease steadily for up to a million years before ceasing entirely. Kohala (Big Island), Lanai (Lanai), and Waianae (Oahu) are considered extinct volcanoes, in the erosional stage of development; Koolau (Oahu) and West Maui (Maui) volcanoes are extinct volcanoes in the rejuvenation stage—after lying dormant for hundreds of thousands of years, they began erupting again, but only once every several thousand years.

There is currently an active undersea volcano to the south and east of the Big Island called Kamaehu that has been erupting regularly. If it continues its current pattern, it should breach the ocean's surface in tens of thousands of years.

Hawaii's Flora and Fauna

More than 90% of native Hawaiian flora and fauna are endemic (they evolved into unique species here), like the koa tree and the yellow hibiscus. Long-dormant volcanic craters are perfect hiding places for rare native plants. The silversword, a rare cousin of the sunflower, grows on Hawaii's three tallest peaks: Haleakala, Mauna Kea, and Mauna Loa, and nowhere else on Earth. Ohia trees—thought to be the favorite of Pele, the volcano goddess—bury their roots in fields of once-molten lava, and one variety sprouts ruby pom-pom-like lehua blossoms. The deep yellow petals of ilima (once reserved for royalty) are tiny discs, which make elegant lei.

But most of the plants you see while walking around aren't Hawaiian at all, and came from Tahitian, Samoan, or European visitors. Plumeria is ubiquitous; alien orchids run rampant on the Big Island; bright orange relatives of the ilima light up the mountains of Oahu. Although these flowers are not native, they give the Hawaiian lei their color and fragrance.

Hawaii's state bird, the nene goose, is making a comeback from its former endangered status. It roams freely in parts of Maui, Kauai, and the Big Island. Rare Hawaiian monk seals breed in the northwestern Islands. With only 1,500 left in the wild, you probably won't catch many lounging on the beaches, although they have been spotted on the shores of Kauai in recent years. Spinner dolphins and sea turtles can be found off the coast of all the Islands; and every year from November to April, the humpback whales migrate past Hawaii in droves.

HAWAIIAN PEOPLE AND THEIR CULTURE

By 2013, Hawaii's population was more than 1.3 million with the majority of residents living on Oahu. Ten percent are Hawaiian or other Pacific Islander, almost 40% are Asian American, 9% are Latino, and about 26% Caucasian. Nearly a fifth of the population lists two or more races, making Hawaii the most diverse state in the United States.

Among individuals 18 and older, about 89% finished high school, half attained some college, and 29% completed a bachelor's degree or higher.

The Role of Tradition

The kingdom of Hawaii was ruled by a spiritual class system. Although the *alii*, or chief, was believed to be the direct descendent of a deity or god, high priests (*kahuna*) presided over every aspect of life, including *kapu* (taboos), which strictly governed the commoners.

Each part of nature and ritual was connected to a deity: Kane was the highest of all deities, symbolizing sunlight and creation; Ku was the god of war; Lono represented fertility, rainfall, music, and peace; Kanaloa was the god of the underworld or darker spirits. Probably the most well known by outsiders is Pele, the goddess of fire.

The kapu not only provided social order, they also swayed the people to act with reverence for the environment. Any abuse was met with extreme punishment—often death—as it put the land and people's *mana*, or spiritual power, in peril.

Ancient deities play a huge role in Hawaiian life today—not just in daily rituals, but in the Hawaiians' reverence for their land. Gods and goddesses tend to be associated with particular parts of the land, and most of them are connected with

many places, thanks to the body of stories built up around each.

One of the most important ways the ancient Hawaiians showed respect for their gods and goddesses was through the hula. Various forms of the hula were performed as prayers to the gods and as praise to the chiefs. Performances were taken very seriously, as a mistake was thought to invalidate the prayer, or even to offend the god or chief in question. Hula is still performed both as entertainment and as prayer; it is not uncommon for a hula performance to be included in an official government ceremony.

Who Are the Hawaiians Today?

To define the Hawaiians in a page, let alone a paragraph, is nearly impossible. Those considered to be indigenous Hawaiians are descendants of the ancient Polynesians who crossed the vast ocean and settled Hawaii. According to the government, there are Native Hawaiians or native Hawaiians (note the change in capitalization), depending on a person's background.

Federal and state agencies apply different methods to determine Hawaiian lineage, from measuring blood percentage to mapping genealogy. This has caused turmoil within the community, because it excludes many who claim Hawaiian heritage. It almost guarantees that, as races intermingle, even those considered Native Hawaiian now will eventually disappear on paper, displacing generations to come.

Modern Hawaiian Culture

Perfect weather aside, Hawaii might be the warmest place anyone can visit. The Hawaii experience begins and ends with *aloha*, a word that envelops love, affection, and mercy, and has become a salutation for hello and good-bye. Broken down, *alo* means "presence" and *ha* means "breath"—the presence of breath. It's to live with love and respect for self and others with every breath. Past the manicured resorts and tour buses, aloha is a moral compass that binds all of Hawaii's people.

Hawaii is blessed with some of the most unspoiled natural wonders, and aloha extends to the land, or *aina*. Hawaiians are raised outdoors and have strong ties to nature. They realize as children that the ocean and land are the delicate sources of all life. Even ancient gods were embodied by nature, and this reverence has been passed down to present generations who believe in *kuleana*, their privilege and responsibility.

Hawaii's diverse cultures unfold in a beautiful montage of customs and arts—from music, to dance, to food. Musical genres range from slack key to *Jawaiian* (Hawaiian reggae) to *hapa-haole* (Hawaiian music with English words). From George Kahumoku's Grammy-worthy laid-back strumming to the late Iz Kamakawiwoole's "Somewhere over the Rainbow" to Jack Johnson's more mainstream tunes, contemporary Hawaiian music has definitely carved its ever-evolving niche.

The Merrie Monarch Festival celebrates more than 50 years of worldwide hula competition and education. The fine-dining culinary scene, especially in Honolulu, has a rich tapestry of ethnic influences and talent. But the real gems are the humble hole-in-the-wall eateries that serve authentic cuisines of many ethnic origins in one plate, a deliciously mixed plate indeed.

And perhaps the most striking quality in today's Hawaiian culture is the sense of family, or *ohana*. Sooner or later, almost everyone you meet becomes an uncle or auntie, and it is not uncommon for near-strangers to be welcomed into a home as a member of the family.

Until the last century, the practice of *hanai*, in which a family essentially adopts a child, usually a grandchild, without formalities, was still prevalent. While still practiced to a somewhat lesser degree, the *hanai*, which means to feed or nourish, still resonates within most families and communities.

How to Act Like a Local

Adopting local customs is a firsthand introduction to the Islands' unique culture. So live in T-shirts and shorts. Wear cheap rubber flip-flops, but call them slippers. Wave people into your lane on the highway, and, when someone lets you in, give them a wave of thanks in return. Never, ever blow your horn, even when the pickup truck in front of you is stopped for a long session of "talk story" right in the middle of the road.

Holoholo means to go out for the fun of it—an aimless stroll, ride, or drive. "Wheah you goin', braddah?" "Oh, *holoholo*." It's local speak for Sunday drive, no plan, it's not the destination but the journey. Try setting out without an itinerary. Learn to *shaka*: pinky and thumb extended, middle fingers curled in, waggle sideways. Eat white rice with everything. When someone says, "Aloha!" answer, "Aloha no!" ("And a real big aloha back to you"). And, as the locals say, "No make big body" ("Try not to act like you own the place").

TOP 10 HAWAIIAN FOODS TO TRY

Food in Hawaii is a reflection of the state's diverse cultural makeup and tropical location. Fresh seafood, organic fruits and vegetables, free-range beef, and locally grown products are the hallmarks of Hawaii regional cuisine. Its preparations are drawn from across the Pacific Rim, including Japan, the Philippines, Korea, and Thailand—and "local food" is a cuisine in its own right. Don't miss Hawaiian-grown coffee either, whether it's smooth Kona from the Big Island or coffee grown on other Islands.

Bento Box
The bento box gained popularity back in the plantation days, when workers toiled in the sugarcane fields. No one brought sandwiches to work then. Instead it was a lunch box with the ever-present steamed white rice, pickled *ume* (plum) to preserve the rice, and meats such as fried chicken or fish. Today, many stores sell prepackaged bentos or you may go to an *okazuya* (Japanese deli) with a hot buffet counter and create your own.

Crack Seed
There are dozens of varieties of crack seed in dwindling specialty shops and at the drugstores. Chinese call the preserved fruits and nuts *see mui*, but somehow the Pidgin English version is what Hawaiians prefer. Those who like hard candy and salty foods will love *li hing* mangoes and rock-salt plums, and those with an itchy throat will feel relief from the lemon strips. Peruse large glass jars of crack seed sold in bulk or smaller hanging bags—the latter make good gifts to give to friends back home.

Fresh Ahi or Tako Poke
There's nothing like fresh ahi or *tako* (octopus) *poke* to break the ice at a backyard party, except, of course, the cold beer handed to you from the cooler. The perfect *pupu*, *poke* (pronounced "poh-kay") is basically raw seafood cut into bite-sized chunks and mixed with everything from green onions to roasted and ground *kukui* nuts. Other variations include mixing the fish with chopped round onion, sesame oil, seaweed, and chili pepper water. *Shoyu* (the "local" name for soy sauce) is the constant. These days, grocery stores sell endless poke varieties such as kimchi crab; anything goes, from adding mayonnaise to *tobiko* (caviar). Fish lovers who want to take it to the next level order sashimi, the best cuts of ahi sliced and dipped in a mixture of shoyu and wasabi.

Manapua
Another savory snack is *manapua*, fist-size dough balls fashioned after Chinese *bao* (a traditional Chinese bun) and stuffed with fillings such as *char siu* (Chinese roast pork) and then steamed. Many mom-and-pop stores sell them in commercial steamer display cases along with pork hash and other dim sum. Modern-day fillings include curry chicken.

Malasadas
The Portuguese have contributed much to Hawaii cuisine in the form of sausage, soup, and sweetbread. But their most revered food is *malasadas*, hot, deep-fried doughnuts rolled in sugar. Malasadas are crowd-pleasers—buy them by the dozen, hot from the fryer, placed in brown paper bags to absorb the grease, or bite into gourmet malasadas at restaurants, filled with vanilla or chocolate cream.

Plate Lunch
It would be remiss not to mention the plate lunch as one of the most beloved dishes in Hawaii. It generally includes two scoops of sticky white rice, a scoop of macaroni or macaroni-potato salad,

heavy on the mayo, and perhaps kimchi or *koko* (salted cabbage). There are countless choices of main protein such as chicken *katsu* (fried cutlet), fried mahimahi, and tomato. The king of all plate lunches is the Hawaiian plate. The main item is *laulau* (pork or fish wrapped in taro leaf) or *kalua* pig (cooked in an underground oven, or *imu*) and cabbage along with poi, *lomilomi* salmon (salmon-and-tomato salad), chicken long rice, and sticky white rice.

Saimin

The ultimate hangover cure and the perfect comfort food during Hawaii's mild winters, *saimin* ranks at the top of the list of local favorites. In fact, it's one of the few dishes deemed truly local, having been highlighted in cookbooks since the 1930s. Saimin is an Asian-style noodle soup so ubiquitous it's even on McDonald's menus statewide. In mom-and-pop shops, a large melamine bowl is filled with homemade *dashi*, or broth, and wheat-flour noodles and then topped off with strips of omelet, green onions, bright pink fish cake, and char siu or canned luncheon meat, such as SPAM. Add shoyu and chili pepper water, lift your chopsticks, and slurp away.

Shave Ice

Much more than just a snow cone, shave ice is what locals crave after a blazing day at the beach or a hot-as-Hades game of soccer. If you're lucky, you'll find a neighborhood store that hand-shaves the ice, but it's rare. Either way, the counter person will ask you first if you'd like ice cream and/or adzuki beans scooped into the bottom of the cone or cup. Then they shape the ice into a giant mound and add colorful fruit syrups. First-timers should order the rainbow, of course.

SPAM

Speaking of SPAM, Hawaii's most prevalent grab-and-go snack is SPAM *musubi*. Often displayed next to cash registers at groceries and convenience stores, the glorified rice ball is rectangular, topped with a slice of fried SPAM and wrapped in *nori* (seaweed). Musubi is a bite-size meal in itself. But just like sushi, the rice part hardens when refrigerated. So it's best to gobble it up right after purchase.

Hormel Company's SPAM actually deserves its own recognition—way beyond as a mere musubi topping. About 5 million cans are sold per year in Hawaii, and the Aloha State even hosts a festival in its honor. It's inexpensive protein and goes a long way when mixed with rice, scrambled eggs, noodles or, well, anything. The spiced luncheon meat gained popularity in World War II days, when fish was rationed. Gourmets and those with aversions to salt, high cholesterol, or high blood pressure may cringe at the thought of eating it, but SPAM in Hawaii is here to stay.

Tropical Fruits

Tropical fruits such as apple banana and strawberry papaya are plucked from trees in island neighborhoods and eaten for breakfast—plain or with a squeeze of fresh lime. Give them a try; the apple banana tastes somewhat like an apple, and the strawberry papaya's rosy flesh explains its name. Locals also love to add their own creative touches to exotic fruits. Green mangoes are pickled with Chinese five spice, and Maui Gold pineapples are topped with *li hing mui* (salty dried plum) powder (heck, even margarita glasses are rimmed with it). Green papaya is tossed in a Vietnamese salad with fish paste and fresh prawns.

ONLY IN HAWAII

Traveling to Hawaii is as close as an American can get to visiting another country while staying within the United States. There's much to learn and understand about the state's indigenous culture, the hundred years of immigration that resulted in today's blended society, and the tradition of aloha that has welcomed millions of visitors over the years.

Aloha Shirt

To go to Hawaii without taking an aloha shirt home is almost sacrilege. The first aloha shirts from the 1920s and 1930s—called "silkies"—were classic canvases of art and tailored for the tourists. Popular culture caught on in the 1950s, and they became a fashion craze. With the 1960s came more subdued designs, Aloha Friday was born, and the shirt became appropriate clothing for work, play, and formal occasions. Because of its soaring popularity, cheaper and mass-produced versions became available.

Hawaiian Quilt

Although ancient Hawaiians were already known to produce fine *kapa* (bark) cloth, the actual art of quilting originated from the missionaries. Hawaiians have created designs to reflect their own aesthetic, and bold patterns evolved over time. They can be pricey, because the quilts are intricately made by hand and can take years to finish. These masterpieces are considered precious heirlooms that reflect the history and beauty of Hawaii.

Hula

"Hula is the language of the heart, therefore the heartbeat of the Hawaiian people." —Kalakaua, the Merrie Monarch.

Thousands—from tots to seniors—devote hours each week to hula classes. All of these dancers need some place to show off their stuff, and the result is a network of hula competitions (generally free or very inexpensive) and free performances in malls and other public spaces. Many resorts offer hula instruction.

Luau

The luau's origin, which was a celebratory feast, can be traced back to the earliest Hawaiian civilizations. In the traditional luau, the taboo or *kapu* laws were very strict, requiring men and women to eat separately. Nevertheless, in 1819 King Kamehameha II broke the great taboo and shared a feast with women and commoners, ushering in the modern-era luau. Today, traditional luau usually commemorate a child's first birthday, graduation, wedding, or other family occasion. They also are a Hawaiian experience that most visitors enjoy, and resorts and other companies have incorporated the fire-knife dance and other Polynesian dances into their elaborate presentations.

Nose Flutes

The nose flute is an instrument used in ancient times to serenade a lover. For the Hawaiians, the nose is romantic, sacred, and pure. The Hawaiian word for kiss is *honi*. Similar to an Eskimo's kiss, the noses touch on each side sharing one's spiritual energy or breath. The Hawaiian term *ohe hano ihu* simply translates to "bamboo," from which the instrument is made; "breathe," because one has to gently breathe through it to make soothing music; and "nose," as it is made for the nose and not the mouth.

Popular Souvenirs

Souvenir shopping can be intimidating. There's a sea of island-inspired and often kitschy merchandise, so we'd like to give you a breakdown of popular and fun gifts that you might encounter and consider bringing home. If authenticity is important to you, be sure to check labels and ask shopkeepers. Museum shops are good places for authentic, Hawaiian-made souvenirs.

Fabrics. Purchased by the yard or already made into everything from napkins to bedspreads, modern Hawaiian fabrics make wonderful keepsakes.

Home accessories. Deck out your kitchen or dining room in festive luau style with bottle openers, pineapple mugs, tiki glasses, shot glasses, slipper and surfboard magnets, and salt-and-pepper shakers.

Lauhala products. *Lauhala* weaving is a traditional Hawaiian art. The leaves come from the *hala,* or *pandanus,* tree and are handwoven to create lovely gift boxes, baskets, bags, and picture frames.

Lei and shell necklaces. From silk or polyester flower lei to kukui or puka shell necklaces, lei have been traditionally used as a welcome offering to guests (although the artificial ones are more for fun, since real flowers are always preferable).

Spa products. Relive your spa treatment at home with Hawaiian bath and body products, many of them manufactured with ingredients found only on the Islands.

Vintage Hawaii. You can find vintage photos, reproductions of vintage postcards or paintings, heirloom jewelry, and vintage aloha wear in many specialty stores.

Slack-Key Guitar and the Paniolo
Kihoalu, or slack-key music, evolved in the early 1800s when King Kamehameha III brought in Mexican and Spanish vaqueros to manage the overpopulated cattle that had run wild on the Islands. The vaqueros brought their guitars and would play music around the campfire after work. When they left, supposedly leaving their guitars to their new friends, the Hawaiian *paniolo,* or cowboys, began to infuse what they learned from the vaqueros with their native music and chants, and so the art of slack-key music was born. Today, the paniolo culture thrives where ranchers have settled.

Traditional Canoe
Hawaii's ancestors voyaged across 2,500 miles from Polynesia on board a double-hulled canoe with the help of the stars, the ocean swells, and the flight pattern of birds. The creation of a canoe spanned months and involved many religious ceremonies by the *kahuna kalai waa,* or high priest canoe builder. In 1973, the Polynesian Voyaging Society was founded to rediscover and preserve this ancestral tradition. Since 1975, the group has built and launched the majestic *Hokulea* and *Hawaiiloa,* which regularly travel throughout the South Pacific. In 2014, *Hokulea* began a historic, three-year, around-the-world voyage.

Ukulele
The word *ukulele* literally translates to "the jumping flea" and came to Hawaii in the 1880s by way of the Portuguese and Spanish. Once a fading art form, today it brings international kudos as a solo instrument, thanks to tireless musicians and teachers who have worked hard to keep it by our fingertips.

One such teacher is Roy Sakuma. Founder of four ukulele schools and a legend in his own right, Sakuma and his wife, Kathy, produced Oahu's first Ukulele Festival in 1971. Since then, they've brought the tradition to the Big Island, Kauai, and Maui. The free event annually draws thousands of artists and fans from all over the globe.

HAWAII AND THE ENVIRONMENT

Sustainability—it's a word rolling off everyone's tongues these days. In a place known as the most remote island chain in the world (check your globe), Hawaii relies heavily on the outside world for food and material goods—estimates put the percentage of food arriving on container ships as high as 90. Like many places, though, efforts are afoot to change that. And you can help.

Shop Local Farms and Markets

From Kauai to the Big Island, farmers' markets are cropping up, providing a place for growers to sell fresh fruits and vegetables. There is no reason to buy imported mangoes, papayas, avocadoes, and bananas at grocery stores, when the ones you'll find at farmers' markets are not only fresher but tastier, too. Some markets allow the sale of fresh-packaged foods—salsa, say, or smoothies—and the on-site preparation of food—like *laulau* (pork, beef, and fish or chicken with taro, or luau, leaves wrapped and steamed in *ti* leaves) or roasted corn on the cob—so you can make your run to the market a dining experience.

Not only is the locavore movement vibrantly alive at farmers' markets, but Hawaii's top chefs are sourcing more of their produce—and fish, beef, chicken, and cheese—from local providers as well. You'll notice this movement on restaurant menus featuring Kilauea greens or Hamakua tomatoes or locally caught mahimahi.

And although most people are familiar with Kona coffee farm tours on the Big Island, if you're interested in the growing Slow Food movement in Hawaii, you'll be heartened to know many farmers are opening up their operations for tours—as well as sumptuous meals.

Support Hawaii's Merchants

Food isn't the only sustainable effort in Hawaii. Buying local goods like art and jewelry, Hawaiian heritage products, crafts, music, and apparel is another way to "green up" the local economy. The County of Kauai helps make it easy with a program called **Kauai Made** (⊕ *www. kauaimade.net*), which showcases products made on Kauai, by Kauai people, using Kauai materials. Think of it as the Good Housekeeping Seal of Approval for locally made goods.

Then there are the crafty entrepreneurs who are diverting items from the trash heap by repurposing garbage. Take Oahu's **Muumuu Heaven** (⊕ *www.muumuuheaven. com*). They got their start by reincarnating vintage aloha apparel into hip new fashions.

Choose Green Tour Operators

Conscious decisions when it comes to island activities go a long way to protecting Hawaii's natural world. The **Hawaii Ecotourism Association** (⊕ *www. hawaiiecotourism.org*) recognizes tour operators for, among other things, their environmental stewardship. The **Hawaii Tourism Authority** (⊕ *www. hawaiitourismauthority.org*) recognizes outfitters for their cultural sensitivity. Winners of these awards are good choices when it comes to guided tours and activities.

THE HISTORY OF HAWAII

Hawaiian history is long and complex; a brief survey can put into context the ongoing renaissance of native arts and culture.

The Polynesians

Long before both Christopher Columbus and the Vikings, Polynesian seafarers set out to explore the vast stretches of the open ocean in double-hulled canoes. From western Polynesia, they traveled back and forth between Samoa, Fiji, Tahiti, the Marquesas, and the Society Isles, settling on the outer reaches of the Pacific, Hawaii, and Easter Island, as early as AD 300. The golden era of Polynesian voyaging peaked around AD 1200, after which the distant Hawaiian Islands were left to develop their own unique cultural practices and subsistence in relative isolation.

The Islands' symbiotic society was deeply intertwined with religion, mythology, science, and artistry. Ruled by an *alii*, or chief, each settlement was nestled in an *ahupuaa*, a pie-shaped land division from the uplands where the alii lived, through the valleys and down to the shores where the commoners resided. Everyone contributed, whether it was by building canoes, catching fish, making tools, or farming land.

A United Kingdom

When the British explorer Captain James Cook arrived in 1778, he was revered as a god. With guns and ammunition purchased from Cook, the Big Island chief, Kamehameha the Great, gained a significant advantage over the other alii. He united Hawaii into one kingdom in 1810, bringing an end to the frequent interisland battles that dominated Hawaiian life.

Tragically, the new kingdom was beset with troubles. Native religion was abandoned, and *kapu* (laws and regulations) were eventually abolished. The European explorers brought foreign diseases with them, and within a few short decades the Native Hawaiian population was decimated.

New laws regarding land ownership and religious practices eroded the underpinnings of precontact Hawaii. Each successor to the Hawaiian throne sacrificed more control over the island kingdom. As Westerners permeated Hawaiian culture, Hawaii became more riddled with layers of racial issues, injustice, and social unrest.

Modern Hawaii

In 1893, the last Hawaiian monarch, Queen Liliuokalani, was overthrown by a group of Americans and European businessmen and government officials, aided by an armed militia. This led to the creation of the Republic of Hawaii, and it became a U.S. territory for the next 60 years. The loss of Hawaiian sovereignty and the conditions of annexation have haunted the Hawaiian people since the monarchy was deposed.

Pearl Harbor was attacked in 1941, which pulled the United States immediately into World War II. Tourism, from its beginnings in the early 1900s, flourished after the war and naturally inspired rapid real estate development in Waikiki. In 1959, Hawaii officially became the 50th state. Statehood paved the way for Hawaiians to participate in the American democratic process, which was not universally embraced by all Hawaiians. With the rise of the civil rights movement in the 1960s, Hawaiians began to reclaim their own identity, from language to hula.

WEDDINGS AND HONEYMOONS

There's no question that Hawaii is one of the country's foremost honeymoon destinations. Romance is in the air here, and the white, sandy beaches, turquoise water, swaying palm trees, balmy tropical breezes, and perpetual sunshine put people in the mood for love. It's easy to understand why Hawaii is fast becoming a popular wedding destination as well, especially as the cost of airfare is often discounted, new resorts and hotels entice visitors, and same-sex marriage is now legal in the state. A destination wedding is no longer exclusive to celebrities and the superrich. You can plan a traditional ceremony in a place of worship followed by a reception at an elegant resort, or you can go barefoot on the beach and celebrate at a luau. There are almost as many wedding planners in the Islands as real estate agents, which makes it oh-so-easy to wed in paradise, and then, once the knot is tied, stay and honeymoon as well.

The Big Day

Choosing the Perfect Place. When choosing a location, remember that you really have two choices to make: the ceremony location and where to have the reception, if you're having one. For the former, there are beaches, bluffs overlooking beaches, gardens, private residences, resort lawns, and, of course, places of worship. As for the reception, there are these same choices, as well as restaurants and even luau. If you decide to go outdoors, remember the seasons—yes, Hawaii has seasons. If you're planning a winter wedding outdoors, be sure you have a backup plan (such as a tent), in case it rains. Also, if you're planning an outdoor wedding at sunset—which is very popular—be sure you match the time of your ceremony to the time the sun sets at that time of year. If you choose an indoor spot, be sure to ask for pictures of the location when you're planning. You don't want to plan a pink wedding, say, and wind up in a room that's predominantly red. Or maybe you do. The point is, it should be your choice.

Finding a Wedding Planner. If you're planning to invite more than an officiant and your loved one to your wedding ceremony, seriously consider an on-island wedding planner who can help select a location, help design the floral scheme and recommend a florist as well as a photographer, help plan the menu and choose a restaurant, caterer, or resort, and suggest any Hawaiian traditions to incorporate into your ceremony. And more: Will you need tents, a cake, music? Maybe transportation and lodging? Many planners have relationships with vendors, providing packages—which mean savings.

If you're planning a resort wedding, most have on-site wedding coordinators; however, there are many independents around the Islands and even those who specialize in certain types of ceremonies—by locale, size, religious affiliation, and so on. A simple "Hawaii weddings" Google search will reveal dozens. What's important is that you feel comfortable with your coordinator. Ask for references and call them. Share your budget. Get a proposal—in writing. Ask how long they've been in business, how much they charge, how often you'll meet with them, and how they select vendors. Request a detailed list of the exact services they'll provide. If your idea of your wedding doesn't match their services, try someone else. If you can afford it, you might want to meet the planner in person.

Getting Your License. The good news about marrying in Hawaii is that there is no waiting period, no residency or citizenship requirement, and no blood test or shots are required. You can apply and pay the fee online; however, both the bride and groom must appear together in person before a marriage-license agent to receive the marriage license (the permit to get married). You'll need proof of age—the legal age to marry is 18. (If you're 19 or older, a valid driver's license will suffice; if you're 18, a certified birth certificate is required.) Upon approval, a marriage license is immediately issued and costs $60 (credit cards accepted online and in person; cash only accepted in person). After the ceremony, your officiant will mail the marriage certificate (proof of marriage) to the state. Approximately four months later, you will receive a copy in the mail. (For $10 extra, you can expedite this process; ask your marriage-license agent when you apply.) For more detailed information, visit ⊕ *marriage. ehawaii.gov.*

Also—this is important—the person performing your wedding must be licensed by the Hawaii Department of Health, even if he or she is a licensed officiant. Be sure to ask.

Wedding Attire. In Hawaii, basically anything goes, from long, formal dresses with trains to white bikinis. Floral sundresses are fine, too. For men, tuxedos are not the norm; a pair of solid-colored slacks with a nice aloha shirt is. In fact, tradition in Hawaii for the groom is a beautiful white aloha shirt (they do exist) with slacks or long shorts and a colored sash around the waist. If you're planning a wedding on the beach, barefoot is the way to go.

If you decide to marry in a formal dress and tuxedo, you're better off making your selections on the mainland and hand-carrying them aboard the plane. Yes, it can be a pain, but ask your wedding-gown retailer to provide a special carrying bag. After all, you don't want to chance losing your wedding dress in a wayward piece of luggage.

Local Customs. The most obvious traditional Hawaiian wedding custom is the lei exchange in which the bride and groom take turns placing a lei around the neck of the other—with a kiss. Bridal lei are usually floral, whereas the groom's is typically made of *maile*, a green leafy garland that drapes around the neck and is open at the ends. Brides often also wear a *lei poo*—a circular floral headpiece. Other Hawaiian customs include the blowing of the conch shell, hula, chanting, and Hawaiian music.

The Honeymoon

Do you want champagne and strawberries delivered to your room each morning? A breathtaking swimming pool in which to float? A five-star restaurant in which to dine? Then a resort is the way to go. If, however, you prefer the comforts of a home, try a bed-and-breakfast. A small inn is also good if you're on a tight budget or don't plan to spend much time in your room. On the other hand, maybe you want your own private home in which to romp naked—or just laze around recovering from the wedding planning. Maybe you want your own kitchen so you can whip up a gourmet meal for your loved one. In that case, a private vacation-rental home is the answer. Or maybe a condominium resort. That's another beautiful thing about Hawaii: the lodging accommodations are almost as plentiful as the beaches, and there's one that will perfectly match your tastes and your budget.

LUAU: A TASTE OF HAWAII

The best place to sample Hawaiian food is at a backyard luau. Aunts and uncles are cooking, the pig is from a cousin's farm, the fish is from a brother's boat, and someone plinks a wistful tune on a ukulele.

The luau is such a special event that even locals have to angle for invitations. So unless you're tight with a local family, your choice is most likely between a commercial luau and a Hawaiian restaurant.

Some commercial luau are not particularly authentic; they offer little of the traditional diet and are more about umbrella drinks, spectacle, and fun.

For greater culinary authenticity, folksy experiences, and rock-bottom prices, try a Hawaiian restaurant. Most are located in anonymous storefronts in residential neighborhoods.

Much of what is known today as Hawaiian food would be foreign to a 16th-century Hawaiian. The precontact diet was simple and healthy—mainly raw and steamed seafood and vegetables. Early Hawaiians used earth ovens and heated stones to cook seafood, taro, sweet potatoes, and breadfruit. They seasoned their food with sea salt and ground kukui nuts. Seaweed, fern shoots, sweet potato vines, coconut, banana, sugarcane, and select greens and roots rounded out the diet.

Immigrants added their favorites to the ti leaf–lined table, so now foods as disparate as salt salmon and chicken long rice have become Hawaiian—even though there is no salmon in Hawaii and long rice (cellophane noodles) is Chinese.

AT THE LUAU: KALUA PORK
The heart of any luau is the *imu*, the earth oven in which a whole pig is roasted. The preparation of an imu is

an arduous affair for most families, who tackle it only once a year or so for a baby's first birthday or at Thanksgiving, when many Islanders prefer to imu their turkeys. Commercial luau operations have it down to a science, however.

The Art of the Stone. The key to a proper imu is the *pohaku*, the stones. Imu cook by means of long, slow, moist heat released by special stones that can withstand a hot fire without exploding. Many Hawaiian families keep their imu stones in a pile in the backyard and pass them on through generations.

Pit Cooking. The imu makers first dig a pit about the size of a refrigerator, then lay down *kiawe* (mesquite) wood and stones, and build a white-hot fire that is allowed to burn itself out. The ashes are raked away, and the hot stones covered with banana and ti leaves. Well-wrapped in ti or banana leaves and a net of chicken wire, the pig is lowered onto the leaf-covered stones. *Laulau* (leaf-wrapped bundles of meats, fish, and taro leaves) may also be placed inside. Leaves—ti, banana, even ginger—cover the pig followed by wet burlap sacks (to create steam). The whole is topped with a canvas tarp and left to steam for the better part of a day.

Opening the Imu. This is the moment everyone waits for: The imu is unwrapped like a giant present and the imu keepers gingerly wrestle out the

steaming pig. When it's unwrapped, the meat falls moist and smoky-flavored from the bone.

Which Luau? Most resort hotels have luau on their grounds that include hula, music, and, of course, lots of food and drink. Each island also has at least one "authentic" luau.

MEA AI ONO: GOOD THINGS TO EAT

Laulau. Steamed meats, fish, and taro leaf in ti-leaf bundles: fork-tender, a medley of flavors; the taro resembles spinach.

Lomi Lomi Salmon. Salt salmon in a piquant salad or relish with onions and tomatoes.

Poi. A paste made of pounded taro root, poi may be an acquired taste, but it's a must-try during your visit.

Consider: The Hawaiian Adam is descended from *kalo* (taro). Young taro plants are called *keiki*, or children. Poi is the first food after mother's milk for many Islanders. *Ai*, the word for food, is synonymous with poi in many contexts.

Not only that, we love it. "There is no meat that doesn't taste good with poi," the old Hawaiians said. But you have to know how to eat it: with something rich or powerfully flavored.

ALL ABOUT LEI

Lei brighten every occasion in Hawaii, from birthdays to weddings to baptisms. Artisans weave flowers, ferns, and vines into gorgeous creations that convey an array of heartfelt messages.

"Welcome," "Congratulations," "Good luck," "Farewell," "Thank you," "I love you." When it's difficult to find the right words, a lei can express exactly the right sentiment.

Though lei are usually created from native flora, Niihau, the Forbidden Island, is famous for its exquisite tiny shells made into lei. Some of these shell lei can cost thousands of dollars and are often an exotic jewelry item. Lei are also sometimes constructed of paper, fish teeth, and even candy.

If you happen to be in the Islands around May 1, be sure to seek out the annual May Day celebrations at local schools and parks, because "May Day is Lei Day" in Hawaii. Not a Hawaiian tradition, Lei Day was the brainchild of poet Don Blanding in 1928. Happening during the full blossoming of spring flowers, May Day creations are a feast for the eyes.

WHERE TO BUY LEI

Most airports, supermarkets, and every florist shop in Hawaii sell lei. And you'll always find lei sellers at crafts fairs and outdoor festivals.

LEI ETIQUETTE

Lei are usually presented with a kiss on the cheek. To wear a closed lei, drape it over your shoulders, half in front and half in back. Open lei are worn around the neck, with the ends draped over the front in equal lengths.

Pikake, ginger, and other sweet, delicate blossoms are "feminine" lei. Men opt

1

for cigar, crown flower, and ti leaf lei, which are sturdier and don't emit as much fragrance.

You shouldn't wear a lei before you give it to someone else. Hawaiians believe the lei absorbs your *mana* (spirit); if you give your lei away, you'll be giving away part of your essence.

TYPES OF LEI

Orchid. Growing wild on every continent except Antarctica, orchids comprise the largest family of plants in the world. Of the more than 20,000 species of orchids, only three are native to Hawaii—and they are very rare. The pretty lavender vanda you see hanging by the dozens at local lei stands has probably been imported from Thailand.

Maile. An endemic twining vine with a heady aroma, maile is sacred to Laka, goddess of the hula. In ancient times, dancers wore maile and decorated hula altars with it to honor Laka. Today, "open" maile lei usually are given to men. Instead of ribbon, interwoven lengths of maile are used at dedications of new businesses.

Ilima. Designated by Hawaii's Territorial Legislature in 1923 as the official flower of the island of Oahu, the golden ilima is so delicate it lasts for just a day. Five to seven hundred blossoms are needed to make one garland. Queen Emma, wife of King Kamehameha IV, preferred ilima over all other lei, which may have led to the incorrect belief that they were reserved only for royalty.

Plumeria. Plumeria ranks among the most popular lei in Hawaii because it's fragrant, hardy, plentiful, inexpensive, and requires very little care. Although yellow is the most common color, you'll also find plumeria lei in shades of pink, red, orange, and "rainbow" blends.

Pikake. Favored for its fragile beauty and sweet scent, pikake was introduced from India. In lieu of pearls, many brides in Hawaii adorn themselves with long, multiple strands of white pikake. Princess Kaiulani enjoyed showing guests her beloved pikake and peacocks at Ainahau, her Waikiki home. Interestingly, *pikake* is the Hawaiian word for both the bird and the blossom.

Kukui. The *kukui* (candlenut) is Hawaii's state tree. Early Hawaiians strung the oily kukui nuts together and burned them for light. They also burned the nuts with oil to make an indelible dye and mashed roasted nuts to consume as a laxative. Kukui nut lei may not have been made until after Western contact, when the Hawaiians saw black beads from Europe and wanted to imitate them.

HULA: MORE THAN A FOLK DANCE

Hula has been called "the heartbeat of the Hawaiian people" and "the world's best known, most misunderstood dance." Both are true. Hula isn't just dance. It is storytelling. Today's Hawaii distinguishes between the traditional hula (*kahiko*) and modern hula (*auana*).

Called "an extension of a piece of poetry," hula integrates every important Hawaiian cultural practice: poetry, history, genealogy, craft, plant cultivation, martial arts, religion, and protocol. So when 19th-century Christian missionaries sought to eradicate a practice they considered depraved, they threatened more than just a folk dance.

With public performance outlawed and private hula practice discouraged, hula went underground for decades. The fragile verbal link by which culture was transmitted from teacher to student hung by a thread, as hula's practitioners were a secretive and protected circle.

As if that weren't bad enough, vaudeville, Broadway, and Hollywood got hold of the hula, giving it the glitz treatment in an unbroken line from "Oh, How She Could Wicky Wacky Woo" to "Rock-A-Hula Baby." Hula became shorthand for paradise: fragrant flowers, lazy hours, gorgeous beaches. Ironically, this development assured that hundreds of Hawaiians could make a living performing and teaching hula. Many danced *auana* (modern form) in performance, but taught *kahiko* (traditional), quietly, at home or in hula schools.

Today, language immersion programs have assured a new generation of proficient—and even eloquent—chanters, songwriters, and translators. Visitors can see more traditional hula than at any other time in the last 200 years.

ABOUT THE HULA

At backyard parties, hula is performed in bare feet and street clothes. But in performance, adornments play a key role, as do rhythm-keeping implements such as the *pahu* drum and the *ipu* (gourd).

In hula *kahiko* (traditional style), the usual dress is multiple layers of stiff fabric (often with a pellom lining, which most closely resembles *kapa*, the paperlike bark cloth of the Hawaiians). These wrap tightly around the bosom but flare below the waist to form a skirt. In precontact times, dancers wore only kapa skirts. Men traditionally wear loincloths.

Monarchy-period hula is performed in voluminous muumuu or high-necked muslin blouses and gathered skirts. Men wear white or gingham shirts and black pants.

In hula *auana* (modern), dress for women can range from grass skirts and strapless tops to contemporary tea-length dresses. Men generally wear aloha shirts, but sometimes don grass skirts over pants or even everyday gear.

SURPRISING HULA FACTS

Grass skirts are not traditional; workers from Kiribati (the Gilbert Islands) brought this custom to Hawaii.

Hula *mai* is a traditional hula form in praise of a noble's genitals; the power of the *alii* (royalty) to procreate gave *mana* (spiritual power) to the entire culture.

Hula students in old Hawaii adhered to high standards: scrupulous cleanliness, no sex, daily cleansing rituals, certain food prohibitions, and no contact with the dead. They were fined if they broke the rules.

WHERE TO WATCH HULA

If you're interested in "the real thing," there are annual hula festivals on each island. Check the individual island visitors' bureaus websites (⊕ *www.gohawaii.com*).

For total immersion, check out the weeklong Merrie Monarch Festival in Hilo in early Spring. *Halaus* (schools) from every island and from around the world compete with a common goal of preserving and promoting this sacred art form. If you can't make it to a festival and are in the Islands, check the local TV listings for festival coverage; it's an annual event that spellbinds many island residents.

There are plenty of other hula shows at resorts, lounges, and shopping centers. Ask your hotel concierge for performance information.

CRUISING THE HAWAIIAN ISLANDS

Cruising has become popular in Hawaii. Cruises are a comparatively inexpensive way to see all of Hawaii, and you'll save travel time by not having to check in at hotels and airports on each island. The limited amount of time in each port can be an argument against cruising, but you can make reservations for tours, activities, rental cars, and more aboard the cruise ship. This will also give you more time for sightseeing and shopping at ports.

The larger cruise lines such as Carnival, Princess, and Holland America offer itineraries of 10–16 days departing from the West Coast of the United States, most with stops at all the major Hawaiian Islands. Some cruise lines, such as Crystal, Cunard, and Disney, include ports in Hawaii on around-the-world cruises. All have plenty on board to keep you busy during the 4–5 days that you are at sea between the U.S. mainland and Hawaii.

Cruise ships plying the Pacific from the continental United States to Hawaii are floating resorts complete with pools, spas, rock-climbing walls, restaurants, nightclubs, shops, casinos, children's programs, and much more. Most hold thousands of passengers with an average staff-to-passenger ratio of three to one.

Prices for cruises are based on accommodation type: interior (no window, in an inside corridor); outside (includes a window or porthole); balcony (allows you to go outside without using a public deck); and suite (larger cabin, more amenities and perks). Passages start at about $1,000 per person for the lowest class accommodation (interior) and include room, on-board entertainment, and food. Ocean-view, balcony, and suite accommodations can run up to $6,500 and more per person.

Cruising to Hawaii

Carnival Cruises is great for families, with plenty of kid-friendly activities. Departing from Los Angeles or Vancouver, Carnival's "fun ships" show your family a good time, both on board and on shore (☎ 888/227–6482 ⊕ www.carnival.com). The grand dame of cruise lines, Holland America has a reputation for service and elegance. Their 14-day Hawaii cruises leave from and return to San Diego, with a brief stop at Ensenada (☎ 877/932–4259 ⊕ www.hollandamerica.com). More affordable luxury is what Princess Cruises offers. Although their prices seem a little higher, you get more bells and whistles on your trip (more affordable balcony rooms, more restaurants to choose from, personalized service) (☎ 800/774–6237 ⊕ www.princess.com).

Cruising within Hawaii

Norwegian Cruise Lines (⊕ www.ncl.com) is the only major operator to begin and end cruises in Hawaii. *Pride of Hawaii* (vintage America theme, family focus with lots of connecting staterooms and suites) offers a seven-day itinerary that includes stops on Maui, Oahu, the Big Island, and Kauai. This is the only ship to cruise Hawaii that does not spend days at sea visiting a foreign port, allowing you more time to explore destinations). Ocean conditions in the channels between islands can be a consideration when booking an inter-island cruise on a smaller vessel such as the one operated by **Un-Cruise Adventures** (⊕ www.un-cruise.com)—a stately yacht accommodating only 36 passengers. This yacht's small size allows it to dock at less frequented islands such as Molokai and Lanai. The cruise is billed as "all inclusive"—your passage includes shore excursions, water activities, and a massage.

EXPLORING KAUAI

SEEING THE NAPALI COAST

If you're coming to Kauai, Napali ("cliffs" in Hawaiian) is a major must-see. More than 5 million years old, these sea cliffs rise thousands of feet above the Pacific, and every shade of green is represented in the vegetation that blankets their lush peaks and folds. At their base, there are caves, secluded beaches, and waterfalls to explore.

The big question is how to explore this gorgeous stretch of coastline. You can't drive to it, through it, or around it. You can't see Napali from a scenic lookout. You can't even take a mule ride to it. The only way to experience its magic is from the sky, the ocean, or the trail. ⇨ *For information on Napali Coast tour operators see the Boat Tours section in the Water Sports and Tours chapter and the Aerial Tours section in the Golf, Hiking, and Outdoor Activities chapter.*

FROM THE SKY
Seeing Napali by helicopter is breathtaking. You may snap a few pictures (not too many or you'll miss the eyes-on experience!), nudge a friend or spouse, and point at a whale breeching in the ocean, but mostly you stare, mouth agape. There is simply no other way to take in the immensity and greatness of Napali but from the air. Helicopter companies depart from the north, east, and west side of the island. Most are based in Lihue, near the airport. If you want more adventure—and air—choose one of the helicopter companies that flies with the doors off. Some companies offer flights without music. Know the experience you want ahead of time. Your pilot shares history, legend, and lore. If you miss something, speak up: pilots love to show off their island knowledge.

2

Good to know. Wintertime rain grounds some flights; plan your trip early in your stay in case the flight gets rescheduled.

Is this for me? Helicopter trips are the most expensive way to see Napali—as much as $300 for an hour-long tour. Claustrophobic? Choose a boat tour or hike. It's a tight squeeze in the helicopter, especially in one of the middle seats. Short on time? A helicopter tour is a great way to see the island.

What you might see. Nualolo Kai (an ancient Hawaiian fishing village) with its fringed reef; the 300-foot Hanakapiai Falls; a massive sea arch formed in the rock by erosion; the 11-mile Kalalau Trail threading its way along the coast; the amazing striations of *aa* and *pahoehoe* lava flows that helped push Kauai above the sea.

FROM THE OCEAN

You'll breathe ocean air, feel spray on your face, and see pods of spinner dolphins, green sea turtles, flying fish, and, if you're lucky, a rare Hawaiian monk seal.

Three journeys. There are three different ways to view Napali from the ocean. There's a mellow pleasure-cruise catamaran that allows you to kick back and sip a mai tai; an adventurous raft (Zodiac) tour inside sea caves under waterfalls, with the option of snorkeling; or a daylong outing in a kayak, which can be a real workout, but then you can say you paddled 16 miles of

coastline. Napali stretches from Kee Beach in the north to Polihale Beach on the West Side. If your departure point is Kee, you are already headed toward the lush Hanakapiai Valley.

Good to know. For snorkel tours, choose a morning rather than an afternoon tour—preferably during a summer visit—when seas are calmer. If you're on a budget, choose a non-snorkeling tour. If you want to see whales, December through March is the best time. If you're staying on the North Shore or East Side, embark from the North Shore. If you're staying on the South Shore, it might not be worth your time to drive to the north, so head to the West Side.

Is this for me? Boat tours are several hours long, so if you're short on time, a helicopter tour is a better alternative. Prone to seasickness? A large boat can be surprisingly rocky, so be prepared.

What you might see. Waiahuakua Sea Cave, with a waterfall coming through its roof; tons of marine life, including dolphins, green sea turtles, flying fish, and humpback whales, especially in February and March; waterfalls—especially if your trip is after a heavy rain.

FROM THE TRAIL

If you want to be one with Napali—feeling the soft red earth beneath your feet, picnicking on the beaches, and touching the lush vegetation—hiking the Kalalau Trail is the way to do it.

Most people hike only the first 2 miles of the 11-mile trail and turn around at Hanakapiai. This 4-mile round-trip hike takes three to four hours. It starts at sea level and doesn't waste any time gaining elevation. (Take heart—the uphill lasts only a mile and tops out at 400 feet; then it's downhill all the way.) At the half-mile point, the trail curves west and the folds of Napali Coast unfurl. After the 1-mile mark the trail begins its drop into Hanakapiai. You'll pass a couple of streams of water trickling across the trail, and maybe some banana trees, ginger plants, the native uluhe fern, and the Hawaiian ti plant. Finally the trail swings around the eastern ridge of Hanakapiai for your first glimpse of the valley and then switchbacks down the mountain. You'll have to boulder-hop across the stream to reach the beach.

Good to know. Wear comfortable, amphibious shoes. Unless your feet require extra support, wear a self-bailing sort of shoe (for stream crossings) that doesn't mind mud. Don't wear heavy, waterproof hiking boots. During winter the trail is often muddy, and sometimes it's completely inaccessible. Don't hike after heavy rain—flash floods are common. If you plan to hike the entire 11-mile trail you'll need a permit to go past Hanakapiai.

Is this for me? Of all the ways to see Napali (with the exception of kayaking the coast), this is the most active. You need to be in decent shape. In winter this hike might not be an option due to flooding—whereas you can take a helicopter year-round.

What you might see. Big dramatic surf right below your feet; amazing vistas of the Pacific; the spectacular Hanakapiai Falls; if you have a permit, don't miss Hanakoa Falls, less than ½ mile off the trail; wildlife, including goats and pigs; zany-looking ohia trees, with aerial roots and long, skinny, serrated leaves known as *hala*.

2

Updated by
Charles E.
Roessler

Even a nickname like "The Garden Island" fails to do justice to Kauai's beauty. Verdant trees grow canopies over the few roads, and brooding mountains are framed by long, sandy beaches, coral reefs, and sheer sea cliffs. Pristine trade winds moderate warm daily temperatures while offering comfort for deep, refreshing sleep through gentle nights.

The main road tracing Kauai's perimeter takes you past much more scenery than would seem possible on one small island. Chiseled mountains, thundering waterfalls, misty hillsides, dreamy beaches, lush vegetation, and small towns make up the physical landscape. Perhaps the most stunning piece of scenery is a place no road will take you—the breathtakingly beautiful Napali Coast, which runs along the northwest side of the island.

For adventure seekers, Kauai offers everything from difficult hikes to helicopter tours. The island has top-notch spas and golf courses, and its beaches are known to be some of the most beautiful in the world. Even after you've spent days lazing around drinking mai tais or kayaking your way down a river, there's still plenty to do, as well as see: plantation villages, a historic lighthouse, wildlife refuges, a fern grotto, a colorful canyon, and deep rivers are all easily explored.

■TIP➜ While exploring the island, try to take advantage of the many roadside scenic overlooks and pull over to take in the constantly changing view. Don't try to pack too much into one day. Kauai is small, but travel is slow. The island's sights are divided into four geographic areas, in clockwise order: the North Shore, the East Side, the South Shore, and the West Side.

GEOLOGY

Kauai is the oldest and northernmost of the main Hawaiian Islands. Five million years of wind and rain have worked their magic, sculpting fluted sea cliffs and whittling away at the cinder cones and caldera that prove its volcanic origin. Foremost among these is Waialeale, one of the wettest spots on Earth. Its approximate 450-inch annual rainfall feeds the mighty Wailua River, the only navigable waterway in Hawaii. The

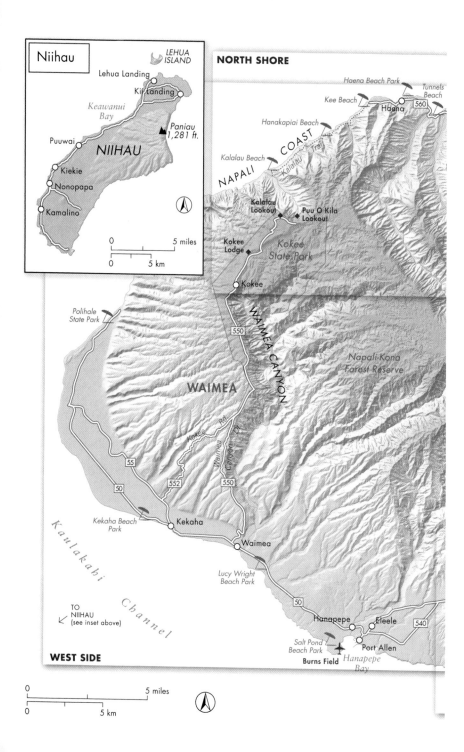

Niihau

LEHUA ISLAND

Lehua Landing

Kii Landing

Keawanui Bay

Puuwai

NIIHAU

Paniau
1,281 ft.

Kiekie

Nonopapa

Kamalino

0   5 miles

0   5 km

Haena Beach Park

Kee Beach

Tunnels Beach

Haena

560

Hanakapiai Beach

COAST

Kalalau Beach

NAPALI

Kalalau Trail

Kalalau
Lookout

Puu O Kila
Lookout

Kokee
Lodge

*Kokee
State Park*

Kokee

Polihale
State Park

550

WAIMEA CANYON

*Napali-Kona
Forest Reserve*

WAIMEA

Kokee Rd

Waimea Canyon Dr

552

550

55

50

Kekaha Beach
Park

Kekaha

Waimea

Kaulakahi Channel

Lucy Wright
Beach Park

50

Hanapepe

Eleele

540

TO
NIIHAU
(see inset above)

Salt Pond
Beach Park

Port Allen

Burns Field

*Hanapepe
Bay*

0   5 miles

0   5 km

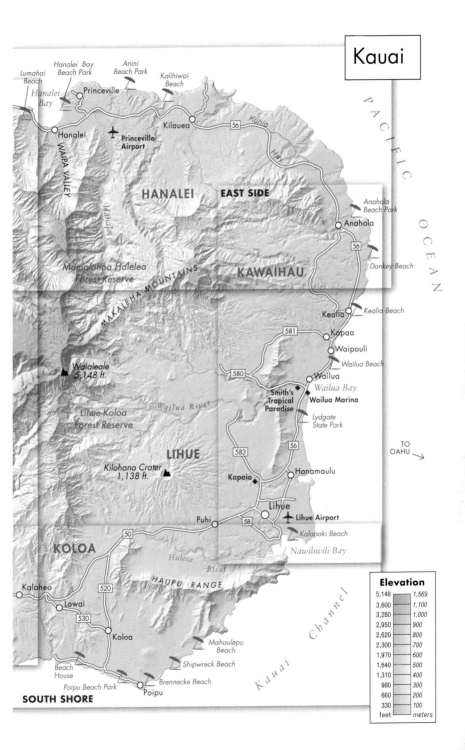

Kauai

Lumahai Beach
Hanalei Bay Beach Park
Anini Beach Park
Kalihiwai Beach
Hanalei Bay
Princeville
Hanalei
Kilauea
Princeville Airport
56
Kuhio Hwy

WAIPA VALLEY
Hanalei

HANALEI

EAST SIDE

Mamalahoa Halelea Forest Reserve

MAKALEHA MOUNTAINS

KAWAIHAU

PACIFIC OCEAN

Anahola Beach Park
Anahola
56
Donkey Beach

Kealia Beach
Kealia
581
Kapaa
Waipouli
Wailua Beach
580
Wailua
Smith's Tropical Paradise
Wailua Bay
Wailua Marina
Lydgate State Park

Waialeale 5,148 ft.

Lihue-Koloa Forest Reserve

Wailua River

LIHUE

Kilohana Crater 1,138 ft.

583
56

Kapaia
Hanamaulu

Lihue
Lihue Airport

Puhi
58

TO OAHU →

Kalapaki Beach
Nawiliwili Bay

KOLOA
50

Huleia River

HAUPU RANGE

Kalaheo
Lawai
520
530
Koloa

Mahaulepu Beach
Shipwreck Beach

Beach House
Poipu Beach Park
Brennecke Beach
Poipu

Channel

Kauai

SOUTH SHORE

Elevation

feet		meters
5,148		1,569
3,600		1,100
3,280		1,000
2,950		900
2,620		800
2,300		700
1,970		600
1,640		500
1,310		400
980		300
660		200
330		100
feet		meters

vast Alakai Swamp soaks up rain like a sponge, releasing it slowly into the watershed that gives Kauai its emerald sheen.

FLORA AND FAUNA

Kauai offers some of the best birding in the state, due in part to the absence of the mongoose. Many nene (the endangered Hawaiian state bird) reared in captivity have been successfully released here, along with an endangered forest bird called the puaiohi. The island is also home to a large colony of migratory nesting seabirds and has two refuges protecting endangered Hawaiian waterbirds. Kauai's most noticeable fowl, however, is the wild chicken. A cross between jungle fowl (*moa*) brought by the Polynesians and domestic chickens and fighting cocks that escaped during the last two hurricanes, they are everywhere, and the roosters crow when they feel like it, not just at dawn. Consider yourself warned.

HISTORY

Kauai's residents have had a reputation for independence since ancient times. Called "The Separate Kingdom," Kauai alone resisted King Kamehameha's charge to unite the Hawaiian Islands. In fact, it was only by kidnapping Kauai's king, Kaumualii, and forcing him to marry Kamehameha's widow that the Garden Isle was joined to the rest of Hawaii. That spirit lives on today as Kauai residents try to resist the lure of tourism dollars captivating the rest of the Islands. Local building tradition maintains that no structure be taller than a coconut tree, and Kauai's capital, Lihue, is still more small town than city.

GUIDED TOURS

Guided tours are convenient; you don't have to worry about finding a parking spot or getting admission tickets. Certified tour guides have taken special classes in Hawaiian history and lore. On the other hand, you won't have the freedom to proceed at your own pace, nor will you have the ability to take a detour trip if something else catches your attention.

Aloha Kauai Tours. You get *way* off the beaten track on these four-wheel-drive van excursions. Choose from several options, including the half-day *Backroads Tour* covering mostly haul-cane roads behind the locked gates of Grove Farm Plantation, and the half-day *Rainforest Tour*, which follows the Wailua River to its source, Mt. Waialeale. The expert guides are some of the best on the island. Rates are $80. ⊠ *1702 Haleukana St., for check-in, Puhi* ☎ *808/245–6400, 800/452–1113* ⊕ *www.alohakauaitours.com* ✉ *$80.*

Roberts Hawaii Tours. The *Round-the-Island Tour*, sometimes called the *Waimea Canyon–Fern Grotto Tour*, gives a good overview of half the island, including Fort Elisabeth and Opaekaa Falls. Guests are transported in air-conditioned, 25-passenger minibuses. The $96 trip includes a boat ride up the Wailua River to the Fern Grotto and a visit to the lookouts above Waimea Canyon. They also offer a *Kauai Movie Tour* for $109. ⊠ *3-4567 Kuhio Hwy., Hanamaulu* ☎ *808/245–9101, 800/831–5541* ⊕ *www.robertshawaii.com* ✉ *From $96.*

Waimea Historic Walking Tour. Led by a *kupuna*, a respected Hawaiian elder, this two-hour tour begins promptly at 8:30 am, every Monday

Talk about remote: Beautiful Kalalau beach is at the end of an 11-mile trail through the incredible Napali Coast State Wilderness.

at the West Kauai Visitor Center. While sharing her personal remembrances, Aletha Kaohi leads an easy walk that explains Waimea's distinction as a recipient of the 2006 National Trust for Historic Preservation Award. The tour is free, but a reservation is required. ⊠ *9565 Kaumualii Highway, Waimea (Kauai County)* ☎ *808/338–1332* ✉ *Free.*

VISITOR INFORMATION
For information about hiking and camping permits and rules and regulations for the Napali Coast visit the Division of State Parks section of ⊕ *hawaii.gov website.*

Division of State Parks. ⊠ *3060 Eiwa St., Suite 306, Lihue* ☎ *808/274–3444* ⊕ *www.hawaii.gov.*

THE NORTH SHORE

The North Shore of Kauai includes the environs of Kilauea, Princeville, Hanalei, and Haena. Traveling north on Route 56 from the airport, the coastal highway crosses the Wailua River and the busy towns of Wailua and Kapaa before emerging into a decidedly rural and scenic landscape, with expansive views of the island's rugged interior mountains. As the two-lane highway turns west and narrows, it winds through spectacular scenery and passes the posh resort community of Princeville before dropping down into Hanalei Valley. Here it narrows further and becomes a federally recognized scenic roadway, replete with one-lane bridges (the local etiquette is for six or seven cars to cross at a time, before yielding to those on the other side), hairpin turns, and heart-stopping coastal vistas.

The road ends at Kee, where the ethereal rain forests and fluted sea cliffs of Napali Coast Wilderness State Park begin.

In winter Kauai's North Shore receives more rainfall than other areas of the island. Don't let this deter you from visiting. The clouds drift over the mountains of Namolokama creating a mysterious mood and then, in a blink, disappear, rewarding you with mountains laced with a dozen waterfalls or more. The views of the mountain—as well as the sunsets over the ocean—from the St. Regis Bar, adjacent to the lobby of the St. Regis Princeville Resort, are fantastic.

The North Shore attracts all kinds—from celebrities to surfers. In fact, the late Andy Irons, three-time world surfing champion, along with his brother Bruce and legend Laird Hamilton grew up riding waves along the North Shore.

HANALEI, HAENA, AND WEST

Haena is 40 miles northwest of Lihue; Hanalei is 5 miles southeast of Haena.

Crossing the historic one-lane bridge into Hanalei reveals old-world Hawaii, including working taro farms, poi making, and evenings of throwing horseshoes at Black Pot Beach Park—found unmarked (as many places are on Kauai) at the east end of Hanalei Bay Beach Park. Although the current real-estate boom on Kauai has attracted mainland millionaires to build estate homes on the few remaining parcels of land in Hanalei, there's still plenty to see and do. It's *the* gathering place on the North Shore. Restaurants, shops, and people-watching here are among the best on the island, and you won't find a single brand name, chain, or big-box store around—unless you count surf brands like Quiksilver and Billabong.

The beach and river at Hanalei offer swimming, snorkeling, body boarding, surfing, and kayaking. Those hanging around at sunset often congregate at the Hanalei Pavilion, where a husband-and-wife-slack-key-guitar-playing combo makes impromptu appearances. There's an old rumor, since quashed by the local newspaper, the *Garden Island*, that says Hanalei was the inspiration for the song "Puff the Magic Dragon," performed by the 1960s singing sensation Peter, Paul & Mary. Even with the newspaper's clarification, some tours still point out the shape of the dragon carved into the mountains encircling the town.

Once you pass through Hanalei town, the road shrinks even more as you skirt the coast and pass through Haena. Blind corners, quick turns, and one-lane bridges force slow driving along this scenic stretch across the Lumahai and Wainiha valleys.

GETTING HERE AND AROUND

There is only one road leading beyond Princeville to Kee Beach at the western end of the North Shore: Route 560. Hanalei's commercial stretch fronts this route, and you'll find parking at the shopping compounds on each side of the road. After Hanalei, parking is restricted to two main areas, Haena Beach Park and a new lot at Haena State Park, and there are few pullover areas along Route 560. Traffic and especially

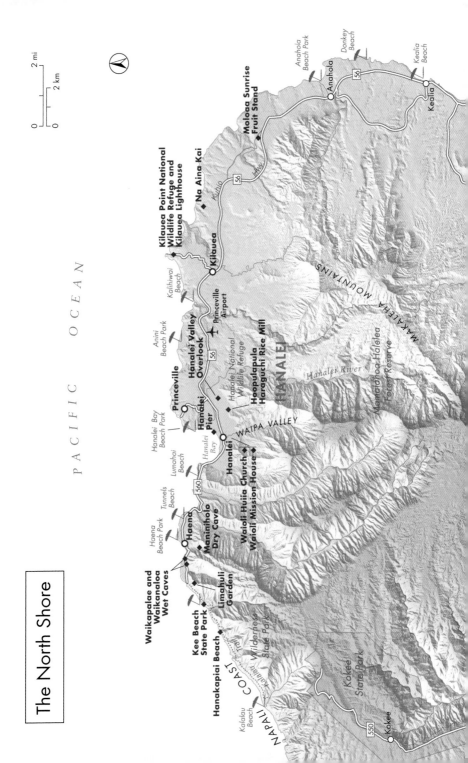

The North Shore

2 mi
2 km

PACIFIC OCEAN

Kilauea Point National
Wildlife Refuge and
Kilauea Lighthouse

Na Aina Kai

Moloaa Sunrise
Fruit Stand

Anahola Beach Park

Donkey Beach

Kealia Beach

Anahola

56

Kealia

Kuhio Hwy

Kilauea

56

Kalihiwai Beach

Princeville Airport

Anini Beach Park

Hanalei Valley Overlook

56

Princeville

Hanalei Bay Beach Park

Hanalei Pier

Hanalei National Wildlife Refuge

Hoopulapula Haraguchi Rice Mill

HANALEI

Hanalei River

Mamalahoa-Halelea Forest Reserve

MAKALEHA MOUNTAINS

Hanalei Bay

Lumahai Beach

560

Hanalei

WAIPA VALLEY

Waioli Huiia Church
Waioli Mission House

Tunnels Beach

Haena Beach Park

Haena

Maniniholo Dry Cave

Waikapalae and Waikanaloa Wet Caves

Kee Beach State Park

Limahuli Garden

Hanakapiai Beach

Kalalau Beach

NAPALI COAST

Kalalau Trail

Alakai Wilderness State Park

Kokee State Park

550

Kokee

parking have become major concerns as the North Shore has gained popularity, so be prepared to be patient.

TOP ATTRACTIONS

Hanalei Valley Overlook. Dramatic mountains and a patchwork of neat taro farms bisected by the wide Hanalei River make this one of Hawaii's loveliest sights. The fertile Hanalei Valley has been planted in taro since perhaps AD 700, save for a century-long foray into rice that ended in 1960. (The historic Haraguchi Rice Mill is all that remains of that era.) Many taro farmers lease land within the 900-acre Hanalei National Wildlife Refuge, helping to provide wetland habitat for four species of endangered Hawaiian water birds. ⊠ *Rte. 56, across from Foodland, Princeville.*

Limahuli Garden. Narrow Limahuli Valley, with its fluted mountain peaks and ancient stone taro terraces, creates an unparalleled setting for this botanical garden and nature preserve. Dedicated to protecting native plants and unusual varieties of taro, it represents the principles of conservation and stewardship held by its founder, Charles "Chipper" Wichman. Limahuli's primordial beauty and strong *mana* (spiritual power) eclipse the extensive botanical collection. It's one of the most gorgeous spots on Kauai and the crown jewel of the National Tropical Botanical Garden, which Wichman now heads. Call ahead to reserve a guided tour, or tour on your own. Be sure to check out the quality gift shop and revolutionary compost toilet, and be prepared to walk a somewhat steep hillside. ⊠ *5-8291 Kuhio Hwy., Haena* ☎ *808/826–1053* ⊕ *www.ntbg. org* ⊠ *Self-guided tour $20, guided tour $40 (reservations required)* ☺ *Tues.–Sat. 9:30–4.*

WORTH NOTING

Hanalei Pier. Built in 1892, the historic Hanalei Pier is a landmark seen from miles across the bay. It came to fame when it was featured in the award-winning 1957 movie *South Pacific*. Kids use it as a diving board, fishers fish, picnickers picnic. It's a great spot for a leisurely stroll and attracts a gathering every sunset. ⊠ *Weke Rd., Princeville.*

Hoopulapula Haraguchi Rice Mill. Rice grew in the taro fields of Hanalei Valley for almost 80 years—beginning in the 1880s and ending in the early 1960s. Today, this history is embodied in the Haraguchi family, whose ancestors threshed, hulled, polished, separated, graded, and bagged rice in their 3,500-square-foot rice mill, which was demolished once by fire and twice by hurricanes. Rebuilt to the exacting standards of the National Register of Historic Places, the mill—and neighboring taro fields—is now open for tours on a very limited schedule mainly due to endangered bird-nesting areas. The family still farms taro on the onetime rice paddies and also operates the Hanalei Taro & Juice kiosk in Hanalei town. Reservations are required for the tour, which currently runs on Wednesday. ⊠ *5-5070 Kuhio Hwy., next to Kayak Kauai, Hanalei* ☎ *808/651–3399* ⊕ *haraguchiricemill.org* ⊠ *$87.*

Maninholo Dry Cave. Kauai's North Shore caves echo an enchanting, almost haunting, alternative to sunny skies and deep blue seas. Steeped in legend, Maninholo Dry Cave darkens and becomes more claustrophobic as you glide across its sandy floor, hearing the drips down the

Hanalei Bay attracts big-wave surfers in the winter and then becomes a calm haven for swimmers in the summer.

walls and wondering at its past. Legend has it that Maniniholo was the head fisherman of the Menehune—Kauai's quasi-mythical first inhabitants. After gathering too much food to carry, his men stored the excess in the dry cave overnight. When he returned in the morning, the food had vanished and he blamed the imps living in the cracks of the cave. He and his men dug into the cliff to find and destroy the imps, leaving behind the cave. Across the highway from Maniniholo Dry Cave is Haena State Park. ⊠ *Rte. 560, Haena.*

Waikapalae and Waikanaloa Wet Caves. These wet caves are smaller (and wetter) than Maniniholo but are still visually worth a short jaunt. Said to have been dug by Pele, goddess of fire, these watering holes used to be clear, clean, and great for swimming. Now stagnant, they're nevertheless a photogenic example of the many haunting natural landmarks of Kauai's North Shore. Waikanaloa is visible right beside the highway, near the end of the road. Waikapalae is back a few hundred yards and is accessed by a five-minute uphill walk. ⊠ *Western end of Rte. 560, Haena.*

Waioli Huiia Church. Designated a National Historic Landmark, this little church—affiliated with the United Church of Christ—doesn't go unnoticed right alongside Route 560 in downtown Hanalei, and its doors are often wide open (from 9 to 5, give or take) inviting inquisitive visitors in for a look around. Like the Waioli Mission House behind it, it's an exquisite representation of New England architecture crossed with Hawaiian thatched buildings. During Hurricane Iniki's visit in 1992, which brought sustained winds of 160 mph and wind gusts up to 220 mph, this little church was lifted off its foundation but, thankfully, lovingly restored. Services are held at 10 am on Sunday with many hymns sung in Hawaiian and often accompanied by piano and ukulele. ⊠ *5-5363A Kuhio Hwy., Hanalei* ☎ *808/826–6253* ⊕ *www.hanaleichurch.org.*

Waioli Mission House. This 1837 home was built by missionaries William and Mary Alexander. Its tidy New England architecture and formal koa-wood furnishings epitomize the prim and proper missionary influence, while the informative guided tours offer a fascinating peek into the private lives of Kauai's early white residents. Half-hour guided tours are available for a $10 requested donation on Tuesday, Thursday, and Saturday from 9 to 3. ■TIP→ If no one is there when you arrive, don't despair; just ring the bell by the chimney. ⊠ *Kuhio Hwy., Hanalei* ☎ *808/245–3202* ⊕ *www.grovefarm.org* 🎫 *$10* 🕑 *Tues., Thurs., and Sat. 9–3.*

PRINCEVILLE AND KILAUEA

Princeville is 4 miles northeast of Hanalei; Kilauea is 5 miles east of Princeville.

Built on a bluff offering gorgeous sea and mountain vistas, including Hanalei Bay, Princeville is the creation of a 1970s resort development. The area is anchored by a few large hotels, world-class golf courses, and lots of condos and time-shares.

Five miles down Route 56, a former plantation town, Kilauea maintains its rural flavor in the midst of unrelenting gentrification encroaching all around it. Especially noteworthy are its historic lava-rock buildings, including **Christ Memorial Episcopal Church** on Kolo Road and, on Keneke and Kilauea Road (commonly known as Lighthouse Road), the Kong Lung Company, which is now an expensive shop.

GETTING HERE AND AROUND

There is only one main road through the Princeville resort area, so maneuvering a car here can be a nightmare. If you're trying to find a smaller lodging unit, be sure to get specific driving directions. Parking is available at the Princeville Shopping Center at the entrance to the resort. Kilauea is about 5 miles east on Route 56. There's a public parking lot in the town center as well as parking at the end of Kilauea Road for access to the lighthouse.

TOP ATTRACTIONS

Fodor'sChoice ★ **Kilauea Point National Wildlife Refuge and Kilauea Lighthouse.** A beacon for sea traffic since it was built in 1913, this National Historic Landmark celebrated its centennial in 2013 and has the largest clamshell lens of any lighthouse in the world. It's within a national wildlife refuge, where thousands of seabirds soar on the trade winds and nest on the steep ocean cliffs. Seeing endangered nene geese, white- and red-tailed tropic birds, and more (all identifiable by educational signboards) as well as native plants, dolphins, humpback whales, huge winter surf, and gorgeous views of the North Shore are well worth the modest entry fee. The gift shop has a great selection of books about the island's natural history and an array of unique merchandise, with all proceeds benefiting education and preservation efforts. ⊠ *Kilauea Lighthouse Rd., Kilauea* ☎ *808/828–1413* ⊕ *www.kilaueapoint.org, www.fws.gov/kilaueapoint* 🏷️*$5, under 15 free* ☼ *Tues.–Sat. 10–4.*

Fodor's Choice
★

Na Aina Kai. Joyce and Ed Doty's love for plants and art spans 240 acres and includes many different gardens, a hardwood plantation, a canyon, lagoons, a Japanese teahouse, a poinciana maze, a waterfall, and access to a sandy beach. Throughout are more than 160 bronze sculptures, reputedly one of the nation's largest collections. One popular feature is a children's garden with a 16-foot-tall Jack and the Beanstalk bronze sculpture, gecko maze, tree house, kid-size train, and, of course, a tropical jungle. Located in a residential neighborhood and hoping to maintain good neighborly relations, the garden, which is now a nonprofit organization, limits tours (guided only). Tour lengths vary widely, from 1½ to 5 hours. Reservations are required. ⊠ *4101 Wailapa Rd., Kilauea* ☎ *808/828–0525* ⊕ *www.naainakai.org* 🏷️*Starts at $35.*

WORTH NOTING

Moloaa Sunrise Fruit Stand. Don't let the name fool you; they don't open at sunrise (more like 7:30 am, so come here after you watch the sun rise elsewhere). And it's not just a fruit stand. Breakfast is light and includes bagels, granola, smoothies, coffee, espresso, cappuccino, latte, and, of course, tropical-style fresh juices (pineapple, carrot, watermelon, guava, even sugarcane, in season). This is also a great spot to get out and stretch, take in the mountain view, and pick up sandwiches to go. Select local produce is available, although the variety is often not as good as at the island's farmers' markets. What makes this fruit stand different is the fresh, natural ingredients like multigrain breads and *nori* (seaweed) wraps. ⊠ *6011 Koolau Rd., at Kuhio Hwy., Kilauea* ☎ *808/822–1441* ☼ *Mon.–Sat. 7:30–5, Sun. 9–3.*

NAPALI COAST

Napali Coast is considered the jewel of Kauai, and for all its greenery, it would surely be an emerald. After seeing the coast, many are at a loss for words, because its beauty is so overwhelming. Others resort to poetry. Pulitzer Prize–winning poet W. S. Merwin wrote a book-length poem, *The Folding Cliffs,* based on a true story set in Napali. *Napali* means "the cliffs," and while it sounds like a simple name, it's quite an apt description. The coastline is cut by a series of small valleys, like fault lines, running to the interior, with the resulting cliffs seeming to bend back on themselves like an accordion-folded fan made of green velvet. More than 5 million years old, these sea cliffs rise thousands of feet above the Pacific, and every shade of green is represented in the vegetation that blankets their lush peaks and folds. At their base there are caves, secluded beaches, and waterfalls to explore.

Let's put this in perspective: even if you had only one day on Kauai, we'd still recommend heading to Napali Coast on Kauai's northwest side. Once you're there, you'll soon realize why no road traverses this series of folding-fan cliffs. That leaves three ways to experience the coastline—by air, by water, or on foot. We recommend all three, in this order: air, water, foot. Each one gets progressively more sensory.(⇨ *See also the Napali feature at the beginning of this chapter.*) A helicopter tour is your best bet if you're strapped for time. We recommend Jack Harter Helicopters or Safari Helicopters (⇨ *see Aerial Tours in the Golf, Hiking, and Outdoor Activities chapter for more information*). Boat tours are great for family fun; and hiking, of course, is the most budget-friendly option.

Whatever way you choose to visit Napali, you might want to keep this awe-inspiring fact in mind: at one time, thousands of Hawaiians lived self-sufficiently in these valleys.

GETTING HERE AND AROUND

Napali Coast runs 15 miles from Kee Beach, one of Kauai's more popular snorkeling spots, on the island's North Shore to Polihale State Park, the longest stretch of beach in the state, on the West Side of the island.

How do you explore this gorgeous stretch of coastline? You can't drive to it, through it, or around it. You can't see Napali from a scenic lookout. You can't even take a mule ride to it. The only way to experience its magic is from the sky, the ocean, or the trail. The Kalalau Trail can be hiked from the "end of the road" at Kee Beach where the trailhead begins in Haena State Park at the northwest end of Kuhio Highway (Route 56). There's no need to hike the entire 11 miles to get a full experience, especially if you just hike the first 2 miles into Hanakapiai Beach and another 2 miles up that valley. ⇨ *For information on Napali Coast tour operators see the Boat Tours section in the Water Sports and Tours chapter and the Aerial Tours section in the Golf, Hiking, and Outdoor Activities chapter.*

TOP ATTRACTIONS

Kee Beach State Park. This stunning, and often extremely overcrowded beach marks the start of the majestic Napali Coast. The 11-mile **Kalalau Trail** begins near the parking lot, drawing day hikers and backpackers. Another path leads from the sand to a stone hula platform dedicated to **Laka,** the goddess of hula, which has been in use since ancient times. This is a sacred site that should be approached with respect; it's inappropriate for visitors to leave offerings at the altar, which is tended by students in a local hula *halau* (school). Local etiquette suggests observing from a distance. Most folks head straight for the sandy beach and its dreamy lagoon, which is great for snorkeling when the sea is calm. ⊠ *Western end of Rte. 560, Haena.*

WORTH NOTING

Hanakapiai Beach. Hanakapiai Beach is a small jewel you'll discover after the first 2 miles of the Napali Trail and crossing the stream. It's a beauty, with fine sand, a feeling of isolation, and a tropical stream valley to explore. Unfortunately, the beach is only swimmable in summer under the right conditions as there is often a dangerous shore break. And, at all times of the year, it's a sweep-away beach, since it is not protected as a bay would be. For relaxation, sunning, and as a solid refresher on your hiking journey, Hanakapiai offers a welcome and stunning respite. **Best for:** sunset; solitude. **Amenities:** toilets. ⊠ *Hanalei ✛ Trailhead is at the end of Rte. 560, 7 miles west of Hanalei.*

THE EAST SIDE

The East Side encompasses Lihue, Wailua, and Kapaa. It's also known as the Coconut Coast, as there was once a coconut plantation where today's aptly named Coconut Marketplace is located. A small grove still exists on both sides of the highway. *Mauka*, a fenced herd of goats keeps the grass tended; on the *makai* side, you can walk through the grove, although it's best not to walk directly under the trees—falling coconuts can be dangerous. Lihue is the county seat, and the whole East Side is the island's center of commerce, so early-morning and late-afternoon drive times (or rush hour) can get very congested. (Because there's only one main road, if there's a serious traffic accident the entire roadway may be closed, with no way around. Not to worry; it's a rarity.)

KAPAA AND WAILUA

Kapaa is 16 miles southeast of Kilauea; Wailua is 3 miles southwest of Kapaa.

Old Town Kapaa was once a plantation town, which is no surprise—most of the larger towns on Kauai once were. Old Town Kapaa is made up of a collection of wooden-front shops, some built by plantation workers and still run by their progeny today. Kapaa houses the two biggest grocery stores on the island, side by side: Foodland and Safeway. It also offers plenty of dining options for breakfast, lunch, and dinner, and gift shopping. If the timing is right, plan to cruise the town on the first Saturday evening of each month when the bands are playing and the town's wares are on display. To the south, Wailua comprises a few restaurants and shops, a few midrange resorts along the coastline, and a housing community *mauka*.

GETTING HERE AND AROUND

Turn to the right out of the airport at Lihue for the road to Wailua. Careful, though—the zone between Lihue and Wailua has been the site of many car accidents. Two bridges—under which the very culturally significant Wailua River gently flows—mark the beginning of Wailua. It quickly blends into Kapaa; there's no real demarcation. Pay attention and drive carefully, always knowing where you are going and when to turn off.

TOP ATTRACTIONS

FAMILY **Opaekaa Falls.** The mighty Wailua River produces many dramatic waterfalls, and Opaekaa (pronounced oh-pie-kah-ah) is one of the best. It plunges hundreds of feet to the pool below and can be easily viewed from a scenic overlook with ample parking. Opaekaa means "rolling shrimp," which refers to tasty native crustaceans that were once so abundant they could be seen tumbling in the falls. Do not attempt to hike down to the pool. ■TIP➜ **Just before reaching the parking area for the waterfalls, turn left into a scenic pullout for great views of the Wailua River valley and its march to the sea.** ⊠ *Kuamoo Rd., Wailua (Kauai County)* ⊹ *From Rte. 56, turn mauka onto Kuamoo Rd. and drive 1½ miles.*

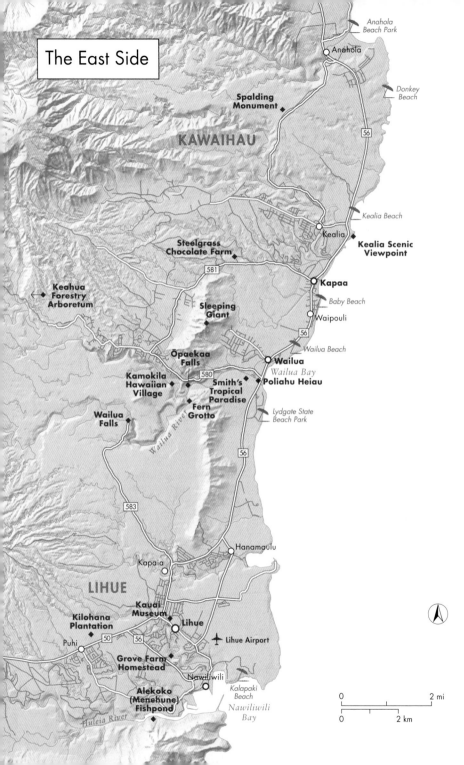

The East Side

Anahola Beach Park

Anahola

Donkey Beach

Spalding Monument

KAWAIHAU

56

Kealia Beach

Steelgrass Chocolate Farm

Kealia

Kealia Scenic Viewpoint

581

Kapaa

Keahua Forestry Arboretum

Baby Beach

Sleeping Giant

Waipouli

56

Ōpaekaa Falls

Wailua Beach

580

Wailua

Wailua Bay

Kamokila Hawaiian Village

Smith's Tropical Paradise

Poliahu Heiau

Fern Grotto

Lydgate State Beach Park

Wailua Falls

Wailua River

56

583

Hanamaulu

Kapaia

LIHUE

Kauai Museum

Kilohana Plantation

Lihue

Puhi

50

56

Lihue Airport

Grove Farm Homestead

Nawiliwili

Alekoko (Menehune) Fishpond

Kalapaki Beach

Nawiliwili Bay

Huleia River

0   2 mi

0   2 km

Poliahu Heiau. Storyboards near this ancient *heiau* (sacred site) recount the significance of the many sacred structures found along the Wailua River. It's unknown exactly how the ancient Hawaiians used Poliahu Heiau—one of the largest pre-Christian temples on the island—but legend says it was built by the Menehune because of the unusual stonework found in its walled enclosures. From this site, drive downhill toward the ocean to *pohaku hanau*, a two-piece birthing stone said to confer special blessings on all children born there, and *pohaku piko*, whose crevices were a repository for umbilical cords left by parents seeking a clue to their child's destiny, which reportedly was foretold by how the cord fared in the rock. Some Hawaiians feel these sacred stones shouldn't be viewed as tourist attractions, so always treat them with respect. Never stand or sit on the rocks or leave any offerings. ⊠ *Rte. 580, Kuamoo Rd., Wailua (Kauai County)*.

> ## ROADSIDE VENDORS
>
> Lei. Tropical flowers. Corn. Rambutan. Avocados. Huli huli chicken. Kalua pig. It's not uncommon to run across individuals selling flowers, produce, and food on the side of the road. Some are local farmers trying to make a living; others are people fund-raising for the local canoe club. Don't be afraid to stop and buy. Most are friendly and enjoy chatting.

FAMILY **Wailua Falls.** You may recognize this impressive cascade from the opening sequences of the *Fantasy Island* television series. Kauai has plenty of noteworthy waterfalls, but this one is especially gorgeous, easy to find, and easy to photograph. ⊠ *Maalo Rd., off Rte. 580, Lihue*.

WORTH NOTING

Fern Grotto. The Fern Grotto has a long history on Kauai. For some reason, visitors seem to like it. Perhaps it's the serenity of just cruising up and down the river accompanied by Hawaiian music. The grotto itself is nothing more than a yawning lava tube swathed in lush fishtail ferns 3 miles up the Wailua River. Though it was significantly damaged after Hurricane Iniki in 1992 and again after heavy rains in 2006, the greenery has completely recovered. Smith's Motor Boat Services is the only way to legally see the grotto. You can access the entrance with a kayak, but if boats are there, you may not be allowed to land. ⊠ *Rte. 56, just south of Wailua River, Kapaa* ☎ *808/821–6893* ⊕ *smithskauai. com* ⊟ *$20* ⊘ *Daily departures 9:30–3:30*.

FAMILY **Kamokila Hawaiian Village.** The village is dramatically ensconced at the base of a steep, long, winding road right down to the Wailua River. In the days of King Kaumualii, it made the perfect hideout to tuck away his war canoes in this crook of the river. Today, there's a replica Hawaiian village in place of war canoes—numerous thatched-roof structures and abundant plant life along with traditional Hawaiian games. Yet, the lack of human activity here makes it seem abandoned, which may be why Hollywood found it an appealing location for the movie *Outbreak*. Visitors can rent canoes for the day and paddle up to the Fern Grotto or Secret Falls. ⊠ *5443 Kuamoo Rd., Kapaa* ☎ *808/823–0559* ⊕ *www.villagekauai.com* ⊟ *$5* ⊘ *Daily 9–5*.

Keahua Forestry Arboretum. Tree-lined and grassy, this is a perfect spot for a picnic—and there are lots of picnic tables scattered throughout the parklike setting. A shallow, cascading stream makes for a fun spot for kids to splash, although the water's a bit chilly. A 1-mile walking trail meanders through mango, monkeypod, and exquisite rainbow eucalyptus trees. This is an exceptionally peaceful place—good for yoga and meditation—that is, unless the resident roosters decide to crow. ■ TIP➜ If it looks like rain, don't follow the road across the stream; it often floods, and could leave you stranded on one side. ⊠ *Kuamoo Rd., Wailua (Kauai County)* ⊙ *Daily dawn–dusk.*

Kealia Scenic Viewpoint. This ocean overlook is perfect for spotting whales during their winter migration. In fact, on three Saturdays in winter, the Hawaiian Islands Humpback Whale National Marine Sanctuary conducts its annual whale count from this spot, one of several around the island. The lookout was rebuilt and doubled in size a few years ago, and it's now easy to hop on the cement bike and walking path just below for a coastal stroll or ride. Most days you can see clear to Lihue and beyond. If you packed them, bring your binoculars. ⊠ *Rte. 56, between mile markers 9 and 10, Kapaa.*

Sleeping Giant. Although its true name is Nounou, this landmark mountain ridge is better known as the Sleeping Giant because of its resemblance to a very large man sleeping on his back. Legends differ on whether the giant is Puni, who was accidentally killed by rocks launched at invading canoes by the Menehune, or Nunui, a gentle creature who has not yet awakened from the nap he took centuries ago after building a massive temple and enjoying a big feast. ⊠ *Rte. 56, about 1 mile north of Wailua River, Kapaa.*

FAMILY **Smith's Tropical Paradise.** Nestled next to Wailua Marina along the mighty Wailua River, this 30-acre botanical and cultural garden offers a glimpse of exotic foliage, including fruit orchards, a bamboo rain forest, and tropical lagoons. Take the tram and enjoy a narrated tour or stroll along the mile-long pathways during the luau. It's a popular spot for wedding receptions and other large events, and its nightly luau is one of the island's oldest and best. ⊠ *3-5971 Kuhio Hwy., just south of Wailua River, Kapaa* 🕾 *808/821–6895* ⊕ *smithskauai.com.*

Spalding Monument. The Colonel Zephaniah Spalding monument commemorates the Civil War veteran who purchased this splendid property overlooking an area from Anahola to Kapaa in 1876 and soon established what became the Kealia Sugar Plantation. Turn onto Kealia Road just after mile marker 10 for an off-the-beaten-track scenic detour. Immediately on your right are a small post office and a food truck and, on your left, rodeo grounds often in use on summer weekends. The road ascends, and 2½ miles later you'll reach a grassy area with the concrete remains of a onetime monument. It's a nice spot to picnic or to simply gaze at the nearby grazing horses. If you're an early riser, this is a great spot to watch the sun rise; if not, check the local newspaper for the next full moon and bring a bottle of wine. It's possible to continue on for another very bumpy 2 miles, where you'll reconnect with Highway 56

One of the best places for a luau is here at Smith's Tropical Paradise.

near the town of Anahola, but your bike or car will not thank you for it. You're better off doubling back. ⊠ *Kealia Rd., Kapaa.*

Steelgrass Chocolate Farm. Hawaii is the only state in the country where *theobroma cacao* grows. As every chocolate connoisseur knows, the tree that grows the precious seed that becomes chocolate is the cacao tree. The Lydgates are on a mission to grow enough cacao on their family farm with the hope that one day they will produce an identifiable Kauai homegrown chocolate. For now, you can tour this organic farm (in addition to cacao, they grow vanilla, timber, bamboo, and many tropical fruits) and learn how chocolate is made,"from branch to bar," as they put it. The three-hour tour includes, of course, plenty of chocolate tastings. Reservations are required for the morning tour, which begins Monday, Wednesday, and Friday at 9 am. Children 12 and under are free. ⊠ *5730 Olohena Rd., Kapaa* ☎ *808/821–1857* ⊕ *www.steelgrass.org* 🎫 *$75; children under 12 free* ☉ *Mon., Wed., and Fri. at 9 am for tours only.*

LIHUE

7 miles southwest of Wailua.

The commercial and political center of Kauai County, which includes the islands of Kauai and Niihau, Lihue is home to the island's major airport, harbor, and hospital. This is where you can find the state and county offices that issue camping and hiking permits and the same fast-food eateries and big-box stores that blight the mainland. The county is seeking help in reviving the downtown; for now, once your business is done, there's little reason to linger in lackluster Lihue.

GETTING HERE AND AROUND

Route 56 leads into Lihue from the north and Route 50 comes here from the south and west. The road from the airport (where Kauai's car rental agencies are) leads to the middle of Lihue. Many of the area's stores and restaurants are on and around Rice Street, which also leads to Kalapaki Bay and Nawiliwili Harbor.

TOP ATTRACTIONS

Kauai Museum. Maintaining a stately presence on Rice Street, the historic museum building is easy to find. It features a permanent display, "The Story of Kauai," which provides a competent overview of the Garden Island and Niihau, tracing the Islands' geology, mythology, and cultural history. Local artists are represented in changing exhibits in the second-floor Mezzanine Gallery. The expanded gift shop alone is worth a visit, with a fine collection of authentic Niihau shell lei, feather hatband lei, hand-turned wooden bowls, reference books, and other quality arts, crafts, and gifts—many of them locally made. ⊠ *4428 Rice St., Lihue* ☎ *808/245-6931* ⊕ *www.kauaimuseum.org* ☜ *$10* ۞ *Mon.–Sat. 10–5.*

WORTH NOTING

Alekoko (Menehune) Fishpond. No one knows just who built this intricate aquaculture structure in the Huleia River. Legend attributes it to the Menehune, a mythical—or real, depending on who you ask—ancient race of people known for their small stature, industrious nature, and superb stoneworking skills. Volcanic rock was cut and fit together into massive walls 4 feet thick and 5 feet high, forming an enclosure for raising mullet and other freshwater fish that has endured for centuries. ⊠ *Hulemalu Rd., Niumalu.*

Grove Farm Homestead. Guided tours of this carefully restored 80-acre country estate offer a fascinating and authentic look at how upper-class Caucasians experienced plantation life in the mid-19th century. The tour focuses on the original home, built by the Wilcox family in 1860 and filled with a quirky collection of classic Hawaiiana. You can also see the workers' quarters, farm animals, orchards, and gardens that reflect the practical, self-sufficient lifestyle of the island's earliest Western inhabitants. Tours of the homestead are conducted twice a day, three days a week. To protect the historic building and its furnishings, tours may be canceled on very wet days. ■TIP➔ With a six-person limit per tour, reservations are essential. ⊠ *4050 Nawiliwili Rd., Lihue* ☎ *808/245-3202* ⊕ *www.grovefarm.org* ☜ *$20 requested donation* ۞ *Tours Mon., Wed., and Thurs. at 10 and 1.*

FAMILY **Kilohana Plantation.** This estate dates back to 1850, shortly after the "Great Mahele"—the division of land by the Hawaiian people. Plantation manager Albert Spencer Wilcox developed it as a working cattle ranch, and his nephew, Gaylord Parke Wilcox, took over in 1936, building Kauai's first mansion. Today the 16,000-square-foot, Tudor-style home houses specialty shops, art galleries, the Koloa Rum Co. and Gaylord's, a pretty restaurant with courtyard seating. Nearly half the original furnishings remain, and the gardens and orchards were

SUNSHINE MARKETS

If you want to rub elbows with the locals and purchase fresh produce and flowers at reasonable prices, head for Sunshine Markets, also known as Kauai's farmers' markets. These busy markets are held weekly, usually in the afternoon, at locations all around the island. They're good fun, and they support neighborhood farmers. Arrive a little early, bring dollar bills to speed up transactions and your own shopping bags to carry your produce, and be prepared for some pushy shoppers. Farmers are usually happy to educate visitors about unfamiliar fruits and veggies, especially when the crowd thins. For schedules and information on Sunshine Markets, call ☎ 808/241–6303; and check out Kauai's government website at ⊕ www.kauai.gov.

East Side Sunshine Markets
✉ Vidinha Stadium, Lihue, ½ mile south of airport on Rte. 51, ☯ Fri. 3 pm. ✉ Kapaa, turn mauka on Rte. 581/Olohena Rd. for 1 block, ☯ Wed. 3 pm.

North Shore Sunshine Markets
✉ Waipa, mauka of Rte. 560 north of Hanalei after mile marker 3, Hanalei, ☯ Tues. 2 pm. ✉ Kilauea Neighborhood Center, on Keneke St., Kilauea, ☯ Thurs. 4:30 pm. ✉ Hanalei Community Center, ☯ Sat. 9:30 am.

South Shore Sunshine Markets
✉ Ballpark, Koloa, north of intersection of Koloa Road and Rte. 520, ☯ Mon. noon.

West Side Sunshine Markets
✉ Kalaheo Community Center, on Papalina Rd. just off Kaumualii Hwy., Kalaheo, ☯ Tues. 3 pm. ✉ Hanapepe Park, Hanapepe, ☯ Thurs. 3 pm. ✉ Kekaha Neighborhood Center, Elepaio Rd., Kekaha, ☯ Sat. 9 am.

replanted according to the original plans. You can tour the grounds for free, or take a short train ride and learn the agricultural story of Kauai while viewing a working farm. ✉ *3-2087 Kaumualii Hwy., Lihue* ☎ *808/245–5608* ⊕ *www.kilohanakauai.com* ☞ *Train tours for adults are $19, children $14.*

THE SOUTH SHORE

As you follow the main road south from Lihue, the landscape becomes lush and densely vegetated before giving way to drier conditions that characterize Poipu, the South Side's major resort area. Poipu owes much of its popularity to a steady supply of sunshine and a string of sandy beaches, although the beaches are smaller and more covelike than those on the West Side. With its extensive selection of accommodations, services, and activities, the South Shore attracts more visitors than any other area of Kauai. It also attracted developers with big plans for the onetime sugarcane fields that are nestled in this region and enveloped by mountains. There are few roads in and out, and local residents are concerned about increased traffic as well as noise and dust pollution as a result of chronic construction. If you're planning to stay on the South Side, be sure to ask if your hotel, condo, or vacation rental will be impacted by the development during your visit.

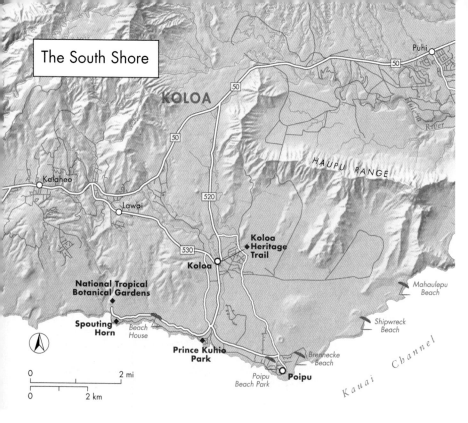

KOLOA

Puhi

HAUPU RANGE

Kalaheo

Lawai

Koloa
◆ Heritage
Trail

Koloa

National Tropical
Botanical Gardens

Mahaulepu
Beach

Spouting
Horn   Beach
House

Shipwreck
Beach

Prince Kuhio
Park

Brennecke
Beach

Poipu
Beach Park   Poipu

Kauai   Channel

0   2 mi

0   2 km

Both Poipu and nearby Koloa (site of Kauai's first sugar mill) can be reached via Route 520 (Maluhia Road) from the Lihue area. Route 520 is known locally as Tree Tunnel Road, due to the stand of eucalyptus trees lining the road that were planted at the turn of the 20th century by Walter Duncan McBryde, a Scotsman who began cattle ranching on Kauai's South Shore. The canopy of trees was ripped to literal shreds twice—in 1982 during Hurricane Iwa and again in 1992 during Hurricane Iniki. And, true to Kauai, both times the trees grew back into an impressive tunnel. It's a distinctive way to announce, "You are now on vacation," for there's a definite feel of leisure in the air here. There's still plenty to do—snorkel, bike, walk, horseback ride, take an ATV tour, surf, scuba dive, shop, and dine—everything you'd want on a tropical vacation. From the west, Route 530 (Koloa Road) slips into downtown Koloa, a string of fun shops and restaurants, at an intersection with the only gas station on the South Shore.

KOLOA

11 miles southwest of Lihue.

Hawaii's lucrative foray into sugar was born in this sleepy town, where the first sugar was milled back in 1830. You can still see the mill's old stone smokestack. Little else remains, save for the charming

2

plantation-style buildings that have kept Koloa from becoming a tacky tourist trap for Poipu-bound visitors. The original small-town character has been preserved by converting historic structures along the main street into boutiques, restaurants, and shops. Placards describe the original tenants and life in the old mill town. Look for Koloa Fish Market, which offers poke and sashimi takeout, and Progressive Expressions, a popular local surf shop.

WORTH NOTING

Koloa Heritage Trail. Throughout the South Shore, you'll find brass plaques with details of 14 historical stops along the 10-mile Koloa Heritage Trail—bike it, hike it, or drive it, your choice. You'll learn about Koloa's whaling history, sugar industry, ancient Hawaiian cultural sites, the island's volcanic formation, and more. Pick up a free self-guided trail map at most any shop in Koloa town. ⊠ *Koloa.*

POIPU

2 miles southeast of Koloa.

Thanks to its generally sunny weather and a string of golden-sand beaches dotted with oceanfront lodgings, Poipu is a top choice for many visitors. Beaches are user-friendly, with protected waters for *keiki* (children) and novice snorkelers, lifeguards, restrooms, covered pavilions, and a sweet coastal promenade ideal for leisurely strolls. Some experts have even ranked Poipu Beach Park number one in the nation. It depends on your preferences, of course, though it certainly does warrant high accolades.

GETTING HERE AND AROUND

Poipu is the one area on Kauai where you could get by without a car, though that could mean an expensive taxi ride from the airport and limited access to other parts of the island. To reach Poipu by car, follow Poipu Road south from Koloa. After the traffic circle, the road curves to follow the coast, leading to some of the popular South Shore beaches.

WORTH NOTING

National Tropical Botanical Gardens (*NTBG*). Tucked away in Lawai Valley, these gardens include lands and a cottage once used by Hawaii's Queen Emma for a summer retreat. Trams depart on the half hour to transport people from the visitor center to the gardens. The rambling 252-acre McBryde Gardens has a number of new exhibits to help visitors learn about biodiversity and plants collected throughout the tropics on self-guided tours. It is known as a garden of "research and conservation." The 100-acre Allerton Gardens, which can be visited only on a guided tour, artfully displays statues and water features that were originally developed as part of a private estate. Reservations are required to visit both gardens. The visitor center has a high-quality gift shop with botany-theme merchandise. Besides harboring and propagating rare and endangered plants from Hawaii and elsewhere, NTBG functions as a scientific research and education center. The organization also operates gardens in Limahuli, on Kauai's North Shore, and in Hana, on Maui's east shore, as well as one in Florida. ⊠ *4425 Lawai Rd., Poipu* ☎ *808/742–2623* ⊕ *www.ntbg.org* ✉ *McBryde self-guided tour $30, Allerton guided tour $45* ☺ *Trams depart between 9 am and 3 pm.*

Brennecke's Beach Broiler. Stop in at Brennecke's Beach Broiler, a longtime fixture on the beach in Poipu. After a day of sun, this is a perfect spot to chill out with a mango margarita or mai tai, paired with a yummy pupu platter. ✉ *2100 Hoone Rd., Poipu* ☏ *808/742-7588* ⊕ *www.brenneckes.com.*

Prince Kuhio Park. A triangle of grass behind the Prince Kuhio condominiums honors the birthplace of Kauai's beloved Prince Jonah Kuhio Kalanianaole. Known for his kind nature and good deeds, he lost his chance at the throne when Americans staged an illegal overthrow of Queen Liliuokalani in 1893 and toppled Hawaii's constitutional monarchy. This is a great place to view wave riders surfing a popular break known as PKs and to watch the sun sink into the Pacific. ✉ *Lawai Rd., Poipu.*

Spouting Horn. If the conditions are right, you can see a natural blowhole in the reef behaving like Old Faithful, shooting saltwater high into the air and making a cool, echoing sound. It's most dramatic during big summer swells, which jam large quantities of water through an ancient lava tube with great force. Vendors hawk inexpensive souvenirs and collectibles in the parking lot. You may find good deals on shell jewelry, but some vendors also carry exotic Niihau-shell creations with prices up to $12,000. ✉ *End of Lawai Rd., Poipu.*

THE WEST SIDE

Exploring the West Side is akin to visiting an entirely different world. The landscape is dramatic and colorful: a patchwork of green, blue, black, and orange. The weather is hot and dry, the beaches are long, the sand is dark. Niihau, a private island and the last remaining place in Hawaii where Hawaiian is spoken exclusively, can be glimpsed offshore. This is rural Kauai, where sugar is making its last stand and taro is still cultivated in the fertile river valleys. The lifestyle is slow, easy, and traditional, with many folks fishing and hunting to supplement their diets. Here and there modern industry has intruded into this pastoral scene: huge generators turn oil into electricity at Port Allen; seed companies cultivate experimental crops of genetically engineered plants in Kekaha and Waimea; the navy launches rockets at Mana to test the "Star Wars" missile defense system; and NASA mans a tracking station in the wilds of Kokee. It's a region of contrasts that simply shouldn't be missed.

Heading west from Lihue or Poipu, you pass through a string of tiny towns, plantation camps, and historic sites, each with a story to tell of centuries past. There's Hanapepe, whose coastal salt ponds have been harvested since ancient times; Kaumakani, where the sugar industry still clings to life; Fort Elisabeth, from which an enterprising Russian tried to take over the island in the early 1800s; and Waimea, where Captain Cook made his first landing in the Islands, forever changing the face of Hawaii.

From Waimea town you can head up into the mountains, skirting the rim of magnificent Waimea Canyon and climbing higher still until you reach the cool, often-misty forests of Kokee State Park. From the vantage point at the top of this gemlike island, 3,200 to 4,200 feet above sea level, you can gaze into the deep, verdant valleys of the North Shore and Napali Coast. This is where the "real" Kauai can still be found: the native plants, insects, and birds that are found nowhere else on Earth.

HANAPEPE

15 miles west of Poipu.

In the 1980s Hanapepe was fast becoming a ghost town, its farm-based economy mirroring the decline of agriculture. Today it's a burgeoning art colony with galleries, crafts studios, and a lively art-theme street fair on Friday nights. The main street has a new vibrancy enhanced by the restoration of several historic buildings. The emergence of Kauai coffee as a major West Side crop, and expanded activities at Port Allen, now the main departure point for tour boats, also gave the town's economy a boost.

GETTING HERE AND AROUND

Hanapepe, locally known as Kauai's "biggest little town," is just past the Eleele Shopping Center on the main highway (Route 50). A sign leads you to the town center, where street parking is easy and there's an enjoyable walking tour.

TOP ATTRACTIONS

Hanapepe Swinging Bridge. This bridge may not be the biggest adventure on Kauai, but it's enough to make your heart hop. It's considered a historic suspension bridge even though it was rebuilt in 1996 after the original was destroyed—like so much of the island—by Hurricane Iniki. What is interesting about this bridge is that it's not just for show; it actually provides the only access to taro fields across the Waimea River. If you're in the neighborhood, it's worth a stroll. ⊠ *Off Hanapepe Rd., next to Banana Patch Studios parking lot, Hanapepe.*

Hanapepe Valley and Canyon Lookout. This dramatic divide and fertile river valley once housed a thriving Hawaiian community of taro farmers, with some of the ancient fields still in cultivation today. From the lookout, you can take in the farms on the valley floor with the majestic mountains as a backdrop. ⊠ *Rte. 50, Hanapepe.*

WORTH NOTING

Hanapepe Walking Tour. This 1½-mile self-guided walking tour takes you to 14 different plaques with historic photos and stories mounted on buildings throughout Hanapepe town. Businesses and shops in town sell a map of the tour for $2; however, you can often pick one up free with a coupon found in many guidebooks on promotional-brochure rack stands. ⊠ *Hanapepe town.*

Kauai Coffee Visitor Center and Museum. Two restored camp houses, dating from the days when sugar was the main agricultural crop on the Islands, have been converted into a museum, visitor center, and gift shop. About 3,100 acres of McBryde sugar land have become Hawaii's largest coffee plantation, producing more than 50% of the state's beans. You can walk among the trees, view old grinders and roasters, watch a video to learn how coffee is processed, sample various estate roasts, and check

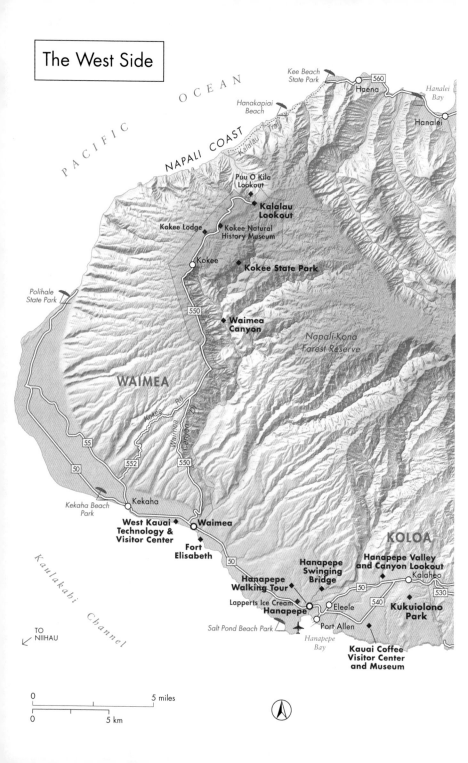

The West Side

PACIFIC OCEAN

Kee Beach
State Park

Haena · 560

Hanalei
Bay

Hanalei

Hanakapiai
Beach

NAPALI COAST

Kalalau Trail

Puu O Kila
Lookout

**Kalalau
Lookout**

Kokee Lodge ◆ · Kokee Natural
History Museum

○ Kokee

◆ **Kokee State Park**

Polihale
State Park

550

◆ **Waimea
Canyon**

*Napali-Kona
Forest Reserve*

WAIMEA

Kokee Rd.

Waimea Canyon Dr.

55

552

550

Kekaha Beach
Park

○ Kekaha

50

West Kauai ◆
**Technology &
Visitor Center**

◆ **Waimea**

KOLOA

**Fort
Elisabeth**

50

**Hanapepe
Swinging
Bridge**

**Hanapepe Valley
and Canyon Lookout**

Kalaheo ○

**Hanapepe
Walking Tour**

50

540

530

Kaulakahi Channel

Lapperts Ice Cream
Hanapepe

◆ Eleele

**Kukuiolono
Park**

TO
NIIHAU

Salt Pond Beach Park

Port Allen

*Hanapepe
Bay*

**Kauai Coffee
Visitor Center
and Museum**

| 0 | | 5 miles |
| 0 | | 5 km |

out the gift store. The center offers a 15-minute self-guided tour with well-marked signs through a small coffee grove as well as free guided tours daily. From Kalaheo, take Highway 50 in the direction of Waimea Canyon (west) and veer left onto Highway 540. It's 2½ miles from the Highway 50 turnoff. ⊠ *870 Halawili Rd., Kalaheo* ☎ *808/335–0813* ⊕ *www.kauaicoffee.com* 🔒 *Free* ☉ *Daily 9–5.*

QUICK BITES
Lappert's Ice Cream. It's not ice cream on Kauai if it's not Lappert's Ice Cream. Guava, mac nut, pineapple, mango, coconut, banana—Lappert's is the ice-cream capital of Kauai. Warning: even at the factory store in Hanapepe, the prices are no bargain. But, hey, you gotta try it. ⊠ *1-3555 Kaumualii Hwy., Hanapepe* ☎ *808/335-6121* ⊕ *www.lappertshawaii.com.*

Kukuiolono Park. Translated as "Light of the God Lono," Kukuiolono has serene Japanese gardens, a display of significant Hawaiian stones, and spectacular panoramic views. This quiet hilltop park is one of Kauai's most scenic areas and an ideal picnic spot. There's also a small golf course. ⊠ *Papalina Rd., Kalaheo* ☎ *808/332–9151* 🔒 *Free* ☉ *Daily 6:30–6:30.*

WAIMEA AND WAIMEA CANYON

Waimea is 7 miles northwest of Hanapepe; Waimea Canyon is approximately 10 miles northeast of Waimea.

Waimea is a serene, pretty town that has the look of the Old West and the feel of Old Hawaii, with a lifestyle that's decidedly laid-back. It's an ideal place for a refreshment break while sightseeing on the West Side. The town has played a major role in Hawaiian history since 1778, when Captain James Cook became the first European to set foot on the Hawaiian Islands. Waimea was also the place where Kauai's King Kaumualii acquiesced to King Kamehameha's unification drive in 1810, averting a bloody war. The town hosted the first Christian missionaries, who hauled in massive timbers and limestone blocks to build the sturdy Waimea Christian Hawaiian and Foreign Church in 1846. It's one of many lovely historic buildings preserved by residents who take great pride in their heritage and history.

North of Waimea town, via Route 550, you'll find the vast and gorgeous Waimea Canyon, also known as the Grand Canyon of the Pacific. The spectacular vistas from the lookouts along the road culminate with an overview of Kalalau Valley. There are various hiking trails leading to the inner heart of Kauai. A camera is a necessity in this region.

GETTING HERE AND AROUND

Route 50 continues northwest to Waimea and Kekaha from Hanapepe. You can reach Waimea Canyon and Kokee State Park from either town—the way is clearly marked. Some pull-off areas on Route 550 are fine for a quick view of the canyon, but the designated lookouts have bathrooms and parking.

TOP ATTRACTIONS

Fort Elisabeth. The ruins of this stone fort, built in 1816 by an agent of the imperial Russian government named Anton Scheffer, are reminders of the days when Scheffer tried to conquer the island for his homeland, or so one story goes. Another claims that Scheffer's allegiance lay with King Kaumualii, who was attempting to regain leadership of his island nation from the grasp of Kamehameha the Great. The crumbling walls of the fort are not particularly interesting, but the signs loaded with historical information are. ⊠ *Rte. 50, Waimea (Kauai County).*

Kalalau Lookout. At the end of the road, high above Waimea Canyon, Kalalau Lookout marks the start of a 1-mile (one way) hike to **Puu o Kila Lookout.** On a clear day at either spot, you can see a dreamy landscape of gaping valleys, sawtooth ridges, waterfalls, and turquoise seas, where whales can be seen spouting and breaching during the winter months. If clouds block the view, don't despair—they tend to blow through fast, giving you time to snap that photo of a lifetime. You may spot wild goats clambering on the sheer, rocky cliffs, and white tropic birds. If it's very clear to the northwest, look for the shining sands of Kalalau Beach, gleaming like golden threads against the deep blue of the Pacific. ⊠ *Waimea Canyon Dr. ✛ 4 miles north of Kokee State Park.*

Kokee State Park. This 4,345-acre wilderness park is 3,600 feet above sea level, an elevation that affords you breathtaking views in all directions and a cooler, wetter climate. You can gain a deeper appreciation of the island's rugged terrain and dramatic beauty from this vantage point. Large tracts of native ohia and koa forest cover much of the land, along with many varieties of exotic plants. Hikers can follow a 45-mile network of trails through diverse landscapes that feel wonderfully remote—until the tour helicopters pass overhead. ⊠ *Hwy. 50, 15 miles north of Kekaha, Kekaha* ⊕ *kokee.org.*

Kokee Natural History Museum. When you arrive at Kokee State Park, Kokee Natural History Museum is a great place to start your visit. The friendly staff is knowledgeable about trail conditions and weather, while informative displays and a good selection of reference books can teach you more about the unique attributes of the native flora and fauna. You may also find that special memento or gift you've been looking for. ⊠ *Rte. 550, Kokee* ☎ *808/335–3353* ⊕ *kokee.org* ✉ *Donations accepted* ☉ *Daily 9–4.*

QUICK
BITES

Kokee Lodge. There's only one place to buy food and hot drinks in Kokee State Park, and that's the dining room of rustic Kokee Lodge. It's known for its Portugese bean soup and corn bread, of all things. Peruse the gift shop for T-shirts, postcards, or campy Kokee memorabilia. ⊠ *Kokee State Park, 3600 Kokee Rd., mile marker 15, Kokee* ☎ *808/335–6061* ⊕ *www.thelodgeatkokee.net* ☉ *No dinner.*

Fodor'sChoice
★

Waimea Canyon. Carved over countless centuries by the Waimea River and the forces of wind and rain, Waimea Canyon is a dramatic gorge nicknamed the "Grand Canyon of the Pacific"—but not by Mark Twain, as many people mistakenly think. Hiking and hunting trails wind through the canyon, which is 3,600 feet deep, 2 miles wide, and 10

DID YOU KNOW?

It's possible to see vast stretches of the Kalalau Valley from Kokee State Park, which is about 4,000 feet above sea level.

miles long. The cliff sides have been sharply eroded, exposing swatches of colorful soil. The deep red, brown, and green hues are constantly changing in the sun, and frequent rainbows and waterfalls enhance the natural beauty. This is one of Kauai's prettiest spots, and it's worth stopping at both the **Puu ka Pele** and **Puu Hinahina** lookouts. Clean public restrooms and parking are at both lookouts. ⊠ *Hwy. 550 (Kokee Rd.), Waimea (Kauai County)* ☎ *808/274–3444* ⊕ *dlnr.hawaii.gov/dsp/ parks/kauai/.*

WORTH NOTING

West Kauai Technology & Visitor Center. Cultural information and local exhibits highlight this museum-style resource center in the middle of Waimea town. Weekly events include historic walks and lei making with reservations required. This small center has a gift shop with island-made items, Niihau shell jewelry, books, and more. ⊠ *9565 Kaumualii Hwy., (Rte. 50), Waimea (Kauai County)* ☎ *808/338–1332* 🖅 *Free* ⊙ *Weekdays 10–4.*

3

BEACHES

Updated by
Joan Conrow

Kauai may be nicknamed the Garden Island, but with more sandy beaches per mile of coastline than any other Hawaiian Island, it could easily be called the Sandy Island as well. Totaling more than 50 miles, Kauai's beaches make up 44% of the island's shoreline—almost twice that of Oahu, second on this list.

It is, of course, because of Kauai's age as the eldest sibling of the inhabited Hawaiian Islands, allowing more time for water and wind erosion to break down rock and coral into sand.

But not all of Kauai's beaches are the same. Each beach is unique unto itself. Conditions and scenery can change throughout the day and certainly throughout the year, transforming, say, a tranquil, lakelike ocean setting in summer into monstrous waves drawing internationally ranked surfers from around the world in winter.

There are sandy beaches, rocky beaches, wide beaches, narrow beaches, skinny beaches, and alcoves. Generally speaking, surf kicks up on the North Shore in winter and the South Shore in summer, although summer's southern swells aren't nearly as frequent or as big as the northern winter swells that attract those surfers. Kauai's longest and widest beaches are found on the North Shore and West Side and are popular with beachgoers, although during winter's rains, everyone heads to the drier South Shore and West Side. The East Side beaches tend to be narrower and have onshore winds less popular with sunbathers, yet fishers abound. Smaller coves are characteristic of the South Shore and attract all kinds of water lovers year-round, including monk seals.

In Hawaii, all beaches are public, but their accessibility varies greatly. Some require an easy ½-mile stroll, some require a four-wheel-drive vehicle, others require boulder-hopping, and one takes an entire day of serious hiking. And then there are those "drive-in" beaches adjacent to parking areas. Kauai is not Disneyland, so don't expect much signage to help you along the way. One of the top-ranked beaches in the whole world—Hanalei—doesn't have a single sign in town directing you to the beach. Furthermore, the majority of Kauai's beaches on Kauai's vast coastline are remote, offering no facilities. It's important to note that drownings are common on Kauai, in part because many beaches have no lifeguards and tricky ocean conditions. When in doubt, stay out. ■TIP➔ **If you want the convenience of restrooms, picnic tables, lifeguards, and the like, stick to county beach parks.**

THE NORTH SHORE

If you've ever dreamed of Hawaii—and who hasn't—you've dreamed of Kauai's North Shore. *Lush*, *tropical*, and *abundant* are just a few words to describe this rugged and dramatic area. And the views to the sea aren't the only attraction—the inland views of velvety-green valley folds and carved mountain peaks will take your breath away. Rain is the reason for all the greenery on the North Shore, and winter is the rainy season. Not to worry, though; it rarely rains *everywhere* on the island at one time. ■TIP➔ **The rule of thumb is to head south or west when it rains in the north.**

The waves on the North Shore can be big—and we mean huge—in winter, drawing crowds to witness nature's spectacle. By contrast, in summer the waters can be completely serene.

HANALEI, HAENA, AND WEST

Fodor's Choice **Haena Beach Park.** This is a drive-up beach park popular with campers
★ year-round. The wide bay here—named Makua—is bordered by two large reef systems creating favorable waves for skilled surfers during peak winter conditions. In July and August, waters at this same beach usually are as calm as a lake. Entering the water can be dangerous in winter when the big swells roll in. ■TIP➔ **During the summer months only, this is a premier snorkeling site on Kauai.** It's not unusual to find a food vendor parked here selling sandwiches and drinks out of a converted bread van. **Amenities:** lifeguards; parking; showers; toilets; food and drink. **Best for:** walking; snorkeling; surfing. ✉ *Near end of Rte. 560, across from "Dry Cave", Haena.*

Hanakapiai Beach. If you're not up for the full 11-mile haul to Kalalau Beach, you can explore Napali Coast via a 2-mile hike to Hanakapiai Beach, which fronts a tropical valley. It'll take about two hours, and you'll have plenty of company on the trail. This is no longer a secluded beach, although it is still wilderness, and you'll find no amenities except pit toilets. The ocean here is what locals like to call "confused," and Hanakapiai Bay has been the site of numerous drownings. In the winter, surf often eats up the beach, exposing lava-rock boulders backing the sand. Be cautious when crossing the stream that runs through the valley, as it can quickly flood, stranding hikers on the wrong side. This has resulted in helicopter rescues and even deaths, as people are swept out to sea while attempting to cross. **Amenities:** toilets. **Best for:** sunset. ✉ *Kalalau Trail, end of Rte. 560, 7 miles west of Hanalei, Hanalei* ⊕ *www.hawaiistateparks.org.*

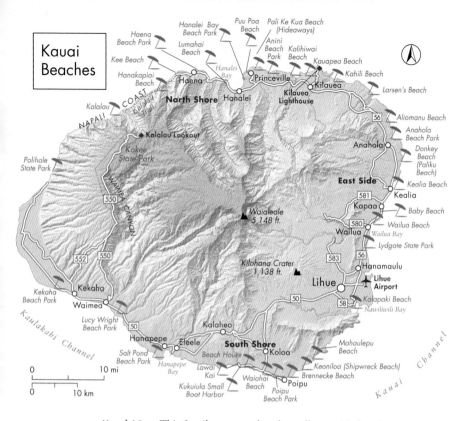

Kauai
Beaches

Haena
Beach Park
Kee Beach
Hanakapiai
Beach
Kalalau
NAPALI COAST
Kalalau Trail
Kalalau Lookout
Kokee
State Park
Polihale
State Park
WAIMEA CANYON
550
552 550
Kekaha
Beach Park Kekaha
Waimea
Lucy Wright
Beach Park 50
Kaulakahi Channel
Hanapepe
Salt Pond
Beach Park Hanapepe
Bay
Kukuiula Small
Boat Harbor
Eleele
Beach House
Lawai
Kai

Haena
Lumahai
Beach
Hanalei
Bay
North Shore Hanalei

Hanalei Bay
Beach Park
Puu Poa
Beach
Anini
Beach
Park
Princeville
Kilauea
Lighthouse

Pali Ke Kua Beach
(Hideaways)

Kalihiwai
Beach Kauapea Beach
Kahili Beach
Kilauea Larsen's Beach

56 Aliomanu Beach
Anahola
Beach Park
Anahola Donkey
Beach
(Paliku
Beach)
Kealia Beach

East Side 581 Kealia
Kapaa Baby Beach
580 Wailua Beach
Wailua Wailua Bay
Lydgate State Park

Waialeale
5,148 ft.

Kilohana Crater
1,138 ft.
56
583
Hanamaulu

Lihue Lihue
Airport

50 Kalapaki Beach
58 Nawiliwili Bay

Kalaheo

South Shore Koloa
Waiohai
Beach Poipu
Poipu
Beach Park

Mahaulepu
Beach

Keoniloa (Shipwreck Beach)
Brennecke Beach
Poipu

Kauai Channel

0   10 mi
0   10 km

FAMILY **Hanalei Bay.** This 2-mile crescent beach cradles a wide bay in a setting
Fodor's Choice that is quintessential Hawaii. The sea is on one side, and behind you
★ are the mountains, often ribboned with waterfalls and changing color
in the shifting light. In winter, Hanalei Bay boasts some of the biggest
onshore surf breaks in the state, attracting world-class surfers, and the
beach is plenty wide enough for sunbathing and strolling. In summer,
the bay is transformed—calm waters lap the beach, sailboats moor
in the bay, and outrigger-canoe paddlers ply the sea. Pack the cooler,
haul out the beach umbrellas, and don't forget the beach toys, because
Hanalei Bay is worth scheduling for an entire day, maybe two. Several
county beach parks, some with pavilions, can be found along the bay.
Amenities: lifeguards; parking; showers; toilets. **Best for:** surfing; swimming; walking; sunsets. ✉ *Weke Rd., Hanalei.*

Fodor's Choice **Kalalau.** Located at the end of the trail with the same name, Kala-
★ lau is a remote beach in the spectacular Napali Coast State Wilderness Park. Reaching it requires an arduous 11-mile hike along sea cliff
faces, through steaming tropical valleys, and across sometimes-raging
streams. Another option is to paddle a kayak to the beach—summer
only, though; otherwise the surf is way too big. The beach is anchored
by a *heiau* (a stone platform used as a place of worship) on one end
and a waterfall on the other. The safest time to come is summer, when

the trail is dry and the beach is wide, cupped by low, vegetated sand dunes and a large walk-in cave on the western edge. Day hikes into the valley offer waterfalls, freshwater swimming pools, and wild, tropical fruits. Though state camping permits are required, the valley often has a significant illegal crowd, which has strained park facilities and degraded much of its former peaceful solitude. Helicopter overflights are near-constant in good weather. **Amenities:** none. **Best for:** sunset; nudists; walking. ⊠ *Trailhead starts at end of Rte. 560, 7 miles west of Hanalei* ⊕ *www.hawaiistateparks.org.*

Kee Beach. Highway 560 on the North Shore literally dead-ends at this beach, pronounced kay-eh. This is also the start of the famous Kalalau Trail, and a culturally significant area to Native Hawaiians, who still use an ancient *heiau* dedicated to hula. (It's not appropriate to hang out on the grass platform or leave offerings there.) The setting is gorgeous, with Makana (a prominent peak that Hollywood dubbed "Bali Hai" in the blockbuster musical *South Pacific*) dramatically imposing itself on the lovely coastline and lots of lush tropical vegetation. The small beach is protected by a reef—except during high surf—creating a small sandy-bottom lagoon that's a popular snorkeling spot. There can be a strong current in winter. Unfortunately, it's so heavily visited that parking is difficult, if not impossible. Expect to park quite a distance from the beach. It's a great place to watch the sunset lighting up Napali Coast. **Amenities:** lifeguards; parking; showers, toilets. **Best for:** swimming; snorkeling; sunset; walking. ⊠ *End of Rte. 560, 7 miles west of Hanalei.*

Lumahai Beach. Famous as the beach where Nurse Nellie washed that man right out of her hair in *South Pacific*, Lumahai's setting is picturesque, with a river and ironwood grove on the western end, and stands of hala (pandanus) trees and black lava rock on the eastern side. In between is a long stretch of thick olivine-flecked sand that can be wide or narrow, depending on surf. It can be accessed in two places from the highway; one involves a steep hike from the road. The ocean can be very dangerous here, with a snapping shore break year-round and monster swells in the winter. The current can be strong near the river. Parking is very limited along the road, or in a rough dirt lot near the river. **Amenities:** none. **Best for:** solitude; walking; sunset. ⊠ *On winding section of Rte. 560, near mile marker 5, Hanalei.*

PRINCEVILLE AND KILAUEA

FAMILY **Anini Beach Park.** A great family park, Anini features one of the longest and widest fringing reefs in all Hawaii, creating a shallow lagoon that is good for snorkeling and kids splashing about. It is safe in all but the highest of winter surf. The reef follows the shoreline for some 2 miles and extends 1,600 feet offshore at its widest point. There's a narrow ribbon of sandy beach and lots of grass and shade, as well as a county campground at the western end and a small boat ramp. **Amenities:** parking; showers; toilets; lifeguard. **Best for:** walking; swimming; sunrise. ⊠ *Anini Rd., off Rte. 56, Princeville.*

Kahili Beach (*Rock Quarry*). You wouldn't know it today, but this beach on Kilauea Bay was once an interisland steamer landing and a rock quarry. Today, it's a fairly quiet beach, although when the surf closes out many other North Shore surf spots, the break directly offshore from Kilauea Stream near the abandoned quarry is still rideable. For the regular oceangoer, summer's your best bet, although the quickly sloping ocean bottom makes for generally treacherous swimming. The stream estuary is quite beautiful, and the ironwood trees and false kamani growing in the generous sand dunes at the rear of the beach provide protection from the sun. It's a wonderful place to observe seabirds. **Amenities:** none. **Best for:** surfing; walking; solitude. ⊠ *Off Wailapa Rd., turn left on dirt road and follow to the end, Kilauea.*

Kalihiwai Beach. A winding road leads down a cliff face to picture-perfect Kalihiwai Beach, which fronts a bay of the same name. It's another one of those drive-up beaches, so it's very accessible. Most people park under the grove of ironwood trees, near the stream, where young kids like to splash and older kids like to body board. Though do beware: the stream carries leptospirosis, a potentially lethal bacteria that can enter through open cuts. In winter months, beware of a treacherous shore break. Summer is the only truly safe time to swim. There's a local-favorite winter surf spot off the eastern edge of the beach, for advanced surfers only. The toilets here are the portable kind, and there are no showers. **Amenities:** parking; toilets. **Best for:** surfing; swimming; walking. ⊠ *Kalihiwai Rd., on Kilauea side of Kalihiwai Bridge, Kilauea.*

Kauapea Beach (*Secret Beach*). This beach went relatively unknown—except by local fishermen, of course—for a long time, hence the common reference to it as "Secret Beach." You'll understand why once you stand on the coarse white sands of Kauapea and see the solid wall of rock that runs the length of the beach, making it fairly inaccessible. For the hardy, there is a steep hike down the western end. From there, you can walk for a long way in either direction in summer. During winter, big swells cut off access to sections of the beach. You may witness dolphins just offshore, and it's a great place to see seabirds, as the Kilauea Point National Wildlife Refuge and its historic lighthouse lie at the eastern end. Nudity is not uncommon. A consistent onshore break makes swimming here typically dangerous. **Amenities:** parking. **Best for:** solitude; walking; sunrise. ⊠ *Kalihiwai Rd., just past turnoff for Kilauea, Kilauea.*

Larsen's Beach. The long, wide fringing reef here is this beach's trademark. The waters near shore are generally too shallow for swimming; if you go in, wear a rash guard to protect against prickly sea urchins and sharp coral on the bottom. This area is known for its tricky currents, especially during periods of high surf, and has been the site of numerous drownings. It can be dangerous to snorkel here. There's some nudity at the western end. Accessing this long strand of coarse, white sand requires hiking down a steep, rocky trail. Slippery when wet. **Amenities:** parking. **Best for:** solitude; sunrise; walking. ⊠ *Off Koolau Rd., look for dirt road and "beach access" sign, Kilauea.*

Pali Ke Kua Beach (*Hideaways Beach*). This is actually two very small pocket beaches separated by a narrow rocky point. The beach area itself is narrow and can all but disappear in wintertime. However, in summer, the steep, rocky trail (don't trust the rusty handrails and rotting ropes) that provides access reduces the number of beachgoers, at times creating a deserted beach feel. Winter's high surf creates dangerous conditions. ■TIP→ Don't attempt the trail after a heavy rain—it turns into a mudslide. **Amenities:** parking. **Best for:** surfing; sunset. ⊠ *End of Ka Haku Rd., on dirt trail between parking lot and condominium complex, Princeville.*

Puu Poa Beach. The coastline along the community of Princeville is primarily made up of sea cliffs with a couple of pockets of beaches. The sea cliffs end with a long, narrow stretch of beach just east of the Hanalei River and at the foot of the St. Regis Princeville Resort. Public access is via 100-plus steps around the back of the hotel; hotel guests can simply take the elevator down to sea level. The beach itself is subject to the hazards of winter's surf, narrowing and widening with the surf height. On calm days, snorkeling is good thanks to a shallow reef system pocked with sand. Sometimes a shallow sandbar extends across the river to Black Pot Beach Park, part of the Hanalei Beach system, making it easy to cross the river. On high-surf days, the outer edge of the reef near the river draws internationally ranked surfers. The resort's pool is off-limits to nonguests, but the restaurants and bars are not. **Amenities:** food and drink; parking. **Best for:** surfing; snorkeling; sunset. ⊠ *End of Ka Haku Rd., off Rte. 560, Princeville.*

> ## COUNTY AND STATE BEACH PARKS
>
> If restrooms, covered picnic areas, showers, and easy accessibility are important to you, stick to these county and state beach parks:
>
> ■ Anahola Beach Park
>
> ■ Anini Beach Park
>
> ■ Haena State Park
>
> ■ Hanalei Beach Park
>
> ■ Kekaha Beach Park
>
> ■ Kukuiula Landing
>
> ■ Lydgate State Park
>
> ■ Salt Pond Beach Park

THE EAST SIDE

The East Side of the island is considered the "windward" side, a term you'll often hear in weather forecasts. It simply means the side of the island receiving onshore winds. The wind helps break down rock into sand, so there are plenty of beaches here. Unfortunately, only a few of those beaches are protected, so many are not ideal for beginning ocean-goers, though they are perfect for long sunrise ambles. On super-windy days, kiteboarders sail along the east shore, sometimes jumping waves and performing acrobatic maneuvers in the air.

BEACH SAFETY ON KAUAI

Hawaii's world-renowned, beautiful beaches can be extremely dangerous at times due to large waves and strong currents—so much so that the state rates wave hazards using three signs: a yellow square (caution), a red stop sign (high hazard), and a black diamond (extreme hazard). Signs are posted and updated three times daily or as conditions change.

Visiting beaches with lifeguards is strongly recommended, and you should swim only when there's a normal caution rating. Never swim alone or dive into unknown water or shallow breaking waves. If you're unable to swim out of a rip current, tread water and wave your arms in the air to signal for help.

Even in calm conditions, there are other dangerous things in the water to be aware of, including razor-sharp coral, jellyfish, eels, and sharks, to name a few.

Jellyfish cause the most ocean injuries, and signs are sometimes posted along beaches when they're present. Reactions to a sting are usually mild (burning sensation, redness, welts); however, in some cases they can be severe (breathing difficulties). If you're stung, pick off the tentacles, rinse the affected area with water, and apply ice.

The chances of getting bitten by a shark in Hawaiian waters are very low; sharks attack swimmers or surfers three or four times per year. Of the 40 species of sharks found near Hawaii, tiger sharks are considered the most dangerous because of their size and indiscriminate feeding behavior. They're easily recognized by their blunt snouts and vertical bars on their sides.

Here are a few tips to reduce your shark-attack risk:

■ Swim, surf, or dive with others at beaches patrolled by lifeguards.

■ Avoid swimming at dawn, dusk, and night, when some shark species may move inshore to feed.

■ Don't enter the water if you have open wounds or are bleeding.

■ Avoid murky waters, harbor entrances, areas near stream mouths (especially after heavy rains), channels, or steep drop-offs.

■ Don't wear high-contrast swimwear or shiny jewelry.

■ Don't swim near dolphins, which are often prey for large sharks.

■ If you spot a shark, leave the water quickly and calmly; never provoke or harass a shark, no matter how small.

The website *oceansafety.ancl.hawaii. edu/* provides statewide beach hazard maps as well as weather and surf advisories.

KAPAA AND WAILUA

Aliomanu Beach. This narrow beach is lined with homes, most of them set back a bit and screened with vegetation that blocks access along the sand in a number of places when the surf is up or tide is high. The waters off Aliomanu Beach are protected by the fringing reef 100 yards or so out to sea, and there are pockets for swimming. However, currents can be tricky, especially near the stream tucked in the beach's elbow toward the northern end, and at the river mouth on the southern end

No matter what time of year you visit Kauai, there's a good chance you'll have a beach all to yourself.

that demarcates neighboring Anahola Beach. This beach is in Hawaiian Homelands and is frequently used by fishermen and local families for camping. **Amenities:** parking. **Best for:** solitude; sunrise. ⊠ *Aliomanu Rd., north of mile marker 14, Anahola.*

Anahola Beach Park. Anahola is part of the Hawaiian Homelands on Kauai, so Anahola Beach Park is definitely a locals' hangout, especially for families with small children. The shallow and calm water at the beach road's end is tucked behind a curving finger of land and perfect for young ones. As the beach winds closer to the river mouth, there's less protection and a shore break favorable for body boarders if the trades are light or *kona* (south) winds are present. The long, sandy beach is nice for a morning or evening stroll. **Amenities:** parking; lifeguards; showers; toilets. **Best for:** swimming; walking; surfing. ⊠ *Anahola Rd., south of mile marker 14, Anahola.*

FAMILY **Baby Beach.** There aren't many safe swimming beaches on Kauai's East Side; however, this one usually ranks highly with parents because there's a narrow, lagoonlike area between the beach and the near-shore reef perfect for small children. In winter, watch for east and northeast swells that would make this not such a safe option. There are no beach facilities—no lifeguards—so watch your babies. There is an old-time shower spigot (cold water only) along the roadside available to rinse the salt water. **Amenities:** showers; parking. **Best for:** swimming; sunrise. ⊠ *Moanakai Rd., Kapaa.*

Donkey Beach (*Paliku Beach*). This beach gets its unusual name from the Lihue Plantation Company, which once kept a herd of mules and donkeys in the pasture adjacent to the beach. If the waves are right, body boarders and surfers might be spotted offshore. However, the waters here are rough and not recommended for swimming and snorkeling. Instead, we suggest a morning walk along the easy trail that overlooks the beach, starting at the northern end of Kealia Beach. **Amenities:** none. **Best for:** surfing; solitude; sunrise. ⊠ *Rte. 56, north of Kealia Kai subdivision, Kealia.*

Kealia Beach. A half-mile long and adjacent to the highway heading north out of Kapaa, Kealia Beach attracts body boarders and surfers year-round. It's a favorite with locals and visitors alike. Kealia is not generally a great beach for swimming, but it's a place to sunbathe and enjoy the beach scene. The waters are usually rough and the waves crumbly due to an onshore break (no protecting reef) and northeasterly trade winds. A scenic lookout on the southern end, accessed off the highway, is a superb location for saluting the morning sunrise or spotting whales during winter. A level, paved trail with small, covered pavilions runs along the coastline here, and is very popular for walking and biking. **Amenities:** lifeguard; parking; showers; toilets. **Best for:** surfing; swimming; walking; sunrise. ⊠ *Rte. 56, at mile marker 10, Kealia.*

FAMILY **Lydgate State Park.** This is by far the best family beach park on Kauai. The waters off the beach are protected by a hand-built breakwater, creating two boulder-enclosed saltwater pools for safe swimming and snorkeling most of the year. The smaller of the two pools is perfect for *keiki* (children). Behind the beach is Kamalani Playground; children of all ages—that includes you—enjoy the swings, lava-tube slides, tree house, and more. Picnic tables abound in the park, and pavilions for day use and overnight camping are available by permit. The Kamalani Kai Bridge is a second playground, south of the original. (The two are united by a bike and pedestrian path that is part of the coastal multiuse path.) ■ **TIP→ This park system is perennially popular; the quietest times to visit are early mornings and weekdays. Amenities:** lifeguards; parking; showers; toilets. **Best for:** partiers; walking; swimming; sunrise. ⊠ *Leho Dr., just south of Wailua River, Wailua (Kauai County).*

Wailua Beach. At the mouth of Hawaii's only navigable river, Wailua Beach has considerable cultural significance. At the river's mouth, petroglyphs carved on boulders are sometimes visible during low surf and tide conditions. Surfers and stand-up paddlers enjoy this beach, and many families spend the weekend days under the Wailua Bridge at the river mouth, even hauling out their portable grills and tables to go with their beach chairs. The great news about Wailua Beach is that it's almost impossible to miss; however, parking can be a challenge. The best parking for the north end of the beach is on Papaloa Road behind the Shell station. For the southern end of the beach, park at Wailua River State Park. **Amenities:** parking; showers; toilets. **Best for:** swimming; surfing; walking; windsurfing. ⊠ *Kuhio Hwy., Wailua (Kauai County).*

LIHUE

FAMILY **Kalapaki Beach.** Five minutes south of the airport in Lihue, you'll find this wide, sandy-bottom beach fronting the Kauai Marriott. This beach is almost always safe from rip currents and undertows because it's around the back side of a peninsula, in its own cove. There are tons of activities here, including all the usual water sports—beginning and intermediate surfing, body boarding, bodysurfing, and swimming—plus, there are two outrigger canoe clubs paddling in the bay and the Nawiliwili Yacht Club's boats sailing around the harbor. **Kalapaki** is the only place on Kauai where sailboats—in this case Hobie Cats—are available for rent (at Kauai Beach Boys, which fronts the beach next to Duke's Canoe Club restaurant). Visitors can also rent snorkel gear, surfboards, body boards, and kayaks from Kauai Beach Boys. A volleyball court on the beach is often used by a loosely organized group of local players; visitors are always welcome. ■ TIP→ Beware the stream on the south side of the beach, though, as it often has high bacteria counts. Duke's Canoe Club restaurant is one of only a couple of restaurants on the island actually on a beach; the restaurant's lower level is casual, even welcoming beach attire and sandy feet, perfect for lunch or an afternoon cocktail. **Amenities:** parking; showers; toilets; water sports; food and drink; lifeguard. **Best for:** swimming; surfing; partiers; walking. ⊠ *Off Rice St., Lihue* ⊕ *www.kalapakibeach.org.*

THE SOUTH SHORE

The South Shore's primary access road is Highway 520, a tree-lined, two-lane, windy road. As you drive along it, there's a sense of tunneling down a rabbit hole into another world, à la Alice. And the South Shore is certainly a wonderland. On average, it rains only 30 inches per year, so if you're looking for fun in the sun, this is a good place to start. The beaches, with their powdery-fine sand, are consistently good year-round, except during high surf, which, if it hits at all, will be in summer. If you want solitude, this isn't it; if you want excitement—well, as much excitement as quiet Kauai offers—this is the place for you.

POIPU

Beach House Beach. Don't pack the beach umbrella, beach mats, and cooler for this one. Just your snorkel gear, when the seas are calm. The beach, named after the neighboring Beach House restaurant and on the road to Spouting Horn, is a small slip of sand during low tide and a rocky shoreline when it's high; however, it is conveniently located by the road's edge, and its rocky coastline and somewhat rocky bottom make it great for snorkeling. (As a rule, sandy-bottom beaches are not great for snorkeling. The rocks create safe hiding places and grow the food that fish and other marine life like to eat.) A sidewalk along the coastline on the restaurant side of the beach makes a great vantage point from which to peer into the water and look for *honu*, the Hawaiian green sea turtle. It's also a gathering spot to watch the sun set. ■ TIP→ Make reservations for dinner at the Beach House in advance and time it around sunset. You can park in the public lot across from the beach. **Amenities:** parking; showers; toilets. **Best for:** snorkeling; surfing; sunset. ⊠ *Lawai Rd., off Poipu Rd., Poipu.*

A lush mountain backdrop, a long stretch of sand, and beautiful surf. It all comes together at Hanalei Bay, a quintessential Hawaii beach.

Brennecke Beach. This beach is synonymous on Kauai with board surfing and bodysurfing, thanks to its shallow sandbar and reliable shore break. Because the beach is small and often congested, surfboards are prohibited near shore. The water on the rocky eastern edge of the beach is a good place to see the endangered green sea turtles noshing on plants growing on the rocks. **Amenities:** parking; food and drink. **Best for:** surfing; sunset. ⊠ *Hoone Rd., off Poipu Rd., Poipu.*

Keoniloa Beach (*Shipwreck Beach*). Few—except the public relations specialists at the Grand Hyatt Kauai Resort and Spa, which backs the beach—refer to this beach by anything other than its common name: Shipwreck Beach. Its Hawaiian name means "long beach." Both make sense. It is a long stretch of crescent-shape beach punctuated by stunning sea cliffs on both ends, and, yes, a ship once wrecked here. With its onshore break, the waters off Shipwreck are best for body boarding and bodysurfing; however, the beach itself is plenty big for sunbathing, sand-castle building, Frisbee, and other beach-related fun. The eastern edge of the beach is the start of an interpretive dune walk (complimentary) held by the hotel staff; check with the concierge for dates and times. **Amenities:** parking; showers; toilets; food and drink. **Best for:** surfing; walking; sunrise. ⊠ *Ainako Rd., continue on Poipu Rd. past Hyatt, turn makai on Ainako Rd., Poipu.*

FAMILY **Kukuiula Small Boat Harbor.** This is a great beach to sit and people-watch as diving and fishing boats, kayakers, and canoe paddlers head out to sea. Shore and throw-net fishermen frequent this harbor as well. It's not a particularly large harbor, so it retains a quaint sense of charm, unlike Nawiliwili Harbor or Port Allen. The bay is a nice, protected

BEST BEACHES

He says "to-mah-toe," and she says "to-may-toe." When it comes to beaches on Kauai, the meaning behind that axiom holds true: People are different. What rocks one person's world wreaks havoc for another's. Here are some additional tips on how to choose a beach that's right for you.

BEST FOR FAMILIES
Lydgate State Park, East Side. The kid-designed playground, the protected swimming pools, and Kamalani Bridge guarantee you will not hear these words from your child: "Mom, I'm bored."

Poipu Beach Park, Poipu, South Shore. The *keiki* (children's) pool and lifeguards make this a safe spot for kids. The near-perpetual sun isn't so bad, either.

BEST STAND-UP PADDLING
Anini Beach Park, North Shore. The reef and long stretch of beach give beginners to stand-up paddling a calm place to give this new sport a try. You won't get pummeled by waves here.

Wailua Beach, East Side. On the East Side, the Wailua River bisects the beach and heads inland 2 miles, providing stand-up paddlers with a long and scenic stretch of water before they have to figure out how to turn around.

BEST SURFING
Hanalei Bay Beach Park, North Shore. In winter, Hanalei Bay offers a range of breaks, from beginner to advanced. Surfing legends Laird Hamilton and the Irons Brothers grew up surfing the waters of Hanalei.

Waiohai Beach, South Shore. Surf instructors flock to this spot with their students for its gentle, near-shore break. Then, as students advance, they can paddle out a little farther to an intermediate break—if they dare.

BEST SUNSETS
Kee Beach, North Shore. Even in winter, when the sun sets in the south and out of view, you won't be disappointed here, because the "magic hour," as photographers call the time around sunset, paints Napali Coast with a warm gold light. But it can be tough to find parking here.

Polihale State Park, West Side. This due-west-facing beach may be tricky to get to, but it does offer the most unobstructed sunset views on the island. The fact that it's so remote means you won't have strangers in your photos, but you will want to depart right after sunset or risk getting lost in the dark.

BEST FOR CELEB SPOTTING
Haena Beach Park, North Shore. Behind those gated driveways and heavily foliaged yards that line this beach live—at least, part-time—some of the world's most celebrated music and movie moguls.

Hanalei Bay Beach Park, North Shore. We know we tout this beach often, but it deserves the praise. It's a mecca for everyone—regular joes, surfers, fishers, young, old, locals, visitors, and, especially, the famous. You may also recognize Hanalei Bay from the movie *The Descendants*.

area for limited swimming, but with all the boat traffic kicking up sand and clouding the water, it's probably not good for snorkeling. Outside the breakwater, there is a decent surf spot. **Amenities:** showers; toilets; parking. **Best for:** solitude; swimming; sunrise. ⊠ *Lawai Rd., off Poipu Rd., Poipu.*

Fodor's Choice
★
Lawai Kai. One of the most spectacular beaches on the South Shore is inaccessible by land unless you tour the National Tropical Botanical Garden's Allerton Garden, which we highly recommend. On the tour, you'll see the beach, but you won't visit it. One way to legally access the beach on your own is by paddling a kayak 1 mile from Kukuiula Harbor. However, you have to rent the kayaks elsewhere and haul them on top of your car to the harbor. Also, the wind and waves usually run westward, making the in-trip a breeze but the return trip a workout against Mother Nature. ■**TIP**➜ Do not attempt this beach in any manner during a south swell. **Amenities:** none. **Best for:** solitude; sunrise. ⊠ *4425 Lawai Rd., off Poipu Rd.* ☎ *808/742–2433 for tour information at the National Tropical Botanical Garden's Allerton Garden* ⊕ *http://ntbg.org.*

Fodor's Choice
★
Mahaulepu Beach. This 2-mile stretch of coast, with its sand dunes, limestone hills, sinkholes, and caves is unlike any other on Kauai. Remains of a large, ancient settlement, evidence of great battles, and the discovery of a now-underwater petroglyph field indicate that Hawaiians lived in this area as early as 700 AD. Mahaulepu's coastline is unprotected and rocky, which makes venturing into the ocean hazardous. There are three beach areas with bits of sandy-bottom swimming; however, the best way to experience Mahaulepu is simply to roam, especially at sunrise. ■**TIP**➜ Access to this beach is via private property. The owner allows access during daylight hours, but be sure to depart before sunset or risk getting locked in for the night. **Amenities:** parking. **Best for:** walking; solitude; sunrise. ⊠ *Poipu Rd., past Hyatt Hotel, Poipu.*

FAMILY
Fodor's Choice
★
Poipu Beach Park. The most popular beach on the South Shore is Poipu Beach Park. During calm seas, the snorkeling and swimming are good, and when the surf's up, the bodyboarding and surfing are good, too. Frequent sunshine, grassy lawns, and easy access add to the appeal, especially with families. The beach is frequently crowded and great for people-watching. Even the endangered Hawaiian monk seal often makes an appearance. **Amenities:** lifeguards; parking; showers; toilets; food and drink. **Best for:** swimming; snorkeling; partiers; walking. ⊠ *Hoone Rd., off Poipu Rd., Poipu* ☎ *808/742–7444.*

Waiohai Beach. The first hotel built in Poipu in 1962 overlooked this beach, adjacent to Poipu Beach Park. Actually, there's little to distinguish where one starts and the other begins other than a crescent reef at the eastern end of Waiohai Beach. That crescent, however, is important. It creates a small, protected bay—good for snorkeling and beginning surfers. If you're a beginner, this is the spot. However, when a summer swell kicks up, the near-shore conditions become dangerous; offshore, there's a splendid surf break for experienced surfers. The beach itself is narrow and, like its neighbor, gets very crowded in summer. **Amenities:** parking. **Best for:** surfing; sunrise; sunset. ⊠ *Hoone Rd., off Poipu Rd., Poipu.*

CLOSE UP

Seal-Spotting on the South Shore

When strolling on one of Kauai's lovely beaches, don't be surprised if you find yourself in the rare company of Hawaiian monk seals. These are among the most endangered of all marine mammals, with perhaps fewer than 1,200 remaining. They primarily inhabit the northwestern Hawaiian Islands, although more are showing their sweet faces on the main Hawaiian Islands, especially on Kauai. They're fond of hauling out on the beach for a long snooze in the sun, particularly after a night of gorging on fish. They need this time to rest and digest, safe from predators.

During the past several summers, female seals have birthed young on the beaches around Kauai, where they stay to nurse their pups for upward of six weeks. It seems the seals enjoy particular beaches for the same reasons we do: the shallow, protected waters.

If you're lucky enough to see a monk seal, keep your distance and let it be. Although they may haul out near people, they still want and need their space. Stay several hundred feet away, and forget photos unless you've got a zoom lens. It's illegal to do anything that causes a monk seal to change its behavior, with penalties that include big fines and even jail time. In the water, seals may appear to want to play. It's their curious nature. Don't try to play with them. They are wild animals—mammals, in fact, with teeth.

If you have concerns about the health or safety of a seal, or just want more information, contact the **Hawaiian Monk Seal Conservation Hui** (☎ *808/651-7668* ⊕ *www. kauaiseals.com*).

THE WEST SIDE

The West Side of the island receives hardly enough rainfall year-round to water a cactus, and because it's also the leeward side, there are few tropical breezes. That translates to sunny and hot with long, languorous, and practically deserted beaches. You'd think the leeward waters—untouched by wind—would be calm, but there's no reef system, so the beach drops off quickly and currents are common. Rivers often turn the ocean water murky. ■TIP→ **The best place to gear up for the beaches on the West Side is on the South Shore or East Side.** Although there's some catering to visitors here, it's not much.

HANAPEPE

FAMILY **Salt Pond Beach Park.** A great family spot, Salt Pond Beach Park features a naturally made, shallow swimming pond behind a curling finger of rock where *keiki* (children) splash and snorkel. This pool is generally safe except during a large south swell, which usually occurs in summer, if at all. The center and western edge of the beach is popular with body boarders and bodysurfers. Pavilions with picnic tables offer shade, and there's a campground that tends to attract a rowdy bunch at the eastern end. On a cultural note, the flat stretch of land to the east of the beach is the last spot in Hawaii where ponds are used to harvest salt in the

South Shore beaches have good surf breaks. Head to Poipu Beach for board rentals or lessons.

dry heat of summer. The beach park is popular with locals and it can get crowded on weekends and holidays. **Amenities:** lifeguard; parking; showers; toilets. **Best for:** swimming; sunset; walking. ☒ *Lolokai Rd., off Rte. 50, Hanapepe.*

WAIMEA AND WAIMEA CANYON

Kekaha Beach Park. This is one of the premier spots on Kauai for sunset walks and the start of the state's longest beach. We don't recommend much water activity here without first talking to a lifeguard. The beach is exposed to open ocean and has an onshore break that can be hazardous any time of year. However, there are some excellent surf breaks—for experienced surfers only. Or, if you would like to run or stroll on a beach, this is the one—the hard-packed sand goes on for miles, all the way to Napali Coast, but you won't get past the Pacific Missile Range Facility and its post-9/11 restrictions. Another bonus for this beach is its relatively dry weather year-round. If it's raining where you are, try Kekaha Beach Park. Toilets here are the portable kind. **Amenities:** lifeguards; showers; toilets; parking. **Best for:** sunset; walking; surfing. ☒ *Rte. 50, near mile marker 27, Kekaha.*

Lucy Wright Beach Park. Named in honor of the first native Hawaiian schoolteacher, this beach is on the western banks of the Waimea River. It is also where Captain James Cook first came ashore in the Hawaiian Islands in 1778. If that's not interesting enough, the sand here is not the white, powdery kind you see along the South Shore. It's a combination of pulverized, black lava rock and lighter-colored reef. In a way, it looks a bit like a mix of salt and pepper. Unfortunately, the intrigue of the beach doesn't extend to the waters, which are reddish and murky (thanks to river runoff) and choppy (thanks to an onshore break). Instead, check out the Waimea Landing State Recreation Pier, from which fishers drop their lines. It's located about 100 yards west of the river mouth. **Amenities:** showers; toilets; parking; **Best for:** walking; sunset; surfing. ⊠ *Pokile Rd., off Rte. 50, Waimea (Kauai County).*

Fodor'sChoice ★ **Polihale State Park.** The longest stretch of beach in Hawaii starts in Kekaha and ends about 15 miles away at the start of Napali Coast. At the Napali end of the beach is the 5-mile-long, 140-acre Polihale State Park. In addition to being long, this beach is 300 feet wide in places and backed by sand dunes 50 to 100 feet tall. It is frequently very hot, with minimal shade and scorching sand in summer. Polihale is a remote beach accessed via a rough, 5-mile haul-cane road (four-wheel drive needed in wet weather) at the end of Route 50 in Kekaha. ■ **TIP➔ Be sure to start the day with a full tank of gas and a cooler filled with food and drink.** Though it's a popular camping and day-use beach location, the water here is typically rough and not recommended for recreation. No driving is allowed on the beach. The Pacific Missile Range Facility (PMRF), operated by the U.S. Navy, is adjacent to the beach and access to the coastline in front of the base is restricted. **Amenities:** parking; showers; toilets. **Best for:** walking; solitude; sunset. ⊠ *Dirt road at end of Rte. 50, Kekaha* ☎ *808/587–0300.*

WHERE TO EAT

Updated by
Joan Conrow

On Kauai, if you're lucky enough to win an invitation to a potluck, baby luau, or beach party, don't think twice—just accept. The best grinds (food) are homemade, and so you'll eat until you're full, then rest, eat some more, and make a plate to take home, too.

But even if you can't score a spot at one of these parties, don't despair. Great local-style food is easy to come by at countless low-key places around the island. As an extra bonus, these eats are often inexpensive, and portions are generous. Expect plenty of meat—usually deep-fried or marinated in a teriyaki sauce and grilled *pulehu*-style (over an open fire)—and starches. Rice is standard, even for breakfast, and often served alongside potato-macaroni salad, another island specialty. Another local favorite is *poke,* made from chunks of raw tuna or octopus seasoned with sesame oil, soy sauce, onions, and pickled seaweed. It's a great *pupu* (appetizer) when paired with a cold beer.

Kauai's cultural diversity is apparent in its restaurants, which offer authentic Chinese, Korean, Japanese, Thai, Mexican, Italian, Vietnamese, and Hawaiian specialties. Less specialized restaurants cater to the tourist crowd, serving standard American fare—burgers, pizza, sandwiches, surf-and-turf combos, and so on. Poipu and Kapaa offers the best selection of restaurants, with options for a variety of tastes and budgets; most fast-food joints are in Lihue.

KAUAI DINING PLANNER

EATING-OUT STRATEGY

Where should we eat? With dozens of island eateries competing for your attention, it may seem like a daunting question. But our expert writers and editors have done most of the legwork—the dozens of selections here represent the best eating experience this island has to offer. Find a restaurant quickly—reviews are ordered alphabetically within their geographic area.

WITH KIDS

Hawaii is a kid-friendly destination in many regards, and that includes taking the little ones out to eat with you. Because of the overall relaxed vibe and casual dress here, you won't have to worry too much about your tot's table manners or togs—within reason, of course. Take advantage of treats and eating experiences unique to Hawaii, such as shave ice, sunshine markets (perfect for picnic lunches or beach provisions), and luau.

SMOKING

Smoking is prohibited in all Hawaii restaurants and bars.

RESERVATIONS

It's always a good idea to make reservations when you can, and if you plan to dine at one of Kauai's top eateries, reservations are essential. However, you'll find that many places on the island don't take reservations at all, and service is first come, first served.

WHAT TO WEAR

Just about anything goes on Kauai. At lunch you can dine in a sarong, or T-shirt and shorts, and flip-flops at most places. Dinner is only a slight step up. That said, if you're out for a special occasion and want to don your fanciest duds, no one will look twice.

HOURS AND PRICES

Restaurants on Kauai significantly quiet down by 9 pm; the limited bar scene continues past midnight—but not much past. It seems as if the entire island is in bed before 10 pm to get up early the next day and play. In general, peak dining hours here tend to be on the earlier side, during sunset hours from 6 to 8 pm. A tip of 18% to 20% is standard for good service.

WHAT IT COSTS			
$	$$	$$$	$$$$
AT DINNER under $18	$18–$26	$27–$35	over $35

Prices in the restaurant reviews are the average cost of a main course at dinner or, if dinner is not served, at lunch; taxes and service charges are generally included.

THE NORTH SHORE

Because of the North Shore's isolation, restaurants have enjoyed a captive audience of visitors who don't want to make the long, dark trek into Kapaa town for dinner. As a result, dining in this region has been characterized by expensive fare that isn't especially tasty, either. Fortunately, the situation is slowly improving as new restaurants open and others change hands or menus.

Still, dining on the North Shore can be pricier than other parts of the island, and not especially family-friendly. Most of the restaurants are found either in Hanalei town or the Princeville resorts. Consequently, you'll encounter delightful mountain and ocean views, but just one restaurant with oceanfront dining.

$$$$ ✕ **Bar Acuda.** This hip and pricey tapas bar is a top place in Hanalei in
TAPAS　terms of tastiness, creativity, and pizzazz. Owner-chef Jim Moffat's brief
Fodor's Choice　menu changes regularly: you might find *banderillas* (grilled flank-steak
★　skewers with honey and chipotle-chili oil), local honeycomb with goat
cheese and apple, or seared island fish with macadamia-nut pesto. The
food is often organic and consistently remarkable, but it's the subtly
intense sauces that elevate the cuisine to outstanding. The dining room
is super casual, but chic, with a welcoming bar and a nice porch for
outdoor dining. ⑤ *Average main: $40 ✉ Hanalei Center, 5-5161 Kuhio
Hwy., Hanalei ☎ 808/826–7081 ⊕ www.restaurantbaracuda.com.*

$$ ✕ **Bouchon's.** This second-story grill and sushi bar, previously known
JAPANESE　as Sushi Blues, has a pleasant ambience, with copper tabletops, lovely
views of mountains streaked with waterfalls, and photos of interna-
tional jazz greats lining the staircase. Regular entertainment, a full bar,
and sake menu add to its appeal. The food isn't as inspired as the set-
ting, but the specialty sushi items, such as the Popper Roll, which is
filled with salmon, cream cheese, jalapeno, and avocado, wrapped in
seaweed and tempura fried, are good. Or choose from steaks, fish, and
seafood dishes. ⑤ *Average main: $25 ✉ Ching Young Village, 5-5190
Kuhio Hwy., Hanalei ☎ 808/826–9701 ⊕ www.bouchonshanalei.com.*

$$ ✕ **Hanalei Gourmet.** This spot in Hanalei's restored old schoolhouse
AMERICAN　offers dolphin-safe tuna, low-sodium meats, fresh-baked breads, and
homemade desserts as well as a casual atmosphere where both families
and the sports-watching crowd can feel equally comfortable. Lunch and
dinner menus feature sandwiches, burgers, hearty salads, a variety of
pupus, and nightly specials of fresh local fish. They also will prepare
a picnic and give it to you in an insulated backpack. A full bar and
frequent live entertainment keep things hopping even after the kitchen
closes. Monday and Thursday evenings fill up for fish taco night, which
begins at 6. ⑤ *Average main: $25 ✉ Hanalei Center, 5-5161 Kuhio
Hwy., Hanalei ☎ 808/826–2524 ⊕ www.hanaleigourmet.com.*

$$$$ ✕ **Kauai Grill.** Savor an artful meal created by world-renowned chef
ECLECTIC　Jean-Gorges Vongerichten, surrounded by a dramatic Hanalei Bay scene
Fodor's Choice　that's positively stunning at sunset. Located at the luxurious St. Regis
★　Princeville Resort, Kauai Grill has dark-wood decor and an ornate
chandelier, the centerpiece of the room. The attention here is on the
flavors of robust meat and local, fresh seafood. Meats are simply grilled
and paired with exotic sauces. Specials change frequently and use many
Hawaiian-grown ingredients. Expect attentive service with the feel of an
exclusive nightclub, and an expertly created meal. Vegetarian and gluten-free menus are available. ⑤ *Average main: $45 ✉ St. Regis Princev-
ille, 5520 Ka Haku Rd., Princeville ☎ 808/826–9644 ⊕ www.kauaigrill.
com ⊗ No lunch. Closed Sun. and Mon. ⌂ Reservations essential.*

$$ ✕ **Kilauea Bakery and Pau Hana Pizza.** This bakery is known for its starter
AMERICAN　of Hawaiian sourdough made with guava as well as its specialty piz-
FAMILY　zas topped with eclectic ingredients such as smoked *ono* (a Hawaiian
fish), Gorgonzola-rosemary sauce, barbecued chicken, goat cheese, and
chipotle peppers. Open from 6:30 am, the bakery serves coffee drinks,
delicious fresh pastries, bagels, and breads in the morning. Late ris-
ers beware: breads and pastries sell out quickly on weekends. Pizza

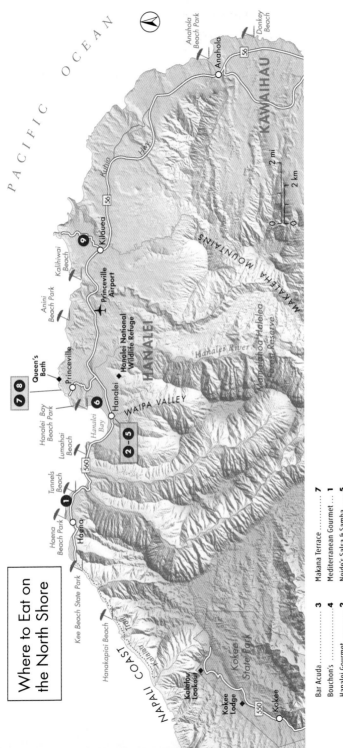

Where to Eat on the North Shore

Bar Acuda **3**
Bouchon's **4**
Hanalei Gourmet **2**
Kauai Grill **8**
Kilauea Bakery
and Pau Hana Pizza **9**

Makana Terrace **7**
Mediteranean Gourmet ... **1**
Neide's Salsa & Samba **5**
Postcards Café **6**

BUDGET-FRIENDLY EATS: NORTH SHORE

It's not easy to find cheap food on the North Shore, but these little eateries serve up dinner for two for under $20.

Foodland. In a pinch, you can pick up pretty good sushi, ready-to-eat hot entrées, deli items, bakery goods, and panini sandwiches at the Foodland grocery store. ⊠ *Princeville Shopping Center, 5–4280 Kuhio Hwy., Princeville,* ☎ *808/826–9880.*

Harvest Market. Health foods, such as rice dishes, soups, and salads, are served in the back of this natural-foods store at the Hanalei Center; takeout only. ⊠ *5-5161 Kuhio Hwy., Hanalei,* ☎ *808/826–0089.*

Neide's Salsa & Samba. This is one of the better low-cost eateries on the North Shore, with tasty Brazilian and Mexican food, which is not commonly found on the island, to take out or eat in an informal garden setting at the Hanalei Center. ⊠ *5-5161 Kuhio Hwy., Hanalei,* ☎ *808/826–1851.*

Tropical Taco. This place is a safe choice for very basic Mexican food, though the prices are high for the cuisine. Take out or limited outdoor seating. ⊠ *5-5088 Kuhio Hwy., Hanalei,* ☎ *808/827–8226,* ⊕ *www.tropicaltaco.com.*

(including a gluten-free dough option), soup, and salads can be ordered for lunch or dinner. Service is leisurely. There's free Wi-Fi and a cute courtyard with covered tables. ⑤ *Average main: $20* ⊠ *Kong Lung Center, 2484 Keneke St., Kilauea* ☎ *808/828–2020.*

$$$$
HAWAIIAN
FAMILY
✕ **Makana Terrace.** Enjoy dining while gazing at a breathtaking panoramic view of Hanalei Bay. There's no doubt it's pricey, but you're paying for the view—sit on the terrace if you can—and for an attentive staff. The focus is on local, Hawaiian-grown foods here, including the fish plate of a fresh Pacific catch, which is your best bet for lunch. For breakfast, feast at an extensive buffet or order à la carte. A fantastic and expensive brunch is the only option on Sunday morning and afternoon. The sushi is a good dinner choice—splurge on the petite fillet and lobster tail (around $58) and time your dinner around sunset for an unforgettable Hawaiian vista. ⑤ *Average main: $40* ⊠ *St. Regis Princeville Resort, 5520 Ka Haku Rd., Princeville* ☎ *808/826–9644* ⊕ *www.stregisprinceville.com* ⊗ *No dinner Tues. and Wed.*

$$$
MEDITERRANEAN
✕ **Mediterranean Gourmet.** A trip to this romantic Middle Eastern oasis pays off after a narrow, cliff-hugging ride along the exquisite North Shore coastline. Owner-chef Imad Beydoun, a native of Beirut, serves multiple hummus appetizers, stuffed grape leaves, baba ghanoush, crispy spinach and lamb *fatayers* (meat pies) alongside traditional favorites like chicken and duck kebab, rib eye, and rosemary rack of lamb. Local fish including ahi, ono, and seasonal catches add Pacific Rim touches when combined with fresh local produce. Lunch makes the most of the oceanfront setting and view. Live music Wednesday, Friday, Saturday, and Sunday evenings. ⑤ *Average main: $30* ⊠ *Hanalei Colony Resort, 5-7130 Kuhio Hwy., Haena* ☎ *808/826–9875* ⊕ *www. kauaimedgourmet.com* ⊗ *Closed Mon.*

$
BRAZILIAN
✕ **Neide's Salsa and Samba.** The only restaurant serving authentic Brazilian food on Kauai, Neide's Salsa and Samba is also one of the most

affordable establishments on the island. The first half of the menu focuses on Mexican food, but it's the Brazilian dishes here that deserve your attention. The *muqueca* is the Brazilian version of the French bouillabaisse or the Spanish paella, but with a touch of coconut milk, opening a whole new bouquet of flavors. The *panquecas* are crepes, filled with vegetables or chicken and then immersed in Neide's secret sauce. If you choose any dish that comes with beans, ask for black beans, a staple of Brazilian cuisine. $ *Average main: $14* ✉ *5-5161 Kuhio Hwy., Hanalei* ☎ *808/826–1851.*

$$ ✕ **Postcards Café.** This plantation-cottage restaurant has a menu full
AMERICAN of seafood but also offers additive-free vegetarian and vegan options. Top menu picks include taro fritters, wasabi-crusted ahi, tandoori, and baked portobello mushrooms. Desserts are made without refined sugar. Try the chocolate silk pie made with barley-malt chocolate, pure vanilla, and creamy tofu with a gingery crust, or even better yet, the warm chocolate volcano. $ *Average main: $21* ✉ *5-5075A Kuhio Hwy., Hanalei* ☎ *808/826–1191* ☾ *No lunch.*

THE EAST SIDE

Since the East Side is the island's largest population center, it makes sense that it should boast a wide selection of restaurants. It's also a good place to get both cheaper meals and the local-style cuisine that residents favor.

Most of the eateries are found along Kuhio Highway between Kapaa and Wailua; a few are tucked into shopping centers and resorts. In Lihue, it's easier to find lunch than dinner because many restaurants cater to the business crowd.

You'll find all the usual fast-food joints in both Kapaa and Lihue, as well as virtually every ethnic cuisine available on Kauai. Although fancy gourmet restaurants are less abundant in this part of the island, there's plenty of good, solid food, and a few stellar attractions. But unless you're staying on the East Side, or passing through, it's probably not worth the long drive from the North Shore or Poipu resorts to eat here.

KAPAA AND WAILUA

In recent years, the most affordable, hip new eateries on the island have opened in Kapaa. Unlike the resort-dominated South and North shores, Kapaa is local, fun, and eclectic, with food trucks on the side of the road, vegetarian venues, and bars serving up artful appetizers. Diversity is the key to this area; there is something for everyone, especially those on a budget.

$$$ ✕ **Bull Shed.** The A-frame structure makes this popular restaurant look
STEAKHOUSE distinctly rustic from the outside. Inside, light-color walls and a full wall of glass highlight an ocean view that is one of the best on Kauai. Come early for a window seat and watch the surf crashing on the rocks while you study the menu. The food is simple, but they know how to do surf and turf. You can try both in one of several combo dinner platters or order fresh island fish and thick steaks individually. Meals include

salad bar. The restaurant is best known for its prime rib and Australian rack of lamb. Longtime visitors and locals love this place, which hasn't changed much in 30 years. Arrive early for the best seats. *Average main: $32* *796 Kuhio Hwy., Kapaa* *808/822–3791, 808/822–1655* *www.bullshedrestaurant.com* *No lunch.*

$$ ECLECTIC **Caffé Coco.** A restored plantation cottage is the casual setting for this island café. It's set back off the highway and surrounded by tropical foliage. The eclectic menu has many vegan, vegetarian, and gluten-free options, and the kitchen uses primarily local ingredients. Outdoor seating in the vine-covered garden is pleasant during nice weather. Acoustic music is offered most evenings, attracting a laid-back local crowd. *Average main: $26* *4-369 Kuhio Hwy., Kapaa* *808/822–7990* *www.caffecocokauai.com* *No lunch.*

$$$ ECLECTIC **The Eastside.** This restaurant lacks ambience, but the service is friendly and attentive, and the food is pretty good. The kale salad with goat cheese and succulent hulihuli chicken are winners, as are any of the fresh fish choices. For dessert, the lilikoi cheesecake and flourless chocolate cake come in huge portions that are best shared. The small bar is a nice place for a specialty cocktail, and there's live music a few nights a week. *Average main: $30* *4-1380 Kuhio Hwy., Kapaa* *808/823–9500* *Closed Sun.*

$ AMERICAN FAMILY **Eggbert's.** If you're big on breakfasts, try Eggbert's, which serves breakfast items until 2 pm daily. This longtime eatery has high volume, so seating and service may be delayed. Popular items are banana pancakes and eggs Benedict in two sizes. And if you'd like a Bloody Mary or mimosa, Eggbert's bar can oblige. Lunch selections include sandwiches, burgers, a pork-and-cabbage plate, and fresh fish. Take-out orders are also available, which some may prefer to the casual open-air dining room. *Average main: $11* *Coconut Marketplace, 4-484 Kuhio Hwy., Kapaa* *808/822–4422* *No credit cards* *No dinner.*

$$ AMERICAN Fodor's Choice ★ **Hukilau Lanai.** Relying heavily on super-fresh island fish and locally grown vegetables, this restaurant offers quality food that is competently and creatively prepared. The nightly fish specials—served grilled, steamed, or sautéed with succulent sauces—shine here. Other sound choices are the savory meat loaf and prime rib. Mac-nut-crusted chicken and a few pasta dishes round out the menu. The ahi poke nachos appetizer is not to be missed, nor is the warm chocolate cake. The spacious dining room looks out to the ocean, and it's lovely to eat at the outdoor tables when the weather is nice. Overall, it's a great choice for value and consistent quality on the East Side. *Average main: $23* *Kauai Coast Resort, Coconut Marketplace, 520 Aleka Loop, Kapaa* *808/822–0600* *www.hukilaukauai.com* *No lunch. Closed Mon.*

$$ ITALIAN **Kauai Pasta.** This simple yet elegant establishment offers some of the best Italian food on the island at moderate prices. Their specials are delicious, and their 10-inch pizzettas make a fine meal for one. The adjacent and chic KP Lounge stays open late, offering a handsome hideout for tasty appetizers, some with Asian spices, such as the crispy calamari with *togarashi*, and soy-lemon aioli. Their signature drink menu has a few gems, including a rosemary-and-ginger margarita, and a basil-and-coconut mojito. There's a branch in Lihue that also serves lunch and dinner. *Average main: $18* *4-939B Kuhio Hwy., Kapaa* *www.kauaipasta.com.*

$ ✕**Kountry Kitchen.** If you like a hearty breakfast, try Kountry Kitchen, a family-friendly restaurant that has a cozy, greasy-spoon atmosphere with friendly service. Breakfast is served all day. Across the street from the library in Kapaa, it's a great spot for omelets, banana pancakes, and eggs Benedict in two sizes. Lunch selections include sandwiches, burgers, and *loco mocos* (a popular local rice, beef, gravy, and eggs concoction). It's very busy at breakfast, so expect a wait on weekends. Take-out orders are also available. $ *Average main: $12* ⊠ *1485 Kuhio Hwy., Kapaa* ☎ *808/822–3511* ⊗ *No dinner.*

AMERICAN
FAMILY

$$ ✕**Lemongrass Grill.** The inside of Kapaa's Lemongrass Grill may remind you of a Pacific Rim–theme rustic tavern, with its stained wood interior, numerous paintings and carvings, and food that is as fresh as it can get. There's something for everybody here: salads, poultry, steaks and ribs, vegetarian fare, and, of course, a wide selection of seafood, all with an island flair. The best choices are the curries and satays. Service is laid-back but friendly, and there's often live, acoustic music. $ *Average main: $25* ⊠ *4-871 Kuhio Hwy., Kapaa* ☎ *808/821–2888* ⊕ *www. lemongrasshawaii.com* ⊗ *No lunch.*

ASIAN FUSION

$ ✕**Papaya's.** Kauai's largest natural-foods market contains a limited, buffet-style café with decent food at low prices. Food items change daily, but there's always a salad bar, and favorites like taro burgers and fish tacos for lunch and dinner, as well as a juice bar, coffee, and muffins. Meals are made with fresh organic lettuce and vegetables, most grown nearby. You can order takeout or eat at a covered table in the courtyard. $ *Average main: $7* ⊠ *Kauai Village Shopping Center, 4-831 Kuhio Hwy., Kapaa* ☎ *808/823–0190* ⊕ *www.papayasnaturalfoods.com.*

AMERICAN

$$ ✕**Restaurant Kintaro.** If you want to eat at a hip restaurant that's a favorite with locals, visit Kintaro. Be prepared to wait on weekends when the dining room and sushi bar are always busy. Try the soft-shell crab roll or the unbeatable Bali Hai bomb, a roll of crab and smoked salmon, baked and topped with wasabi mayonnaise. For a traditional Japanese meal, ask for the tempura combination, complete with fish, shrimp, and vegetables. *Teppanyaki* dinners are meat, seafood, and vegetables flash-cooked on tabletop grills in an entertaining display. Tatami-mat seating is available behind shoji screens that provide privacy for groups. The purple haze, a delicious mix of warm sake and framboise liqueur, is a must-have cocktail. $ *Average main: $22* ⊠ *4-370 Kuhio Hwy., Kapaa* ☎ *808/822–3341* ⊗ *No lunch. Closed Sun.*

JAPANESE
Fodor'sChoice
★

$ ✕**Shivalik Indian Cuisine.** This eatery provides a refreshing alternative to the typical fish and seafood offerings at most of Kauai's restaurants. Boasting no particular Indian regional style, this small-plaza hideaway with a tandoor oven has delicious curried vegetables, chicken dishes, and naan. Their samosas are especially noteworthy. The atmosphere is pleasant and the service is efficient. An all-you-can eat buffet is offered on Wednesday night. $ *Average main: $17* ⊠ *4-771 Kuhio Hwy., Wailua (Kauai County)* ☎ *808/821–2333* ⊗ *Closed Tues.*

INDIAN

$ ✕**Tiki Tacos.** Tiki Tacos is a notch above most Kauai taco joints, with excellent authentic Mexican food at reasonble prices. The meals are made from quality ingredients, many of them organic and locally sourced. The corn tortillas are house-made, and so are the tamales and

MEXICAN

slow-cooked meats. The fish tacos are popular, as are those filled with spicy steak or fire-roasted vegetables. Tacos are about $5 each, and they're very large. Outside tables face a parking lot; inside is a tiny, warm dining room. ⑤ *Average main: $8* ✉ *4-971 Kuhio Hwy., Kapaa* ☎ *808/823–8226.*

$ ✕ **Verde.** Combining classic Mexican food with chili-based sauces and
MEXICAN creations from the chef's home state of New Mexico, Verde's menu includes tostadas, enchiladas, and tacos served with fresh fish or slow-cooked beef or chicken. The seared tuna tacos with red chili aioli and the stacked enchilada, with chicken or beef short ribs smothered in red or green chili sauce, are favorites. The food runs hot and spicy. Beers and margaritas served with premium tequila complement the spicy sauces perfectly. ⑤ *Average main: $13* ✉ *4-1101 Kuhio Hwy., Kapaa* ☎ *808/821–1400* ⊕ *www.verdehawaii.com.*

$ ✕ **Wailua Marina Restaurant.** Offering the island's only river view, this
MODERN marina restaurant—an island fixture for almost 40 years—is a good
HAWAIIAN spot to stop for a quiet, leisurely lunch after a boat ride up the Wailua River to the Fern Grotto, and worth a visit on its own merit. With more than 40 selections, the menu is a mix of comfort food and more sophisticated dishes; portions are gigantic. The chef is fond of stuffing: you'll find stuffed baked pork chops, stuffed chicken baked in plum sauce, and ahi stuffed with crab. The steamed mullet is a classic island dish. ⑤ *Average main: $17* ✉ *Wailua River State Park, Wailua Rd., Wailua (Kauai County)* ☎ *808/822–4311* ⊙ *Closed Mon.*

LIHUE

You will probably find yourself in Lihue at least a few times during your stay. When it comes to restaurants, Lihue isn't especially outstanding. There are some decent restaurants and some good low-cost eateries that feed locals and the business-lunch crowd—but nothing really stellar. If you are in town for lunch, don't pass up some of the authentic local spots.

$ ✕ **Dani's Restaurant.** Kauai residents frequent this large, spare eatery near
HAWAIIAN the Lihue Fire Station for hearty, local-style food at breakfast and lunch.
FAMILY Dani's is a good place to try traditional luau cuisine without commercial luau prices. You can order Hawaiian-style *laulau* (pork and taro leaves wrapped in ti leaves and steamed) or kalua pig, slow roasted in an underground oven. Other island-style dishes include Japanese-prepared *tonkatsu* (pork cutlet) and teriyaki beef, and there's always the all-American New York steak. Omelets are whipped up with fish cake, kalua pig, or seafood; everything is served with rice. ⑤ *Average main: $8* ✉ *4201 Rice St., Lihue* ☎ *808/245–4991* ⊙ *Closed Sun. No dinner.*

$$ ✕ **Duke's Canoe Club.** Surfing legend Duke Kahanamoku is immor-
SEAFOOD talized at this casual bi-level restaurant and bar on Kalapaki Beach. Surfboards, photos, and other memorabilia marking Duke's long tenure as a waterman adorn the walls. You'll find simple fare ranging from fish tacos and stir-fried cashew chicken to hamburgers, served 11 am to 11 pm. Upstairs, at dinner, fresh fish prepared in a variety of styles is the best choice, though the prime rib is a favorite among

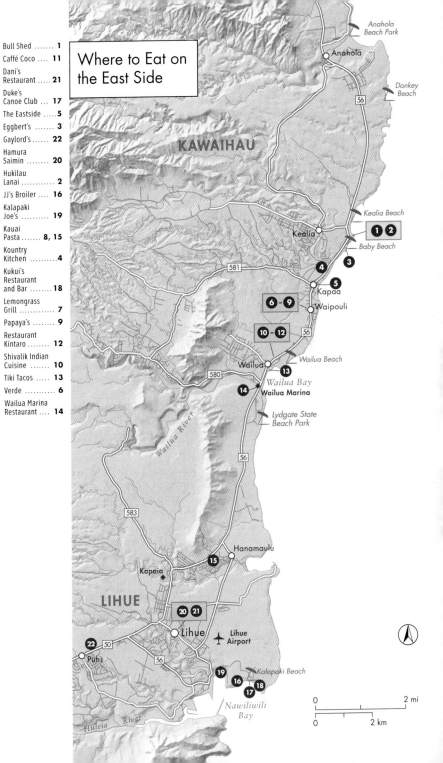

Where to Eat on the East Side

locals. A comprehensive salad bar comes with dinner. Save room for the famous hula pie, a gigantic ice-cream dessert that should be shared by at least two people. Downstairs, at the Barefoot Bar, a happy-hour drink and appetizer is a less expensive way to enjoy the moonrises and ocean views—though it can get pretty crowded. ⑤ *Average main: $25* ✉ *Kauai Marriott Resort & Beach Club, 3610 Rice St., Kalapaki Beach, Lihue* ☎ *808/246–9599* ⊕ *www.dukeskauai.com.*

$$$
ECLECTIC
✗ **Gaylord's.** Located in what was once Kauai's most expensive plantation estate, Gaylord's pays tribute to the elegant dining rooms of 1930s high society. Although the food is satisfying, Gaylord's is primarily about ambience. Tables with candlelight sit on a cobblestone patio that surrounds a fountain and overlooks a wide lawn. The menu is eclectic, ranging from tender seared scallops served in a fennel cream with potato croquettes to buttermilk fried chicken with a thick country gravy. Try the fish-packed cioppino or the tender hoisin-glazed pork short ribs. The pineapple shortcake is a tasty twist on an old favorite. Lunch mostly consists of pricey burgers, crepes, and salads. The lavish Sunday brunch buffet includes an ahi tuna Benedict, blackened steak and eggs, and a waffle station. Before or after dining you can stroll the estate grounds. ⑤ *Average main: $30* ✉ *Kilohana Plantation, 3-2087 Kaumualii Hwy., Puhi* ☎ *808/245–9593* ⊕ *www.gaylordskauai.com* ⊘ *No dinner Sun.*

$
ASIAN
Fodor's Choice
★
✗ **Hamura Saimin.** Folks just love this funky old plantation-style diner. Locals and tourists stream in and out all day long, and neighbor islanders stop in on their way to the airport to pick up take-out orders for friends and family back home. Their famous *saimin* soup is the big draw, and each day the Hiraoka family dishes up about 1,000 bowls of steaming broth and homemade noodles, topped with a variety of garnishes. The barbecued chicken and meat sticks adopt a smoky flavor during grilling. The landmark eatery is also famous for its *lilikoi* (passion fruit) chiffon pie. ■TIP→ This is one of the few Lihue restaurants open late—8:30 pm on weeknights and midnight on Friday and Saturday. ⑤ *Average main: $7* ✉ *2956 Kress St., Lihue* ☎ *808/245–3271* ⊟ *No credit cards.*

$$$
AMERICAN
✗ **JJ's Broiler.** This spacious, low-key restaurant serves hearty fare, with dinner specials such as lobster and Slavonic steak, a broiled sliced tenderloin dipped in buttery wine sauce, and local-style kalua pig and cabbage. The grilled Cajun-style prime rib is also pretty good. On sunny afternoons, ask for a table on the lanai overlooking Kalapaki Bay and

BUDGET-FRIENDLY EATS: EAST SIDE

At these small, local-style eateries, two people can generally eat dinner for less than $20.

Garden Island BBQ and Chinese Restaurant. ✉ *4252-A Rice St., Lihue,* ⊕ *www.gardenislandbbq.com,* ☎ *808/245-8868.*

Hamura Saimin. ✉ *2956 Kress St., Lihue,* ☎ *808/245-3271.*

Papaya's. ✉ *4-831 Kuhio Hwy., Kapaa,* ⊕ *www.papayasnaturalfoods.com,* ☎ *808/823-0190.*

Waipouli Restaurant. ✉ *Waipouli Town Center, 4-771 Kuhio Hwy., Kapaa,* ☎ *808/822-9311.*

SHAVE ICE

Nothing goes down quite as nicely as shave ice on a hot day. This favorite island treat has been likened to a sno-cone, but that description doesn't do a good shave ice justice. Yes, it is ice served up in a cone-shaped cup and drenched with sweet syrup, but the similarities end there. As its name implies, the ice should be feathery light—the texture of snowflakes, not frozen slush. And alongside the standard cherry and grape, you'll find all sorts of exotic island flavorings, such as passion fruit, pineapple, coconut, mango, and, of course, a rainbow mix or snow topping of condensed milk.

Not all shave ice meets these high standards, and when you're hot, even the average ones taste great. But a few places are worth seeking out. On the East Side, the best is **Hawaiian Blizzard** (⊠ *Kapaa Shopping Center, 4-1105 Kuhio Hwy.*), a true shave-ice stand that opens up weekday afternoons next to the Big Save grocery store in Kapaa. In Lihue, try **Halo Halo Shave Ice** in the Harbor Mall Shopping Center (⊠ *3501 Rice St.*). And on the hot, dry West Side, make a beeline for **Jo-Jo's Clubhouse** (⊠ *Mile marker 23, Kaumualii, Hwy. 50*), on the main drag in Waimea. All three places have benches where you can sit and slurp.

try one of the generous salads or appetizers and a drink. The upstairs section is currently only available for private events, but you can still eat at the restaurant's lower level, which is open-air and casual. JJ's is a relaxed place to enjoy lunch, dinner, or just sit at the bar for a drink, with one of the best ocean views in Lihue. ⑤ *Average main: $30* ⊠ *Anchor Cove, 3416 Rice St., Nawiliwili* ☎ *808/246–4422* ⊕ *www. jjsbroiler.com.*

$$ ✕ **Kalapaki Joe's.** The original Kalapaki Joe's has moved from Nawiliwili Harbor to Kukui Grove in Lihue, but it is still the place for sports fans who like a rip-roaring happy hour. The appetizer menu is extensive, or choose from burgers, salads, sandwiches, fish tacos, steaks, ribs, and fresh fish specials. This place is typically packed with a boisterous crowd from late afternoon on into the night. The second-story location has a postcard-perfect view of Kalapaki Bay. ⑤ *Average main: $20* ⊠ *3-2600 Kaumualii Hwy., Lihue* ☎ *808/245–6366* ⊕ *www.kalapakijoes.com.*

AMERICAN

$$ ✕ **Kukui's Restaurant and Bar.** The meals at Kukui's feature Hawaiian, Asian, and contemporary American influences, and the open-air setting makes it a pleasant place to dine. It's very spacious, and not as busy and noisy as the other eateries at the Marriott, making it well suited to families and those who want a relaxed setting. The menu includes slow-roasted prime rib, fresh fish, and pasta dishes. You can also order from the Toro Tei sushi bar, or from the bar menu. A full breakfast buffet is offered every morning, or choose from the à la carte menu. ⑤ *Average main: $25* ⊠ *Kauai Marriott Resort & Beach Club, 3610 Rice St., Kalapaki Beach, Lihue* ☎ *808/245–5050* ⊕ *www.marriott.com.*

ECLECTIC
FAMILY

$ ✕ **Mema Thai Chinese Cuisine.** Some menu items at Mema's reveal a Chinese flair, but the emphasis is on Thai dishes. A host of curries—red, green, yellow, house, and Mema's, which is made with coconut milk and Kaffir-lime leaves—run from mild to mouth-searing. The pad thai is

THAI

Nothing beats shave ice (no, not "shaved" ice) on a hot Hawaiian day.

served with a choice of tofu, chicken, pork, shrimp, or seafood combo. The shrimp summer rolls taste fresh, and the traditional green-papaya salad adds a cool touch for the palate. Though it's a bit shabby and service can be slow, the food is hearty and good. Beware: it tends be hot inside. $ *Average main: $14* ⊠ *3-3204 Kuhi Hwy., Ste. 101, Lihue* ☎ *808/823–0899* ⊘ *No lunch weekends.*

THE SOUTH SHORE

Most South Shore restaurants are more upscale and located within the Poipu resorts. If you're looking for a gourmet meal in a classy setting, the South Shore is where you'll find it. Poipu has a number of excellent restaurants in dreamy settings and decidedly fewer family-style, lower-price eateries.

$$$
ASIAN
Fodor's Choice
★

× **Beach House.** This restaurant partners a dreamy ocean view with impressive cuisine, and is one of the best places on the island for a romantic dinner, open-air lunch, or cocktail and appetizer. Few Kauai experiences are more delightful than sitting at one of the Beach House's outside tables and savoring a delectable meal while the sun sinks into the glassy blue Pacific and surfers slice the waves. Cobble up a meal from tasty sides like crab cakes, sweet-spicy braised pork, arugula–goat cheese salad, and an excellent ceviche. Or pick a wasabi-crusted fresh fish sauté or braised lamb shank with truffle-asparagus risotto. The fire-grilled filet mignon with blue cheese is remarkable. Our dessert favorites include the warm molten chocolate cake, the bananas Foster, and the carrot cake with pineapple, macadamia nuts, and cream cheese

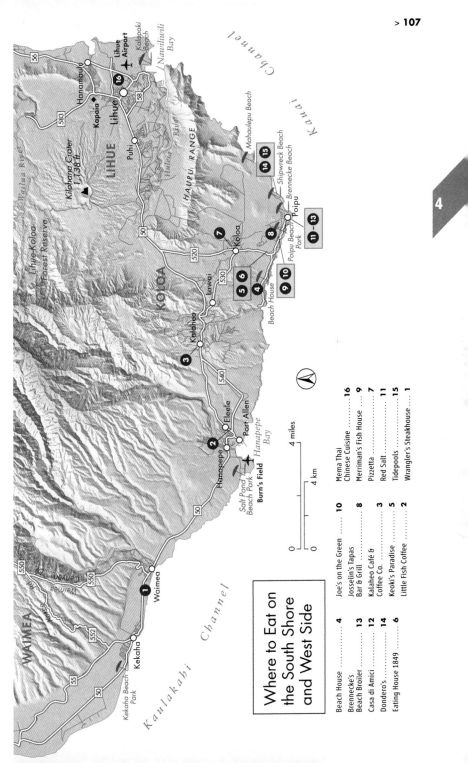

4

Where to Eat on the South Shore and West Side

Beach House **4**	Joe's on the Green **10**
Brennecke's Beach Broiler **13**	Josselin's Tapas Bar & Grill **8**
Casa di Amici **12**	Kalaheo Café & Coffee Co. **3**
Dondero's **14**	Keoki's Paradise **5**
Eating House 1849 ...... **6**	Little Fish Coffee **2**
Mema Thai Chinese Cuisine **16**	
Merriman's Fish House **9**	
Pizzetta **7**	
Red Salt **11**	
Tidepools **15**	
Wrangler's Steakhouse **1**	

frosting. Gluten-free and vegan choices are also available. $ *Average main: $35* ⊠ *5022 Lawai Rd., Koloa* ☎ *808/742–1424* ⊕ *www. the-beach-house.com* ⊸ *Reservations essential.*

$$$ ✕ **Brennecke's Beach Broiler.** Bren-
AMERICAN necke's is decidedly casual and fun, with a busy bar, windows overlooking the beach, and a cheery blue-and-white interior. It specializes in big portions in a wide range of offerings including rib-eye steak, burgers, fish tacos, pasta, shrimp, and the fresh catch of the day. Can't decide? Then create your own combination meal. This place is especially good for happy hour (3 pm to 5 pm and 8:30 pm to closing), as the drink and pupu menus bring the prices closer to reality. The fare is fair, but the ocean view and convenient location compensate for the food's shortcomings. There's a take-out deli with shave ice downstairs. $ *Average main: $27* ⊠ *2100 Hoone Rd., Poipu* ☎ *808/742–7588* ⊕ *www.brenneckes.com.*

$$$ ✕ **Casa di Amici.** Tucked away in a quiet neighborhood above Poipu
ITALIAN Beach, this longtime restaurant has an outside deck open to sweeping ocean views. It boasts an eclectic menu, with a few Asian and Mexican dishes slipped into the original all-Italian lineup. The interior has been freshened up with a remodel, and you can still dine outside with the twinkly lights. Start with the spicy tamales or fried calamari with a lemon-caper sauce. Choices include chicken picatta, ahi with ginger miso, a Thai beef satay risotto, and fettuccine with house-made Italian sausage. For dessert, take the plunge with a baked Hawaii—a chocolate-macadamia-nut brownie topped with coconut and passion-fruit sorbet and flambéed Italian meringue. Volume here can get a bit loud. $ *Average main: $27* ⊠ *2301 Nalo Rd., Poipu* ☎ *808/742–1555* ⊕ *www. casadiamici.com* ⊘ *No lunch.*

$$$ ✕ **Dondero's.** With a beautiful setting, good food, and impeccable ser-
ITALIAN vice, Dondero's is one of Kauai's better restaurants. The inlaid marble
Fodor'sChoice floors, ornate tile work, and Italianate murals that compose the elegant
★ interior at this restaurant compete with a stunning ocean view. The elegant tasting menu features Italian dishes, including homemade pastas, risotto, and flatbread pizza. Try the olive-braised chicken orzo; grilled steak; seafood cioppino with scallops, mussels, fresh fish, lobster, and shrimp; or any of the outstanding pasta, meat, fish, and vegetarian choices. Many menu items are gluten-free, and Black Forest tiramisu is a divine ending to the meal. The food is beautifully executed, and the waitstaff earns special praise for thoughtful, personalized service. It's delightful to sit outside beneath twinkling lights. $ *Average main: $33* ⊠ *Grand Hyatt Kauai Resort and Spa, 1571 Poipu Rd., Poipu* ☎ *808/240–6456* ⊘ *No lunch.*

BUDGET-FRIENDLY: SOUTH SHORE AND WEST SIDE

Grind's Cafe and Espresso. ⊠ Rte. 50, 4469 Waialo Rd., ☎ 808/335–6027, ⊕ www.grindscafe.net.

Puka Dog. ⊠ 2650 Kiahuna Plantation Dr., Koloa, ☎ 808/742–6044, ⊕ www.pukadog.com.

Wong's. ⊠ Kaumuali Hwy., ☎ 808/335–5066, ⊕ www.wongsomoide.com.

The Plate-Lunch Tradition

To experience island history firsthand, step up to the counter at one of Hawaii's ubiquitous "plate lunch" eateries, and order a segmented Styrofoam plate piled with rice, macaroni salad, and maybe a pickled vegetable condiment. On the sugar plantations, Native Hawaiians and immigrant workers from many different countries ate together in the fields, sharing food from their "kaukau kits," the utilitarian version of the Japanese *bento* lunchbox. From this "melting pot" came the vibrant language of pidgin and its equivalent in food: the plate lunch.

Along roadsides, and at beaches and events, you will see food trucks, another excellent venue for sampling plate lunches. These portable restaurants are descendants of "lunch wagons" that began selling food to plantation workers in the 1930s. Try the deep-fried chicken *katsu* (rolled in Japanese panko bread crumbs and spices). The marinated beef teriyaki is another good choice, as is miso butterfish. The noodle soup, *saimin*, with its Japanese fish stock and Chinese red-tinted barbecue pork, is a distinctly local medley. Koreans have contributed spicy barbecue *kalbi* ribs, often served with chili-laden *kimchi* (pickled cabbage). Portuguese bean soup and tangy Filipino *adobo* stew are also favorites. The most popular Hawaiian contribution to the plate lunch is the *laulau*, a mix of meat and fish and young taro leaves, wrapped in more taro leaves and steamed.

$$$ ✕ **Eating House 1849.** Hawaii's culinary superstar, Roy Yamaguchi, has
ASIAN FUSION moved his signature Hawaiian-fusion-cuisine restaurant on Kauai's
Fodor'sChoice South Shore to an updated shopping-center locale that suits the new
★ name and creative fare. Billed as "plantation cuisine," the menu fea-
tures blackened ahi, a delectable open-fire-grilled rib-eye steak, delicious
takes on beef tostadas, and a Reuben sandwich. Pot stickers, lumpia,
calamari, and an array of soups and salads make it easy to cobble
together a hearty tapas-type meal. The food is served in cast-iron skillets
and other casual ware that suit the plantation-style decor. Reservations
are recommended. ⑤ *Average main: $35* ✉ *Shops at Kukuiula, 2829
Ala Kalanikaumaka Rd., No. A-201, Koloa* ☎ *808/742–5000* ⊕ *www.
eatinghouse1849.com* ⊘ *No lunch.*

$ ✕ **Joe's on the Green.** Eat an open-air breakfast, lunch, or early dinner
AMERICAN (it closes at 7 pm) with an expansive vista of Poipu. Located on the
Kiahuna Golf Course, this restaurant boasts such favorites as eggs Bene-
dict, tofu scramble, and banana-macadamia-nut pancakes. For lunch or
dinner, try the quarter-pound hot dog, the Reuben sandwich, the ribs,
or build your own salad. Happy hour, which often features live music,
offers local favorites like *manapua* dumplings and ahi poke, along with
sliders, ribs, and homemade chili nachos. With a casual atmosphere
and generous portions, Joe's is a refreshing alternative to the pricier
hotel brunch venues in this area. ⑤ *Average main: $12* ✉ *2545 Kiahuna
Plantation Dr., Poipu* ☎ *808/742–9696* ⊕ *www.joesonthegreen.com.*

$$$ ✕**Josselin's Tapas Bar & Grill.** Chef Jean-Marie Josselin, one of the pio-
CONTEMPORARY neers of Hawaiian regional cuisine, has a winner with this fun, sophis-
ticated, small-plates restaurant. After the roaming sangria cart rolls up
with concoctions containing lilikoi and lychee, the feast is on. The menu
changes frequently, but expect a wide range of Hawaiian-influenced,
Asian, and Western choices to satisfy all palates. The idea is to share a
variety of choices. The tempura ahi roll with beurre blanc is especially
tasty. Or try the Kauai shrimp-and-duck tacos with pineapple salsa, the
pumpkin ravioli, or the sesame-crusted mahi and braised pork belly
with apple kimchi. The only drawback is the very noisy dining room.
⑤ *Average main: $30* ✉ *Kukuiula shopping center, upstairs, 2829 Ala
Kalanikaumaka St., Poipu* ☎ *808/742–7117* ⊕ *www.josselinstapas.com*
☺ *No lunch.*

$ ✕**Kalaheo Café & Coffee Co.** Folks love this roadside café, especially for
AMERICAN breakfast, though it's good for lunch and a simple dinner, too. It's a
FAMILY casual atmosphere, and is frequently busy, especially on weekend morn-
ings. Order up front and then find a seat inside or out on the lanai.
Favorites include the Kahili Breakfast, scrambled eggs served with Por-
tuguese sausage, ham, and green onions; and the Longboard sandwich,
with fried egg, bacon, lettuce, tomato, and melted provolone cheese.
The dinner menu has some really good salads, ribs, meat loaf, chicken,
fish, burgers, and weekly specials. Lots of local products are used here,
including Anahola Granola, local fish, and Kauai coffee, which you can
buy by the pound. It's a solid choice in an area with limited restaurants.
⑤ *Average main: $17* ✉ *2-2560 Kaumualii Hwy. (Rte. 50), Kalaheo*
☎ *808/332–5858* ⊕ *www.kalaheo.com* ☺ *No dinner Sun. or Mon.*

$$ ✕**Keoki's Paradise.** Built to resemble a dockside boathouse, this active,
ASIAN boisterous place fills up quickly at night thanks to a busy bar and
FAMILY frequent live music. Seafood appetizers span the tide from sashimi to
Thai shrimp sticks, crab cakes, and pot stickers. The day's fresh catch
is available in various styles and sauces, along with scallops, seafood
risotto, and lobster. The *imu*-roasted pork ribs are popular, as is the
prime rib. The ice cream–and–Oreo cookie hula pie is a classic, but the
chocolate crème brûlée should not be overlooked. There's a gluten-free
menu, and lighter fare at the bar. The *keiki* (kids) menu includes tropical
drinks. ⑤ *Average main: $25* ✉ *Poipu Shopping Village, 2360 Kiahuna
Plantation Dr., Koloa* ☎ *808/742–7534* ⊕ *www.keokisparadise.com.*

$$$$ ✕**Merriman's Fish House.** The regional food served up at chef Peter Mer-
MODERN riman's namesake restaurant is enhanced by a sophisticated setting and
HAWAIIAN lovely views from a pretty second-floor dining room. Start at the bar,
where fine wines are offered by the glass, and try the crispy crab cakes or
raw fish poke. The dinner menu states the origin of the fish, lamb, beef,
chicken, and veggies. Wok-charred ahi is the signature dish, though the
butter-poached Keahole lobster and Hanalei taro enchilada also shine.
Smaller portions of two entrées also can be ordered. Lunch and casual
meals are served downstairs, which has a nice outdoor eating area.
⑤ *Average main: $38* ✉ *2829 Ala Kalanikaumaka St., G-149, Poipu*
☎ *808/742–8385* ⊕ *www.merrimanshawaii.com.*

ROMANTIC DINING

For divine sunsets, the **Beach House** (☏ *808/742–1424*), in Koloa, is tops, as it puts you right on the water. **Café Portofino** (☏ *808/245–2121*), at the Kauai Marriott in Lihue, with its second-story view of Kalapaki Bay and harp music, practically caters to couples. Tops overall, though, is **Dondero's** (☏ *808/240–6456*), in Koloa, where the food, service, and elegant setting come together to create a special evening. If it's a nice evening, by all means opt for the veranda.

Be sure to make reservations, and don't plan on pinching pennies. If you're on a budget, pick up some take-out food and spread a blanket on the beach for a memorable sunset picnic and dessert beneath brilliant stars.

4

$ ✕ **Pizzetta.** This family-style Italian restaurant serves up hearty portions of pasta, calzones, and pizza, along with kalua pork and cabbage, grilled fish, and barbecue ribs, all of which can find their way into pizza toppings. Gluten-free crust and pasta are available. The tropical fruit crisp with vanilla gelato is a nice finish. The menu is quite extensive, and the food is generally good. Meals are served in a casual, lively setting, with an open-air deck. Neighborhood delivery is available. $ *Average main: $15* ✉ *5408 Koloa Rd., Koloa* ☏ *808/742–8881* ⊕ *www.pizzettarestaurant.com.*

ITALIAN

FAMILY

$$$ ✕ **Red Salt.** A smart, sophisticated decor and exceptional food paired with professional service make Red Salt a great choice for leisurely fine dining. The seared mahi is enlivened with a mango vinaigrette, while the rack of lamb is basted with a tamarind glaze, and the Wagyu burger is topped with a lobster tail and seared foie gras. The root-beer float is a fun dessert, but the lilikoi-ginger crème brûlée and dark-chocolate macadamia-nut torte are memorable. The presentation is exquisite, making this a feast for the eyes as well as the taste buds. A breakfast buffet also is served. $ *Average main: $32* ✉ *Koa Kea Resort, 2251 Poipu Rd., Koloa* ☏ *808/742–4288* ⊕ *www.koakea.com/dining-at-red-salt/.*

ECLECTIC

Fodor'sChoice

★

$$$$ ✕ **Tidepools.** Of the Grand Hyatt's many notable restaurants, Tidepools is definitely the most tropical and campy, sure to appeal to folks seeking a bit of island-style romance and adventure. Private grass-thatch huts seem to float on a koi-filled pond beneath starry skies while torches flicker in the lushly landscaped grounds nearby. The equally distinctive food has an island flavor that comes from the chef's advocacy of Hawaii regional cuisine and extensive use of Kauai-grown products including fresh herbs from the resort's organic garden. You won't go wrong ordering the soy-ginger-glazed catch of the day, macadamia-nut-crusted mahimahi, or the grilled wild boar rack of ribs. Start with jumbo lump crab cakes or Tahitian ceviche to wake up your taste buds. The tropical fruit tart with coconut streudel is a memorable dessert. $ *Average main: $40* ✉ *Grand Hyatt Kauai Resort and Spa, 1571 Poipu Rd., Poipu* ☏ *808/240–6456* ☉ *No lunch.*

SEAFOOD

THE WEST SIDE

When it comes to dining on the West Side, pickings are mighty slim. Fortunately, the few eateries that are here are generally worth patronizing.

$ ✕ **Little Fish Coffee.** For a wholesome breakfast or lunch on the West Side,
CAFÉ   Little Fish Coffee is the spot. The coffee is good, with each cup individually dripped, and the fresh bagels come with house-made cream cheese. The fruit-and-granola bowls, sandwiches, and wraps are recommendable, too. Smoothies and juices add to the healthy cuisine. This place is small, friendly, funky, and fun, right down to the marking pens that allow you to leave your own graffiti on the bathroom wall. Seating is very limited inside, but the courtyard in the back is a nice spot to dine. ⑤ *Average main: $8* ⊠ *3900 Hanapepe Rd., Eleele* ☎ *808/335–5000* ⊘ *No dinner.*

$$ ✕ **Wrangler's Steakhouse.** Denim-covered seating, decorative saddles, and
STEAKHOUSE   a stagecoach in a loft helped to transform the historic Ako General Store in Waimea into a West Side steak house. You can eat under the stars on the deck out back or inside the old-fashioned, wood-panel dining room. The 16-ounce New York steak comes sizzling, and the rib eye is served with capers. A trip to the tiny salad bar is included. Those with smaller appetites might consider the vegetarian tempura or the ahi served on penne pasta. Local folks love the special lunch: rice, beef teriyaki, and shrimp tempura with kimchi served in a three-tier *kaukau* tin, or lunch pail, just like the ones sugar-plantation workers once carried. There's live music on Saturday night. ⑤ *Average main: $25* ⊠ *9852 Kaumualii Hwy., Waimea (Kauai County)* ☎ *808/338–1218* ⊘ *No lunch Sat. Closed Sun.*

WHERE TO STAY

Updated by Joan Conrow

The Garden Isle has lodgings for every taste, from swanky resorts to rustic cabins, and from family-friendly condos to romantic bed-and-breakfasts. The savvy traveler can also find inexpensive places that are convenient, safe, and accessible to Kauai's special places and activities.

Kauai may seem small on a map, but because it's circular with no through roads, it can take more time than you think to get from place to place. If at all possible, stay close to your desired activities. This way, you'll save time to squeeze in all the things you'll want to do.

Time of year is also a factor. If you're here in winter or spring, consider staying on the South Shore, as the surf on the North Shore and East Side tends to be rough, making many ocean beaches dangerous for swimming or water sports.

Before booking accommodations, think hard about what kind of experience you want to have for your island vacation. There are several top-notch resorts to choose from, and Kauai also has a wide variety of condos, vacation rentals, and bed-and-breakfasts. The Kauai Visitors Bureau provides a comprehensive listing of accommodation choices to help you decide.

KAUAI LODGING PLANNER

HOTELS AND RESORTS

If you want to golf, play tennis, or hang at a spa, stay at a resort. You'll also be more likely to find activities for children at resorts, including camps that allow parents a little time off. The island's hotels tend to be smaller and older, with fewer on-site amenities. The swankiest places to stay on the island are the St. Regis Princeville Resort on the North Shore, where rooms run more than $1,000 per night in high season, and the Grand Hyatt Kauai on the South Shore for a bit less; of course, those with views of the ocean book faster than those without. Many resorts have begun charging a daily "amenities fee" that can add $15 to $30 to the price of the lodging, so be sure to inquire when you make reservations to avoid unpleasant surprises upon checkout.

B&BS AND INNS

The island's bed-and-breakfasts allow you to meet local residents and more directly experience the aloha spirit. Many have oceanfront settings and breakfasts with everything from tropical fruits and juices, Kauai coffee, and macadamia waffles to breads made with local bananas and mangoes. Some have pools, hot tubs, services such as *lomilomi* massage, and breakfasts delivered to your lanai. Some properties have stand-alone units on-site.

CONDOS AND VACATION RENTALS

Condos and vacation rentals on Kauai tend to run the gamut from fabulous luxury estates to scruffy little dives. It's buyer-beware in this largely unregulated sector of the visitor industry, where there's no inspection of properties and many operate without county permits. If you're planning to stay at one of these, ask for their county permit number and be sure to contact the Kauai Visitors Bureau (☎ *800/262–1400*) to see whether any complaints have been made against it. Also be aware that most do not have air-conditioning.

Properties managed by individual owners can be found on online vacation-rental directories such as CyberRentals and Vacation Rentals By Owner, as well as on the Kauai Visitors Bureau's website. There are also several Kauai-based management companies with vacation rentals.

RESERVATIONS

The rule on Kauai—and for Hawaii in general—is to book as far in advance as possible. Rooms go most quickly during holidays, but there really isn't any low season to speak of. Some places allow 24 hours' notice to cancel; others require a week or will penalize you the cost of one night. Most hotels allow children under a certain age to stay in their parents' room at no extra charge, but others charge for them as extra adults; find out the cutoff age for discounts.

PRICES

Prices listed in our hotel reviews are the lowest cost of a standard double room in high season, which generally includes taxes and service charges but not any optional meal plans. Prices for rentals are the lowest per-night cost for a one-bedroom unit in high season.

For expanded lodging reviews and current deals, visit Fodors.com.

WHAT IT COSTS			
$	$$	$$$	$$$$
FOR TWO PEOPLE	under $180	$180–$260	$261–$340	over $340

Hotel prices are for two people in a standard double room in high season. Condo price categories reflect studio and one-bedroom rates.

WHERE TO STAY IN KAUAI

	Local Vibe	Pros	Cons
The North Shore	Properties here have the "wow" factor with ocean and mountain beauty; laid-back Hanalei and Princeville set the high-end pace.	When the weather is good (summer) this side has it all. Epic winter surf, gorgeous waterfalls, and verdant vistas create some of the best scenery in Hawaii.	Frequent winter rain (being green has a cost) means you may have to travel south to find the sun; expensive restaurants and shopping offer few deals.
The East Side	The most reasonably priced area to stay for the practical traveler; lacks the pizzazz of expensive resorts on North and South shores; more traditional beach hotels.	The best travel deals show up here; more direct access to the local population; plenty of decent restaurants with good variety, along with delis in food stores.	Beaches aren't the greatest (rocky, reefy) at many of the lodging spots; congested traffic at times; some crime issues in parks.
The South Shore	Resort central; plenty of choices where the consistent sunshine is perfect for those who want to do nothing but play golf or tennis and read a book by the pool.	Beautiful in its own right; many enchanted evenings with stellar sunsets; summer surf a bit easier for beginners to handle.	Though resorts are lush, surrounding landscape is desertlike with scrub brush; construction can be brutal on peace of mind.
The West Side	There are few options for lodging in this mostly untouristed setting, with contrasts such as the extreme heat of a July day in Waimea to a frozen winter night up in Kokee.	A gateway area for exploration into the wilds of Kokee or for boating trips on Napali Coast; main hub for boat and helicopter trips; outstanding sunsets.	Least convenient side for most visitors; daytime is languid and dry; river runoff can ruin ocean's clarity.

THE NORTH SHORE

The North Shore is mountainous and wet, which accounts for its rugged, lush landscape. Posh resorts and condominiums await you at Princeville, a community with dreamy views, excellent golf courses, and lovely sunsets. It maintains the lion's share of North Shore accommodations—primarily luxury hotel rooms and condos built on a plateau overlooking the sea. Hanalei, a bay-side town in a broad valley, has a smattering of hotel rooms and numerous vacation rentals, many within walking distance of the beach. Prices tend to be high in this resort area. If you want to do extensive sightseeing on other parts of the island, be prepared for a long drive—one that's very dark at night.

$$ 🛎 **Hanalei Bay Resort.** This lovely condominium resort overlooks Hanalei
RESORT   Bay and Napali Coast. **Pros:** beautiful views; tennis courts on property;
FAMILY   children's tennis program; tropical pool; 24-hour fitness center. **Cons:**
steep walkways; long walk to beach. Ⓢ*Rooms from: $189* ✉ *5380
Honoiki Rd., Princeville* ☎ *808/826–6522, 877/507–1428* ⊕ *www.
hanaleibayresort.com* ⤳ *134 units* ⃒⃝ *No meals.*

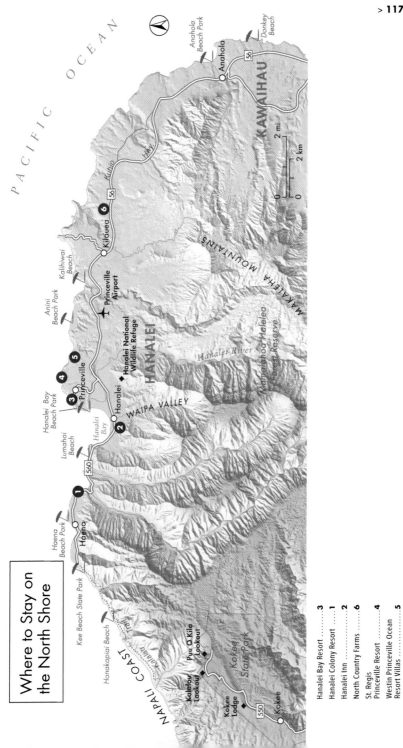

Where to Stay on the North Shore

5

Hanalei Bay Resort **3**
Hanalei Colony Resort **1**
Hanalei Inn **2**
North Country Farms **6**
St. Regis
Princeville Resort **4**
Westin Princeville Ocean
Resort Villas **5**

$$$
HOTEL

⊤ Hanalei Colony Resort. The only true beachfront resort on Kauai's North Shore, Hanalei Colony is a laid-back, go-barefoot kind of resort sandwiched between towering mountains and the sea. **Pros:** oceanfront setting; private, quiet; seventh night free. **Cons:** poor cellphone reception; damp in winter. $ *Rooms from: $340* ⊠ *5-7130 Kuhio Hwy., Haena* ☎ *808/826–6235, 800/628–3004* ⊕ *www.hcr. com* ⤳ *48 units* †○† *No meals.*

> **MOST ROMANTIC RESORTS**
>
> Grand Hyatt Kauai Resort and Spa
>
> Hanalei Bay Resort
>
> Hanalei Colony Resort
>
> Koa Kea Hotel and Resort
>
> St. Regis Princeville Resort

$
RENTAL

⊤ Hanalei Inn. If you're looking for lodgings that won't break the bank a block from gorgeous Hanalei Bay, look no further, as this is literally the only choice among the town's pricey vacation rentals. **Pros:** quick walk to beach, bus stop, and shops; full kitchen. **Cons:** strict cancellation policy; daytime traffic noise; older property. $ *Rooms from: $159* ⊠ *5-5468 Kuhio Hwy., Hanalei* ☎ *808/826–9333, 888/773–4730* ⊕ *www.hanaleiinn.com* ⤳ *4 studios* †○† *No meals.*

$
RENTAL
FAMILY

⊤ North Country Farms. This comfortable lodging is tucked away on a tidy, 4-acre organic fruit, flower, and vegetable farm just east of Kilauea. **Pros:** delightful setting; pick fresh fruit and vegetables; warm and friendly hostess. **Cons:** no beach; no resort-type amenities. $ *Rooms from: $175* ⊠ *4387 Kahili Makai St., Kilauea* ☎ *808/828–1513* ⊕ *www. northcountryfarms.com* ⤳ *1 cottage* †○† *No meals.*

$$$$
RESORT
FAMILY
Fodor's Choice
★

⊤ St. Regis Princeville Resort. Built into the cliffs above Hanalei Bay, this swanky Starwood resort offers expansive views of the sea and mountains, including Makana, the landmark peak immortalized as mysterious Bali Hai island in the film *South Pacific.* **Pros:** great views; excellent restaurants; attractive lobby. **Cons:** minimal grounds; beach not ideal for swimming; extremely expensive. $ *Rooms from: $460* ⊠ *5520 Ka Haku Rd., Princeville* ☎ *877/787–3447, 808/826–9644* ⊕ *www. stregisprinceville.com* ⤳ *201 rooms, 51 suites* †○† *No meals.*

$$$
RESORT

⊤ Westin Princeville Ocean Resort Villas. Spread out over 18½ acres on a bluff above Anini Beach, the Westin Princeville Ocean Resort Villas marries the comforts of condominium living with the top-notch service and amenities of a luxurious hotel resort. **Pros:** on-site mini-market; free parking; kids' program. **Cons:** path to the nearby beach is a steep six- to seven-minute walk and it's not a good swimming beach; whirlpool tub is small. $ *Rooms from: $340* ⊠ *3838 Wyllie Rd., Princeville* ☎ *808/827–8700, 800/827–8801* ⊕ *www.westinprinceville.com* ⤳ *366 units* †○† *No meals.*

THE EAST SIDE

Location, location, location. The East Side, or Coconut Coast, is a good centralized home base if you want to see and do it all. This is one of the few resort areas on Kauai where you can actually walk to the beach, restaurants, and stores from your condo, hotel, or vacation-rental unit. It's not only convenient, but comparatively cheap. You pay less for lodging, meals, services, merchandise, and gas here—mainly because much of the coral-reef coastline isn't as ideal as the sandy-bottom bays that front the fancy resorts. We think the shoreline is just fine. There are pockets in the reef to swim in, and the coast is uncrowded and boasts spectacular views. ■TIP➜ Traffic on the main highway can be bumber-to-bumper in the afternoon. All in all, it's a good choice for families because the prices are right and there's plenty to keep everyone happy and occupied.

> **BEST SPAS**
>
> Grand Hyatt Kauai Resort and Spa, $$$$
>
> Hanalei Colony Resort, $$$
>
> Kauai Beach Resort, $
>
> Kauai Marriott Resort on Kalapaki Beach, $$$
>
> St. Regis Princeville Resort, $$$$

KAPAA AND WAILUA

5

Since Kapaa is the island's major population center, this area, including Waipouli and Wailua, has a lived-in, real-world feel. This is where you'll find some of the best deals on accommodations and a wider choice of inexpensive restaurants and shops than in the resort areas. The beaches here are so-so for swimming but nice for sunbathing, walking, and watching the sun- and moonrise.

The Wailua area is rather compact and much of it can be accessed from a coastal walking and biking path. The resorts here are attractive to middle-class travelers seeking a good bang for their buck. Wailua had a rich cultural significance for the ancient Hawaiians. Their royalty lived here, and ancient sacred grounds, called *heiau*, are clearly marked.

$$$$
RENTAL

⛅ **Aloha Cottages.** Owners Charlie and Susan Hoerner restored a three-bedroom plantation home on Kapaa's Baby Beach to reflect the charm of yesteryear with the conveniences of today. **Pros:** comfortable, home-like ambience; good for large groups; safe children's beach. **Cons:** can be windy at times; not great for swimming. $ *Rooms from: $407* ⊠ *1041 Moana Kai Rd., Kapaa* ☎ *808/823–0933, 877/915–1015* ⊕ *www.alohacottages.com* ⤳ *2 cottages.*

$
HOTEL

⛅ **Aston Islander on the Beach.** A low-rise, Hawaii-plantation-style design gives this 6-acre beachfront property a pleasant, relaxed feeling. **Pros:** convenient location; kids stay free; online rate deals. **Cons:** smallish pool; no restaurant on the property. $ *Rooms from: $122* ⊠ *440 Aleka Pl., Kapaa* ☎ *808/822–7417, 866/774–2924* ⊕ *www.astonhotels.com* ⤳ *198 rooms, 2 suites.*

$$
RESORT

⛅ **Courtyard By Marriott at Coconut Beach.** This popular hotel, one of the few true oceanfront properties on Kauai, sits on a ribbon of sand in Kapaa. **Pros:** convenient location; close to ocean; pleasant grounds. **Cons:** coastline not conducive to swimming; small pool; high daily parking fee. $ *Rooms from: $199* ⊠ *650 Aleka Loop, Kapaa* ☎ *808/822–3455, 800/760–8555* ⊕ *www.marriott.com* ⤳ *311 rooms* ⦿ *No meals.*

$
HOTEL
FAMILY

⛅ **Hotel Coral Reef.** This small hotel has been in business since 1956 and is something of a Kauai beachfront landmark, with clean, comfortable rooms, some with great ocean views. **Pros:** free parking;

oceanfront setting; convenient location. **Cons:** located in a busy section of Kapaa; ocean swimming is marginal. ⑤ *Rooms from: $109* ✉ *4-1516 Kuhio Hwy., Kapaa* ☎ *808/822–4481, 800/843–4659* ⊕ *www.hotelcoralreefresort.com* ⟿ *19 rooms, 2 suites* ⦿¡ *Breakfast.*

$
RENTAL

⚄ **Kapaa Sands.** An old rock etched with Japanese characters known as *kanji* reminds you that the site of this condominium gem was formerly occupied by a Shinto temple. **Pros:** discounts for extended stays; walking distance to shops, restaurants, and beach; turtle and monk seal sightings common. **Cons:** no-frills lodging; small bathrooms; traffic noise in rear units. ⑤ *Rooms from: $135* ✉ *380 Papaloa Rd., Kapaa* ☎ *808/822–4901, 800/222–4901* ⊕ *www.kapaasands.com* ⟿ *24 units* ⦿¡ *No meals.*

$
RENTAL
FAMILY
Fodor's Choice
★

⚄ **Kauai Coast Resort.** Fronting an uncrowded stretch of beach, this three-story primarily time-share resort is convenient and a bit more upscale than nearby properties. **Pros:** central location; nice sunrises; free parking. **Cons:** beach is narrow; ocean not ideal for swimming. ⑤ *Rooms from: $144* ✉ *520 Aleka Loop, Kapaa* ☎ *808/822–3441, 866/678–3289* ⊕ *www.shellhospitality.com* ⟿ *108 units* ⦿¡ *No meals.*

$
HOTEL

⚄ **Kauai Shores.** This oceanfront inn has been transformed into an affordable boutique hotel, thanks to a much-needed renovation of its guest rooms and public spaces, and renamed Kauai Shores under its Aqua Hotels management. **Pros:** convenient location; free Wi-Fi; great sunrises; discount for LGBT travelers. **Cons:** coral reef makes ocean swimming marginal; modest property; minimal amenities. ⑤ *Rooms from: $89* ✉ *420 Papaloa Rd., Kapaa* ☎ *808/822–4951, 800/560–5553* ⊕ *www.kauaishoreshotel.com* ⟿ *200 rooms, 2 suites* ⦿¡ *No meals.*

$$
RENTAL

⚄ **Outrigger at Lae Nani.** Ruling Hawaiian chiefs once returned from ocean voyages to this spot, now host to comfortable condominiums. **Pros:** nice beach; walking distance to playground; attractively furnished. **Cons:** third floor is walk-up; no Wi-Fi; cleaning fee. ⑤ *Rooms from: $219* ✉ *410 Papaloa Rd., Kapaa* ☎ *808/823–1401, 866/956–4262* ⊕ *www.outrigger.com* ⟿ *84 units* ⦿¡ *No meals.*

$
RENTAL

⚄ **Plantation Hale Suites.** These older, plantation-style one-bedroom units have well-equipped kitchenettes and garden lanai and clean, comfortable rooms. **Pros:** friendly staff; three pools; walking distance to shops, restaurant, beach. **Cons:** traffic noise in mountain-view units; coral reef makes ocean swimming challenging. ⑤ *Rooms from: $164* ✉ *525 Aleka Loop, Wailua (Kauai County)* ☎ *808/822–4941, 800/775–4253* ⊕ *www.plantation-hale.com* ⟿ *104 units* ⦿¡ *No meals.*

LIHUE

Lihue is not the most desirable place to stay on Kauai, in terms of scenic beauty, although it does have its advantages, including easy access to the airport. Restaurants and shops are plentiful, and there's lovely Kalapaki Bay for beachgoers. Aside from the Marriott and the Kauai Beach Resort, most of the limited lodging possibilities are smaller and aimed at the cost-conscious traveler.

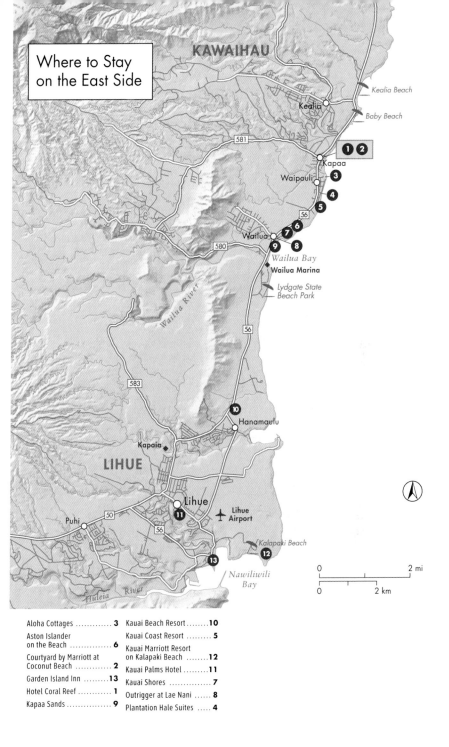

Where to Stay on the East Side

KAWAIHAU

Kealia Beach

Baby Beach

Kealia

581

❶ ❷

Kapaa

Waipouli ❸

❹

❺

56

606

❼ ❻

Wailua ❾ ❽

580

Wailua Bay

Wailua Marina

Lydgate State Beach Park

56

583

❿ Hanamaulu

Kapaia

LIHUE

Lihue

Lihue Airport

Puhi 50 ⓫

56

Kalapaki Beach

⓬

⓭

Nawiliwili Bay

Huleia River

0		2 mi
0		2 km

$ 🏨 **Garden Island Inn.** Budget travel-
HOTEL   ers love this three-story inn near
Kalapaki Bay and Anchor Cove
shopping center. **Pros:** walk to
beach, restaurants, and shops;
good for extended stays and budget travel; air-conditioning. **Cons:**
some traffic noise; near a busy
harbor; limited grounds; no pool.
[$] *Rooms from: $113* ✉ *3445 Wilcox Rd., Kalapaki Beach, Lihue*
☎ *808/245–7227, 800/648–0154* ⊕ *www.gardenislandinn.com* ⤳ *21
rooms* ⦿| *No meals.*

<table>
<tr><td colspan="2">MOST KID-FRIENDLY</td></tr>
<tr><td colspan="2">Grand Hyatt Kauai Resort and Spa</td></tr>
<tr><td colspan="2">Hotel Coral Reef</td></tr>
<tr><td colspan="2">Kauai Marriott Resort on Kalapaki Beach</td></tr>
<tr><td colspan="2">North Country Farms</td></tr>
</table>

$ 🏨 **Kauai Beach Resort.** This plantation-style hotel recently came under the
RESORT   management of Aqua Hotels and Resorts and was given a $14 million
renovation that upgraded the amenities to provide a relaxing, upscale
experience. **Pros:** unique pool; shuttle service to airport; resort amenities. **Cons:** not a good swimming beach; windy at times. [$] *Rooms from:
$176* ✉ *4331 Kauai Beach Dr., Hanamaulu* ☎ *888/805–3843* ⊕ *www.
kauaibeachresorthawaii.com* ⤳ *350 rooms, 7 suites* ⦿| *No meals.*

$$$ 🏨 **Kauai Marriott Resort on Kalapaki Beach.** An elaborate tropical garden,
RESORT   waterfalls right off the lobby, Greek statues and columns, and an enor-
FAMILY   mous 26,000-square-foot swimming pool characterize the grand—and
grandiose—scale of this resort on Kalapaki Beach, which looks out at
the dramatic Haupu Ridge. **Pros:** oceanfront setting; numerous restau-
rants; convenient location; airport shuttle. **Cons:** airport noise; ocean
water quality can be poor at times. [$] *Rooms from: $269* ✉ *3610 Rice
St., Kalapaki Beach, Lihue* ☎ *808/245–5050, 800/220–2925* ⊕ *www.
kauaimarriott.com* ⤳ *356 rooms, 11 suites.*

$ 🏨 **Kauai Palms Hotel.** This low-cost alternative is close to the airport
HOTEL   and priced right for the frugal traveler. **Pros:** friendly staff; inexpen-
sive; centrally located. **Cons:** bare-bones amenities; smallish rooms.
[$] *Rooms from: $89* ✉ *2931 Kalena St., Lihue* ☎ *808/246–0908*
⊕ *www.kauaipalmshotel.com* ⤳ *33 rooms* ⦿| *Breakfast.*

THE SOUTH SHORE

Sunseekers usually head south to the condo-studded shores of Poipu,
where three- and four-story complexes line the coast and the surf is
generally ideal for swimming. As the island's primary resort community,
Poipu has the bulk of the island's accommodations, and more condos
than hotels, with prices in the moderate to expensive range. Although
it accommodates many visitors, its extensive, colorful landscaping and
low-rise buildings save it from feeling dense and overcrowded, and it
has a delightful coastal promenade perfect for sunset strolls. Surpris-
ingly, the South Shore doesn't have as many shops and restaurants
as one might expect for such a popular resort region, but the new
Kukuiula shopping plaza is doing its best to fill the gaps. ■ **TIP➜ The
area's beaches are among the best on the island for families, with sandy
shores, shallow waters, and grassy lawns adjacent to the sand.**

$$$$ ⚇ **Grand Hyatt Kauai Resort and Spa.** Dramatically handsome, this classic
RESORT Hawaiian low-rise is built into the cliffs overlooking an unspoiled coast-
FAMILY line. **Pros:** fabulous pool; excellent restaurants; Hawaiian ambience.
Fodor's Choice **Cons:** poor and somewhat dangerous swimming beach during sum-
★ mer swells; small balconies; $25 daily resort fee. ⑤ *Rooms from: $389
☒ 1571 Poipu Rd., Koloa* ☎ *808/742–1234, 800/633–7313* ⊕ *www.
grandhyattkauai.com* ⥥ *602 rooms, 37 suites* ⦿ *No meals.*

$$ ⚇ **Hideaway Cove.** Hideaway Cove is in a very quiet location, even
RENTAL though it's one block from the ocean's edge in the heart of Poipu. **Pros:**
high-quality furnishings; private lanai; hot tub or Jacuzzi in each unit.
Cons: not on the ocean; cleaning fee. ⑤ *Rooms from: $185* ☒ *2307 Nalo
Rd., Poipu* ☎ *808/635–8785, 866/849–2426* ⊕ *www.hideawaycove.
com* ⥥ *9 units* ⦿ *No meals.*

$ ⚇ **Kauai Cove Cottages.** Three modern studio cottages sit side by side
RENTAL at the mouth of Waikomo Stream, about two blocks from the beach
in a residential neighborhood. **Pros:** clean; great snorkeling nearby.
Cons: not on beach. ⑤ *Rooms from: $159* ☒ *2672 Puuholo Rd., Poipu*
☎ *808/742–2562, 800/624–9945* ⊕ *www.kauaicove.com* ⥥ *3 cottages*
⦿ *No meals.*

$$$$ ⚇ **Koa Kea Hotel and Resort.** This boutique property offers a high-end
RESORT experience without the bustle of many larger resorts, making it a great
Fodor's Choice place to forget it all, and a perfect romantic getaway. **Pros:** incredibly
★ comfortable beds; friendly service; romantic spa. **Cons:** not much for
children. ⑤ *Rooms from: $369* ☒ *2251 Poipu Rd., Koloa* ☎ *808/828–
8888, 888/898–8958* ⊕ *www.koakea.com* ⥥ *121 rooms* ⦿ *No meals.*

$$$ ⚇ **Makahuena at Poipu.** Situated close to the center of Poipu, on a rocky
RENTAL point over the ocean, the Makahuena is near Shipwreck and Poipu
beaches, and it's a better deal for the price than some of the nearby
properties. **Pros:** tennis court; scenic setting; right on the ocean. **Cons:**
no swimming beach; no air-conditioning. ⑤ *Rooms from: $296* ☒ *1661
Pee Rd., Poipu* ☎ *808/742–2482, 800/367–5004* ⊕ *www.castleresorts.
com* ⥥ *78 units* ⦿ *No meals.*

$$ ⚇ **Outrigger Kiahuna Plantation.** This long-time Kauai condo project con-
RENTAL sists of 42 plantation-style, low-rise buildings that arc around a large,
FAMILY grassy field leading to a lovely beach. **Pros:** great sunset and ocean views
are bonuses in some units; convenient to restaurants and shops. **Cons:**
no air-conditioning; some units need updating. ⑤ *Rooms from: $189*
☒ *2253 Poipu Rd., Koloa* ☎ *808/742–6411, 800/542–4862* ⊕ *www.
kauai-kiahuna.com* ⥥ *333 units* ⦿ *No meals.*

$$ ⚇ **Poipu Crater Resort.** These two-bedroom condominium units are fairly
RENTAL spacious, and the large windows and high ceilings add to the sense of
space and light. **Pros:** attractive and generally well kept; pretty setting.
Cons: beach isn't good for swimming; few resort amenities. ⑤ *Rooms
from: $189* ☒ *2330 Hoohu Rd., Poipu* ☎ *808/742–7400* ⥥ *30 units*
⦿ *No meals.*

$$$ ⚇ **Poipu Kapili.** This resort offers spacious one- and two-bedroom condo
RENTAL units that are minutes from Poipu's restaurants and across the street
from a nice beach. **Pros:** units are roomy; good guest services; prop-
erty is small. **Cons:** units are ocean-view but not oceanfront. ⑤ *Rooms*

5

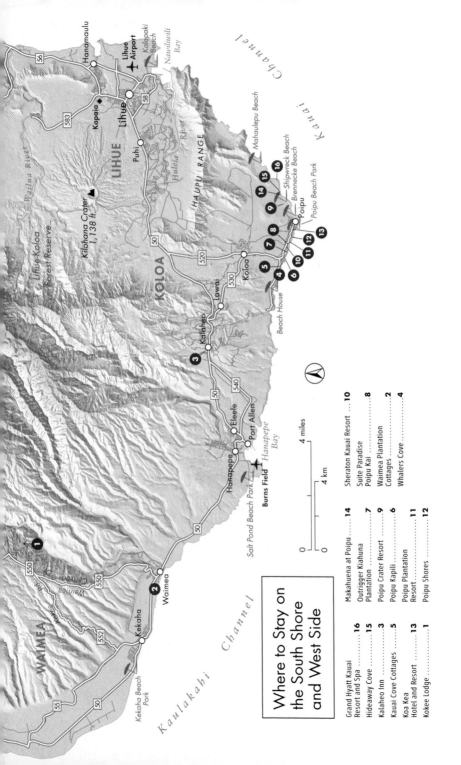

Where to Stay on the South Shore and West Side

Grand Hyatt Kauai
Resort and Spa **16**
Hideaway Cove **15**
Kalaheo Inn **3**
Kauai Cove Cottages **5**
Koa Kea
Hotel and Resort **13**
Kokee Lodge **1**

Makahuena at Poipu........ **14**
Outrigger Kiahuna
Plantation **7**
Poipu Crater Resort **9**
Poipu Kapili **6**
Poipu Plantation
Resort **11**
Poipu Shores **12**

Sheraton Kauai Resort ... **10**
Suite Paradise
Poipu Kai **8**
Waimea Plantation
Cottages **2**
Whalers Cove **4**

from: $275 ✉ *2221 Kapili Rd., Koloa* ☎ *808/742–6449, 800/443–7714* ⊕ *www.poipukapili.com* ↻ *60 units* ⫯⊘ *No meals.*

$ ⛨ **Poipu Plantation Resort.** Plumeria, ti, and other tropical foliage create
B&B/INN a lush landscape for this resort, which rents four rooms in a bed-and-breakfast–style plantation home and nine one- and two-bedroom cottage apartments. **Pros:** attractively furnished; full breakfast at B&B; free Wi-Fi. **Cons:** three-night minimum. **$** *Rooms from: $145* ✉ *1792 Pee Rd., Poipu* ☎ *808/742–6757, 800/634–0263* ⊕ *www.poipubeach.com* ↻ *4 rooms, 9 cottages* ⫯⊘ *Breakfast.*

$$$ ⛨ **Poipu Shores.** Perched on a rocky point above pounding surf, this is
RENTAL a perfect spot for whale- or turtle-watching. **Pros:** every unit faces the water; oceanfront pool; wildlife viewing. **Cons:** units vary widely in style; no resort amenities. **$** *Rooms from: $289* ✉ *1775 Pee Rd., Koloa* ☎ *808/742–7700, 800/367–1912* ⊕ *www.castleresorts.com* ↻ *39 units* ⫯⊘ *No meals.*

$$ ⛨ **Sheraton Kauai Resort.** The Sheraton's ocean-wing accommodations
RESORT are so close to the water you can practically feel the spray of the surf
Fodor's Choice as it hits the rocks below. **Pros:** ocean-view pool; quiet; great restaurant with spectacular views. **Cons:** somewhat businesslike ambience.
★ **$** *Rooms from: $232* ✉ *2440 Hoonani Rd., Poipu Beach, Koloa* ☎ *808/742–1661, 888/488–3535* ⊕ *www.sheraton-kauai.com* ↻ *394 rooms, 11 suites* ⫯⊘ *No meals.*

$$ ⛨ **Suite Paradise Poipu Kai.** Condominiums, many with cathedral ceilings
RENTAL and all with big windows overlooking the lawns, give Suite Paradise the feeling of a spacious, quiet retreat inside and out. **Pros:** close to ocean; full kitchens; good rates for the location. **Cons:** some units don't have air-conditioning; closest beaches not ideal for swimming. **$** *Rooms from: $210* ✉ *1941 Poipu Rd., Koloa* ☎ *808/742–6464, 800/367–8020* ⊕ *www.suite-paradise.com* ↻ *150 units* ⫯⊘ *No meals.*

$$$$ ⛨ **Whalers Cove.** Perched about as close to the water's edge as they can
RENTAL get, these condos are the most luxurious on the South Shore, available in one-, two-, or three-bedroom units. **Pros:** on-site staff; outstanding setting; fully equipped spacious units. **Cons:** rocky beach not ideal for swimming; no air-conditioning. **$** *Rooms from: $366* ✉ *2640 Puuholo Rd., Koloa* ☎ *808/742–7571, 800/225–2683* ⊕ *www. whalerscoveresort.com* ↻ *39 units* ⫯⊘ *No meals.*

THE WEST SIDE

To do a lot of hiking or immerse yourself in the island's history, find a room in Waimea. You won't find many resorts, restaurants, or shops, but you will encounter quiet days, miles of largely deserted beach, and a rural environment.

$ ⛨ **Kalaheo Inn.** It isn't easy to find good lodgings on the southwest side
B&B/INN of the island, but this old-fashioned budget inn does the job in Kalaheo town. **Pros:** some units have kitchens; walking distance to restaurants. **Cons:** no beach; no air-conditioning; poor cell-phone service. **$** *Rooms from: $92* ✉ *4444 Papalina Rd., Kalaheo* ☎ *808/332–6023, 888/332–6023* ⊕ *www.kalaheoinn.com* ↻ *15 units* ⫯⊘ *No meals.*

$

RENTAL

FAMILY

‍☷ **Kokee Lodge.** If you're an outdoors enthusiast, you can appreciate Kauai's mountain wilderness from the 12 rustic cabins that make up this lodge. **Pros:** outstanding setting; more refined than camping; cooking facilities. **Cons:** very austere; no restaurants for dinner; remote. ⑤ *Rooms from: $69* ✉ *3600 Kokee Rd., at mile marker 15, Waimea (Kauai County)* ☎ *808/652–6852* ⊕ *www.thelodgeatkokee.net* ⬎ *12 cabins* ❙◎❙ *No meals.*

$

RENTAL

Fodor's Choice

★

☷ **Waimea Plantation Cottages.** History buffs will adore these relocated and refurbished sugar-plantation cottages, which were originally built in the early 1900s. **Pros:** homey lodging; quiet and low-key; free Wi-Fi. **Cons:** not a white-sand beach; rooms are not luxurious; no air-conditioning. ⑤ *Rooms from: $169* ✉ *9400 Kaumualii Hwy., Box 367, Waimea (Kauai County)* ☎ *808/338–1625, 800/716–6199* ⊕ *www. coasthotels.com* ⬎ *61 cottages* ❙◎❙ *No meals.*

6

NIGHTLIFE AND
PERFORMING ARTS

Updated by
Joan Conrow

Kauai has never been known for its nightlife. It's a rural island, where folks tend to retire early, and the streets are dark and deserted well before midnight. The island does have its nightspots, though, and the after-dark entertainment scene keeps expanding, especially in areas frequented by tourists.

Most of the island's dinner and luau shows are held at hotels and resorts. Hotel lounges are a good source of live music, often with no cover charge, as are a few bars and restaurants around the island.

Check the local newspaper, the *Garden Island*, for listings of weekly happenings. Free publications such as *Kauai Gold, This Week on Kauai,* and *Essential Kauai* also list entertainment events. You can pick them up at Lihue Airport near the baggage claim area, as well as at numerous retail areas on the island.

NIGHTLIFE

For every new venue that opens on Kauai, another one closes, mainly because most island residents tend to retire early. It is, after all, a rural island. But still, there are a number of places to shake your booty, hear local music, and simply enjoy a drink. Nightclubs that stay open until the wee hours are rare on Kauai, and the bar scene is limited. The major resorts generally host their own live entertainment and happy hours. All bars and clubs that serve alcohol must close at 2 am, except those with a cabaret license, which allows them to close at 4 am.

THE NORTH SHORE

BARS AND CLUBS

Hanalei Gourmet. The sleepy North Shore stays awake—until 10:30, that is—each evening in this small, convivial deli and bar inside Hanalei's restored old school building. There's local live Hawaiian, jazz, rock, and folk music on Sunday and Wednesday evening. ⊠ *Hanalei Center, 5-5161*

Kuhio Hwy., Hanalei ☎ *808/826–2524* ⊕ *www.hanaleigourmet.com.*

St. Regis Bar. This spacious and comfortable lounge with a gorgeous view of Hanalei Bay offers drinks daily from 3:30 to 11 and a champagne toast at sunset. Stop by between 5:30 and 10 for *pupu* (hors d'oeuvres), with a popular jazz show from 6:30 to 9 on Sunday night. ⊠ *Princeville Resort, 5520 Ka Haku Rd., Princeville* ☎ *808/826–9644* ⊕ *www.stregisprinceville.com.*

Tahiti Nui. This venerable and funky institution in sleepy Hanalei still offers its famous luau at 5 on Wednesday evenings, even though the venerable owner and founder Auntie Louise Marston has died. Spirits are always high at this popular hangout for locals and visitors alike, which houses live nightly entertainment, usually Hawaiian music. Open until 1 am. ⊠ *5-5134 Kuhio Hwy., Hanalei* ☎ *808/826–6277* ⊕ *www.thenui.com.*

> ## MAI TAIS
>
> Hard to believe, but the cocktail known around the world as the mai tai has been around for more than 50 years. While the recipe has changed slightly over the years, the original formula, created by bar owner Victor J. "Trader Vic" Bergeron, included 2 ounces of 17-year-old J. Wray & Nephew rum over shaved ice, ½ ounce Holland Dekuyper orange curaçao, ¼ ounce Trader Vic's rock candy syrup, ½ ounce French Garier orgeat syrup, and the juice of one fresh lime. Done the right way, this tropical drink still lives up to the name "mai tai!" meaning, "out of this world!"

6

THE EAST SIDE

BARS AND CLUBS

Duke's Barefoot Bar. This is one of the liveliest bars in Nawiliwili. Contemporary Hawaiian music is usually performed at this beachside bar and restaurant every day but Tuesday during "Aloha Hours" from 4 to 6 pm. On Thursday, Friday, and Saturday nights, live music is held from 8:30 to 10:30 pm. ⊠ *Kalapaki Beach, 3610 Rice St., Lihue* ☎ *808/246–9599* ⊕ *www.dukeskauai.com.*

Fodor's Choice **Hukilau Lanai.** This open-air bar and restaurant is on the property of ★ the Kauai Coast Resort but operates independently. Trade winds trickle through the modest little bar, which looks out into a coconut grove. If the mood takes you, go on a short walk to the sea, or recline in big, comfortable chairs while listening to mellow jazz or Hawaiian slack-key guitar. Live music plays from 6 to 9 every night, though the restaurant and bar are closed on Monday. Poolside happy hour runs from 3 to 5. Freshly infused tropical martinis—perhaps locally grown lychee and pineapple or a Big Island vanilla bean infusion—are house favorites. ⊠ *520 Aleka Loop, Wailua (Kauai County)* ☎ *808/822–0600* ⊕ *www.hukilaukauai.com.*

Rob's Good Times Grill. Let loose at this popular restaurant and sports bar, which has live music throughout the week from 4 to 6 pm. Tuesday offers swing dancing from 7:30 to 10 pm, Friday features Hawaiian music, Saturday has late-night club dancing, while Sunday through Thursday go full-on karaoke from 9 pm to 2 am. ⊠ *4303 Rice St., Lihue* ☎ *808/246–0311* ⊕ *www.kauaisportsbarandgrill.com.*

Trees Lounge. This funky bar and restaurant is popular with a middle-aged crowd. It hosts live music nightly that gets people out on the tiny dance floor. It's behind the Coconut Marketplace and next to the Kauai Coast Resort in Kapaa. Closed Sunday. ⊠ *440 Aleka Pl., Kapaa* ☎ *808/823–0600* ⊕ *www.treesloungekauai.com.*

COFFEEHOUSES

The island has few coffeehouses, and even fewer that are open at night, aside from Starbucks in the Kukui Grove, Kauai Village, and Poipu Shopping Village malls.

Fodor'sChoice
★

Caffé Coco. Nestled in a bamboo forest draped in bougainvillea and flowering vines and hidden from view off the Kuhio Highway is a charming little venue where local musicians perform most evenings. Caffé Coco offers *pupu* (appetizers), entrées, and desserts, including vegan, gluten-free options. It may not have a liquor license, but don't let that stop you from enjoying the entertainment in a pleasant outdoor setting; just bring your own wine or beer. It's open until 9 nightly. ⊠ *4-369 Kuhio Hwy., Kapaa* ☎ *808/822–7990* ⊕ *www.caffecocokauai.com.*

THE SOUTH SHORE

BARS AND CLUBS

Keoki's Paradise. A young, energetic crowd makes this a lively spot on Friday and Saturday nights. When the dining room clears out, there's a bit of a bar scene for singles. The bar closes at 10:30 pm. ⊠ *Poipu Shopping Village, 2360 Kiahuna Plantation Dr., Poipu* ☎ *808/742–7534* ⊕ *www.keokisparadise.com.*

Lavas at Poipu Beach. This poolside bar and grill is a great place to be on the South Shore to celebrate sunset with a drink, because the ocean view is unsurpassed. Happy hour is from 3 to 5 pm. ⊠ *Sheraton Kauai Resort, 2440 Hoonani Rd., Poipu* ☎ *808/742–1661* ⊕ *www.sheratonkauai.com/dining.*

PERFORMING ARTS

Although luau remain a primary source of evening fun for families on vacation, there are a handful of other possibilities. There are no traditional dinner cruises, but some boat tours do offer an evening buffet with music along Napali Coast. A few times a year, Women in Theater (WIT), a local women's theater group, performs dinner shows at the Hukilau Lanai in Wailua. You can always count on a performance of *South Pacific* at the Kauai Beach Resort, and the Kauai Community College Performing Arts Center draws well-known artists.

Kauai Community College Performing Arts Center. This is a main venue for island entertainment, hosting a concert music series, visiting musicians, dramatic productions, and special events such as educational forums. ⊠ *3-1901 Kaumualii Hwy., Lihue* ☎ *808/245–8311* ⊕ *www.kauai.hawaii.edu/pac.*

Kauai: Undercover Movie Star

CLOSE UP

Though Kauai has played itself in the movies, most recently starring in *The Descendants* (2011), most of its screen time has been as a stunt double for a number of tropical paradises. The island's remote valleys portrayed Venezuelan jungle in Kevin Costner's *Dragonfly* (2002) and a Costa Rican dinosaur preserve in Steven Spielberg's *Jurassic Park* (1993). Spielberg was no stranger to Kauai, having filmed Harrison Ford's escape via seaplane from Menehune Fishpond in *Raiders of the Lost Ark* (1981).

The fluted cliffs and gorges of Kauai's rugged Napali Coast play the misunderstood beast's island home in *King Kong* (1976), and a jungle dweller of another sort, in *George of the Jungle* (1997), frolicked on Kauai. Harrison Ford returned to the island for 10 weeks during the filming of *Six Days, Seven Nights* (1998), a romantic adventure set in French Polynesia. Part-time Kauai resident Ben Stiller used the island as a stand-in for the jungles of Vietnam in *Tropic Thunder* (2008) and Johnny Depp came here to film some of *Pirates of the Caribbean: On Stranger Tides* (2011). But these are all relatively contemporary movies. What's truly remarkable is that Hollywood discovered Kauai in 1933 with the making of *White Heat*, which was set on a sugar plantation and—like another more memorable movie filmed on Kauai—dealt with interracial love stories.

Then, it was off to the races, as Kauai saw no fewer than a dozen movies filmed on the island in the 1950s, not all of them Oscar contenders. Rita Hayworth starred in *Miss Sadie Thompson* (1953) and no one you'd recognize starred in the tantalizing *She Gods of Shark Reef* (1956).

The movie that is still immortalized on the island in the names of restaurants, real estate offices, a hotel, and even a sushi item is *South Pacific* (1957). (You guessed it, right?) That mythical place called Bali Hai is never far away on Kauai.

In the 1960s Elvis Presley filmed *Blue Hawaii* (1961) and *Girls! Girls! Girls!* (1962) on the island. A local movie tour likes to point out the stain on a hotel carpet where Elvis's jelly doughnut fell.

Kauai has welcomed a long list of Hollywood's A-List: John Wayne in *Donovan's Reef* (1963); Jack Lemmon in *The Wackiest Ship in the Army* (1961); Richard Chamberlain in *The Thorn Birds* (1983); Gene Hackman in *Uncommon Valor* (1983); Danny DeVito and Billy Crystal in *Throw Momma from the Train* (1987); and Dustin Hoffman, Morgan Freeman, Renee Russo, and Cuba Gooding Jr. in *Outbreak* (1995).

Kauai has also appeared on a long list of TV shows and made-for-TV movies, including *Gilligan's Island, Fantasy Island, Starsky & Hutch, Baywatch Hawaii*—even reality TV shows *The Bachelor* and *The Amazing Race 3*.

For the record, just because a movie did some filming here doesn't mean the entire movie was filmed on Kauai. *Honeymoon in Vegas* filmed just one scene here, while the murder mystery *A Perfect Getaway* (2009) was set on the famous Kalalau Trail and featured beautiful Kauaian backdrops but was shot mostly in Puerto Rico.

6

DINNER SHOW

South Pacific Dinner Show. It seems a fitting tribute to see the play that put Kauai on the map. Rodgers and Hammerstein's original *South Pacific* has been playing at the Kauai Beach Resort since 2002. The full musical production, accompanied by a buffet dinner, features local talent. ✉ *Jasmine Ballroom, Kauai Beach Resort, 4331 Kauai Beach Dr., Lihue* ☎ *808/346–6500* ⊕ *www.southpacifickauai.com* ✉ *$86* ⊙ *Wed., doors open at 5:30 pm, show at 6:30.*

FESTIVAL

FAMILY **Bon Festival.** Traditional Japanese celebrations in honor of loved ones who have died are held from late June through August at various Buddhist temples all over the island. It sounds somber, but it's really a community festival of dance. To top it off, you're welcome to participate. Dance, eat, play carnival games, and hear Japanese *taiko* drumming by Kauai youth at one of the Bon folk dances, which take place on temple lawns every Friday and Saturday night from dusk to midnight. Some dancers wear the traditional kimono; others wear board shorts and a tank top. The moves are easy to follow, the event is lively and wholesome, and it's free. A different temple hosts a dance each weekend. Watch the local paper for that week's locale.

LUAU

Although the commercial luau experience is a far cry from the backyard luau thrown by local residents to celebrate a wedding, graduation, or baby's first birthday, they're nonetheless entertaining and a good introduction to the Hawaiian food that isn't widely sold in restaurants. With many, you can watch a roasted pig being carried out of its *imu*, a hole in the ground used for cooking meat with heated stones. Besides the feast, and free mai tais, there's often an exciting dinner show with Polynesian-style music and dancing. It all makes for a fun evening that's suitable for couples, families, and groups, and the informal setting is conducive to meeting other people. Every luau is different, reflecting the cuisine and tenor of the host facility, so compare prices, menus, and entertainment before making your reservation. Most luau on Kauai are offered only on a limited number of nights each week, so plan ahead to get the luau you want. We tend to prefer those *not* held on resort properties, because they feel a bit more authentic.

The luau shows listed below are our favorites.

Grand Hyatt Kauai Luau. What used to be called Drums of Paradise has a new name and a new dance troupe but still offers a traditional luau buffet and an exceptional performance in a garden setting near majestic Keoneloa Bay. ✉ *Grand Hyatt Kauai Resort and Spa, 1571 Poipu Rd., Poipu* ☎ *808/240–6456* ⊕ *www.grandhyattkauailuau.com* ✉ *$108.33* ⊙ *Thurs. and Sun., doors open at 5:45 pm, show begins at 7.*

Luau Kalamaku. Set on historic sugar-plantation land, this luau bills itself as the only "theatrical" luau on Kauai. The luau feast is served buffet style, there's an open bar, and the performers aim to both entertain and

Unlike many luau, Luau Kalamaku is organized like a theatrical performance, telling the story of the settlement of the Hawaiian islands.

educate about Hawaiian culture. Guests sit at tables around a circular stage; tables farther from the stage are elevated, providing unobstructed views. Additional packages offer visitors the opportunity to tour the 35-acre plantation via train, or special romantic perks like a lei greeting and champagne. ⊠ *3-2087 Kaumualii St., Lihue* ☎ *877/622–1780* ⊕ *www.luaukalamaku.com* ✉ *$99* ⊙ *Tues. and Fri. Check-in begins at 5:30, dinner at 6:30, show at 7:30.*

Fodor's Choice
★ **Smith's Tropical Paradise Luau.** A 30-acre tropical garden on the Wailua River provides the lovely setting for this popular luau, which begins with the traditional blowing of the conch shell and *imu* (pig roast) ceremony, followed by cocktails, an island feast, and an international show in the amphitheater overlooking a torch-lighted lagoon. It's fairly authentic and a better deal than the pricier resort events. ⊠ *174 Wailua Rd., Kapaa* ☎ *808/821–6895* ⊕ *www.smithskauai.com* ✉ *$78* ⊙ *Days vary seasonally; 5 pm.*

MUSIC

Check the *Garden Island* for outdoor reggae and Hawaiian-music shows.

Hanalei Slack Key Concerts. Relax to the instrumental music form created by Hawaiian *paniolo* (cowboys) in the early 1800s. Shows are at Hale Halawai Ohana O Hanalei, which is *mauka* (toward the mountains) down a dirt access road across from St. William's Catholic Church (Malolo Road) and then left down another dirt road. Look for a *hale* (house), several little green plantation-style buildings, and the brown double-yurt community center around the gravel parking lot. ✉ *Hanalei Family Community Center, 5-5299 Kuhio Hwy., Hanalei* ☎ *808/826–1469* 🌐 *www.hawaiianslackkeyguitar.com* 🎫 *$15* ⏲ *Fri. at 4, Sun. at 3.*

Kauai Concert Association. This group offers a seasonal program at the Kauai Community College Performing Arts Center that features well-known classical musicians, including soloists and small ensembles. ✉ *3-1901 Kaumualii Hwy., Lihue* ☎ *808/245–7464* 🌐 *www.kauai-concert.org* 🎫 *$30–$65.*

THEATER

Kauai Community Players. This talented local group presents plays throughout the year in its intimate theater. ✉ *4411 Kikowaena St., across from Kauai Community College, Lihue* ☎ *808/245–7700* 🌐 *www.kauaicommunityplayers.org* 🎫 *$20.*

SHOPS AND SPAS

Updated by
Joan Conrow

There aren't a lot of shops and spas on Kauai, but what you will find here are a handful of places very much worth checking out for the quality of their selection of items sold and services rendered. Many shops now make an effort to sell as many locally made products as possible. When buying an item, ask where it was made or even who made it.

Often you will find that a product handcrafted on the island may not be that much more expensive than a similar product made overseas. You can also look for the purple "Kauai Made" sticker many merchants display.

Along with one major shopping mall, a few shopping centers, and a growing number of big-box retailers, Kauai has some delightful mom-and-pop shops and specialty boutiques with lots of character. The Garden Isle also has a large and talented community of artisans and fine artists, with galleries all around the island showcasing their creations. You can find many island-made arts and crafts in the small shops, and it's worthwhile to stop in at crafts fairs and outdoor markets to look for bargains and mingle with island residents.

If you're looking for a special memento of your trip that is unique to Kauai County, check out the distinctive Niihau shell lei. The tiny shells are collected from beaches on Kauai and Niihau, pierced, and strung into beautiful necklaces, chokers, and earrings. It's a time-consuming and exacting craft, and these items are much in demand, so don't be taken aback by the high price tags. Those made by Niihau residents will have certificates of authenticity and are worth collecting. You often can find cheaper versions made by non-Hawaiians at crafts fairs.

Kauai is often touted as the healing island, and local spas try hard to fill that role. With the exception of the Hyatt's ANARA Spa, the facilities aren't as posh as some might want, but it's in the human element that Kauai excels. Many island residents are known for their warmth, kindness, and humility, and you can often find all these attributes in the massage therapists and technicians who work long hours at the resort spas. These professionals take their therapeutic mission seriously; they genuinely want you to experience the island's relaxing, restorative qualities. Private massage services abound on the island, and your spa therapist may offer the same services at a much lower price outside the resort, but if you're looking for a variety of health-and-beauty treatments, an exercise workout, or a full day of pampering, a spa will prove most convenient.

Though most spas on Kauai are associated with resorts, none is restricted to guests only. And there's much by way of healing and wellness to be found on Kauai beyond the traditional spa—or even the day spa. More and more retreat facilities are offering what some would call alternative healing therapies. Others would say there's nothing alternative about them; you can decide for yourself.

Open Hours. Stores are typically open daily from 9 or 10 am to 5 pm, although some stay open until 9 pm, especially those near resorts. Don't be surprised if the posted hours don't match the actual hours of operation at the smaller shops, where owners may be fairly casual about keeping to a regular schedule.

SHOPS

THE NORTH SHORE

The North Shore has three main shopping areas, all in towns off the highway. Hanalei has two shopping centers directly across from each other, which offer more than you would expect in a remote, relaxed town. Princeville Shopping Center is a bustling little mix of businesses, necessities, and some unique, often pricey, shops. Kilauea is a bit more sprawled out and offers a charming, laid-back shopping scene with a neighborhood feel.

AREAS AND SHOPPING CENTERS

Ching Young Village. This popular shopping center looks a bit worn, but that doesn't deter business. Hanalei's only full-service grocery store is here along with a number of other shops useful to locals and visitors, such as a Hawaiian music outlet, jewelry stores, art galleries, a surf shop, variety store, and several restaurants. ⊠ *5-5190 Kuhio Hwy., near mile marker 2, Hanalei* ⊕ *www.chingyoungvillage.com.*

Hanalei Center. Once an old Hanalei schoolhouse, the Hanalei Center is now a bevy of boutiques and restaurants. You can dig through '40s and '50s vintage memorabilia, find Polynesian artifacts, or search for that unusual gift. Buy beach gear as well as island wear and women's clothing. Find a range of fine jewelry and paper art jewelry. There are a full-service salon and a yoga studio in the two-story modern addition to the center, which also houses a small natural foods grocery. ⊠ *5-5161 Kuhio Hwy., near mile marker 2, Hanalei* ☎ *808/826-7677.*

Princeville Shopping Center. The big draws at this small center are a full-service grocery store and a hardware store, but there's also a wine market, bar, a sandal boutique, a small food court, and an ice-cream shop. This is also the last stop for gas and banking on the North Shore. ⊠ *5-4280 Kuhio Hwy., near mile marker 28, Princeville* ☎ *808/826-9497* ⊕ *www.princevillecenter.com.*

GIFTS

Kong Lung Co. Sometimes called the Gump's of Kauai, this gift store sells elegant clothing, exotic glassware, ethnic books, gifts, and artwork—all very lovely and expensive. The shop is housed in a beautiful 1892 stone building in the heart of Kilauea. It's the showpiece of the pretty little Kong Lung Center, where everything from handmade soaps to hammocks can be found. A great bakery and pizzeria round out the offerings, along with an exhibit of historical photos. ✉ *2484 Keneke St., Kilauea* ☎ *808/828–1822* ⊕ *www.konglungkauai.com.*

Village Variety Store. How about a fun beach towel for the folks back home? That's just one of the gifts you can find here, along with shell lei, Kauai shirts, macadamia nuts, and other souvenirs at low prices. The store also has many small, useful items such as envelopes, housewares, and toiletries. ✉ *Ching Young Village, Kuhio Hwy., Hanalei* ☎ *808/826–6077.*

JEWELRY

Crystal & Gems Gallery. Sparkling crystals of every shape, size, type, and color are sold in this small, amply stocked boutique. The knowledgeable staff can help you choose crystals for specific healing purposes. ✉ *4489 Aku Rd., Hanalei* ☎ *808/826–9304* ⊕ *www.crystals-gems.com.*

THE EAST SIDE

KAPAA AND WAILUA

Kapaa is the most heavily populated area on Kauai, so it's not surprising that it has the most diverse shopping opportunities on the island. Unlike the North Shore's retail scene, shops here are not neatly situated in centers; they are spread out along a long stretch of road, with many local retail gems tucked away that you may not find if you're in a rush.

AREAS AND SHOPPING CENTERS

Kauai Village Shopping Center. The buildings of this Kapaa shopping village are in the style of a 19th-century plantation town. **ABC Discount Store** sells sundries; **Safeway** carries groceries and alcoholic beverages; **Papaya's** has health foods and a minimalist café. There's also a great local clothing boutique, **Kauai Crush,** and a **UPS store.** Other shops sell jewelry, art, and home decor. Restaurants include Chinese, vegetarian, and Vietnamese options, and there's also a **Starbucks** and two bars. ✉ *4-831 Kuhio Hwy., Kapaa* ☎ *808/822–3777.*

Kinipopo Shopping Village. Kinipopo is a tiny little center on Kuhio Highway. **Korean Barbeque** fronts the highway, as does **Goldsmith's Kauai Gallery,** which sells handcrafted Hawaiian-style gold jewelry. **Monaco's** has authentic Mexican food, and is the center's biggest draw. There's also a clothing shop, beauty salon, bakery café, and a healing-arts center. ✉ *4-356 Kuhio Hwy., Kapaa* ⊕ *www.kinipopovillage.com.*

Waipouli Town Center. **Foodland** is the focus of this small retail plaza, one of three shopping centers anchored by grocery stores in Kapaa. You can also find a **McDonald's, Fun Factory** video arcade, and **The Coffee Bean,** along with a local-style restaurant. ✉ *4-771 Kuhio Hwy., Kapaa.*

CLOTHING

Deja Vu Surf Hawaii: Kapaa. This family operation has a great assortment of surf wear and clothes for outdoors fanatics, including tank tops, visors, swimwear, and Kauai-style T-shirts. They also carry body boards and water-sports accessories. Good deals can be found at sidewalk sales. ✉ *4-1419 Kuhio Hwy., Kapaa* ☎ *808/822–4401* ⊕ *www.dejavusurf.com.*

Divine Planet. This friendly, hip boutique sells unusual merchandise from India and other exotic Asian locales. Dangly earrings, loose, natural clothing, beads, campy home furnishings, and other eclectic offerings make this fun shop worth a stop. If you miss it here, you can check out the Hanalei location at Ching Young Village, 5–1590 Kuhio Hwy. ✉ *4-831 Kuhio Hwy., Kapaa* ☎ *808/821–1835* ⊕ *www.divine-planet.com.*

Marta's Boat. This charming boutique sells handmade, one-of-a-kind clothing by husband-and-wife team Ambrose and Marta Curry. He creates silk-screen art with nontoxic paint on fabric in his studio next door; then she cuts and sews the fabric into bags and clothing for men, women, and children. ✉ *4-770 Kuhio Hwy., Kapaa* ☎ *808/822–3926* ⊕ *www.martasboat.com.*

GALLERIES

ALOHA Images. ALOHA stands for "Affordable Location of Original Hawaiian Art." A self-proclaimed "candy store for art lovers," it has a large selection of Hawaiian-theme art, ranging from $75 up to the rare $15,000, and owner Ray offers layaway plans to those who request one. ✉ *4504 Kukui St., Kapaa* ☎ *808/821–1382* ⊕ *www.alohaimages.com.*

Kela's Glass Gallery. The colorful vases, bowls, and other fragile items sold in this distinctive gallery are definitely worth viewing if you appreciate quality handmade glass art. It's expensive, but if something catches your eye, they'll happily pack it for safe transport home. They also ship worldwide. ✉ *4-1354 Kuhio Hwy., Kapaa* ☎ *808/822–4527* ⊕ *www.glass-art.com.*

GIFTS

Pagoda. Pagoda is a tiny shop big on exceptional antiques, Hawaiiana, and gifts. The owner, Liane, has been collecting rare finds most of her life and now has a place to showcase them. ✉ *4-369 Kuhio Hwy, Kapaa* ☎ *808/821–2172.*

Vicky's Fabric Shop. This small store is packed full of tropical and Hawaiian prints, silks, slinky rayons, soft cottons, and other fine fabrics. A variety of sewing patterns and notions are featured as well, making it a must-stop for any seamstress, and a great place to buy unique island-made gifts. Check out the one-of-a-kind selection of purses, aloha wear, and other quality hand-sewn items. ✉ *4-1326 Kuhio Hwy., Kapaa* ☎ *808/822–1746* ⊕ *www.vickysfabrics.com.*

HOME DECOR

Otsuka's. Family-owned Otsuka's has a large clientele of visitors, who appreciate the wide selection of unique furniture, artwork, candles, tropical-print pillows, accessories, and knickknacks that can be found here. ✉ *4-1624 Kuhio Hwy., Kapaa* ☎ *808/822–7766* ⊕ *www.otsukas.com* ☾ *Closed Sun. and Mon.*

JEWELRY

Jim Saylor Jewelers. Jim Saylor has been designing beautiful keepsakes for more than 35 years on Kauai. Gems from around the world, including black pearls, diamonds, and more, appear in his unusual settings. ✉ *1318 Kuhio Hwy., Kapaa* ☎ *808/822–3591* ⊙ *Closed Sun.*

Kauai Pearls and Gold. There's a wonderful selection of rare Niihau shell lei at Kauai Pearls and Gold. To appreciate the craftsmanship of these remarkable necklaces and understand the sometimes-high prices (which can range from $20 to $200), be sure to ask how best to care for and preserve them. The store, which has been in business since 1985, also sells a selection of 14-karat gold jewelry and Tahitian black pearls. ✉ *Coconut Marketplace, 4-484 Kuhio Hwy., Kapaa* ☎ *808/822–9361.*

MARKET

Kauai Products Fair. Open daily, the Kauai Products Fair outdoor market features fresh produce, tropical plants and flowers, a red-dirt shirt shop, aloha wear, jewelry, and gifts. ✉ *4-1613 Kuhio Hwy., Kapaa* ☎ *808/246–0988* 🌐 *www.thekauaiproductsfair.com.*

LIHUE

Lihue is the business area on Kauai, as well as home to all the big-box stores (Costco, Home Depot, Walmart, and Big K) and the only real mall. Do not mistake this town as lacking in rare finds, however. Lihue is steeped in history and diversity while simultaneously welcoming new trends and establishments.

AREAS AND SHOPPING CENTERS

Kilohana Plantation. This 16,000-square-foot Tudor mansion contains art galleries, a jewelry store, and the restaurant Gaylord's. Kilohana Plantation is filled with antiques from its original owner, and the restored outbuildings house a craft shop and a Hawaiian-style clothing shop. Train rides on a restored railroad are available, with knowledgeable guides reciting the history of sugar on Kauai. The site is also now the home of Luau Kalamaku and Koloa Rum Company. ✉ *3-2087 Kaumualii Hwy., Lihue* ☎ *808/245–5608.*

Kukui Grove Center. This is Kauai's only true mall. Besides Kmart, anchor tenants are Longs Drugs, Macy's, Ross, Pier One Imports, and Times Supermarket. The mall's stores offer women's clothing, surf wear, art, toys, athletic shoes, jewelry, a hair salon, and locally made crafts. Restaurants range from fast food and sandwiches to Mexican and Korean, with a popular Starbucks and Jamba Juice. The center stage often has entertainment, especially on Friday nights, and there is a farmers' market on Monday. ✉ *3-2600 Kaumualii Hwy., Lihue* ☎ *808/245–7784* 🌐 *www.kukuigrovecenter.com.*

CLOTHING

Hilo Hattie, The Store of Hawaii. This is the big name in aloha wear for tourists throughout the Islands, and Hilo Hattie, the Store of Hawaii has only one store on Kauai. Located a mile from Lihue Airport, come here for cool, comfortable aloha shirts and muumuu in bright floral prints, as well as other souvenirs. Also, be sure to check out the line of Hawaii-inspired home furnishings. ✉ *3252 Kuhio Hwy., Lihue* ☎ *808/245–3404* 🌐 *www.hilohattie.com.*

The gift shop at the Kauai Museum is one of the best places on the island to find reasonably priced local crafts and books.

FOOD SPECIALTIES

Kauai Fruit and Flower Company. At this shop near Lihue and five minutes away from the airport, you can buy fresh Hawaii Gold pineapple, sugarcane, ginger, tropical flowers, coconuts, local jams, jellies, and honey, plus papayas, bananas, and mangoes from Kauai. Some of the fruit at Kauai Fruit and Flower Company cannot be shipped out of state. ✉ *3-4684 Kuhio Hwy., Lihue* ☎ *808/245–1814.*

GIFTS

Fodor's Choice
★

Kapaia Stitchery. Hawaiian quilts made by hand and machine, a beautiful selection of fabrics, quilting kits, and fabric arts fill Kapaia Stitchery, a cute little red plantation-style building. There are also many locally made gifts and quilts for sale in this locally owned store. The staff is friendly and helpful, even though a steady stream of customers keeps them busy. ✉ *3-3551 Kuhio Hwy., Lihue* ☎ *808/245–2281* ⊕ *http://kapaia-stitchery.com.*

Fodor's Choice
★

Kauai Museum. The gift shop at the museum sells some fascinating books, maps, and prints, as well as lovely authentic Niihau shell jewelry, hand-woven *lau hala* hats, and koa wood bowls. Also featured at the Kauai Museum are tapa cloth, authentic *tikis* (hand-carved wooden figurines), as well as other good-quality local crafts and books at reasonable prices. ✉ *4428 Rice St., Lihue* ☎ *808/246–2470* ⊕ *www.kauaimuseum.org.*

HOME DECOR

Two Frogs Hugging. At Two Frogs Hugging, you'll find lots of interesting housewares, accessories, knickknacks, and hand-carved collectibles, as well as baskets and furniture from Indonesia, the Philippines and China.

The shop occupies expansive quarters in the Lihue Industrial Park. ⊠ *3094 Aukele St., Lihue* ☎ *808/246–8777* ⊕ *www.twofrogshugging.com.*

MARKETS

FAMILY   **Kauai Community Market.** This is the biggest and best farmers' market on Kauai, sponsored by the Kauai Farm Bureau at the community college in Lihue, and held on Saturday mornings. You'll find fresh produce and flowers, as well as packaged products like breads, goat cheese, pasta, honey, coffee, soaps, lotions, and more, all made locally. Seating areas are available to grab a snack or lunch from the food booths and lunch wagons set up here. ⊠ *3-1901 Kaumualii Hwy., Lihue* ☎ *808/337–9944* ⊕ *www.kauaicommunitymarket.com.*

THE SOUTH SHORE

The South Shore, like the North Shore, has convenient shopping clusters, including Poipu Shopping Village and the upscale The Shops at Kukuiula. There are many high-priced shops, but some unique clothing and gift selections.

AREAS AND SHOPPING CENTERS

Poipu Shopping Village. Convenient to nearby hotels and condos on the South Shore, the two dozen shops at Poipu Shopping Village sell resort wear, gifts, souvenirs, and art. This complex also has a few food choices, from hot-dog stands to casual restaurants. There are a few upscale and appealing jewelry stores and fun clothing stores. A Tahitian dance troupe performs in the open-air courtyard Monday and Thursday at 4:30 pm. ⊠ *2360 Kiahuna Plantation Dr., Poipu* ☎ *808/742–2831* ⊕ *www.poipushoppingvillage.com.*

The Shops at Kukuiula. This is the South Shore's newest shopping center, with chic, high-end shops, exclusive galleries, several great restaurants and a gourmet grocery store. Check out the Kauai Culinary Market on Wednesday from 3:30 to 6, to see cooking demonstrations, listen to live Hawaiian music, visit the beer and wine garden, and browse wares from local vendors. This attractive open-air, plantation-style center is just beyond the roundabout as you enter Poipu. ⊠ *2829 Kalanikaumaka St., Poipu* ☎ *808/742–9545* ⊕ *www.theshopsatkukuiula.com.*

GALLERIES

Fodor'sChoice   **Galerie 103.** This gallery sells art, but the owners want you to experience
★   it as well. Sparse and dramatic, the main room at Galerie 103 consists of concrete floors and walls of featured pieces, from internationally acclaimed artists and local Kauai ones. Most of the artwork is contemporary or modern with a focus on nature. ⊠ *2829 Kalanikaumaka Rd., Koloa* ☎ *808/742–0103* ⊕ *www.galerie103.com.*

Halelea Gallery. In addition to offering original works by Kauai artists and others, this stylish gallery doubles as a boutique which sells a unique sampling of clothing, jewelry, and gifts made by local designers. A second branch has opened in Hanalei. ⊠ *2829 Kalanikaumaka Rd., Suite K, Koloa* ☎ *808/742–9525* ⊕ *www.haleleagallery.com.*

WEST SIDE

The West Side is years behind the South Shore in development, offering minimal, simple shops with authentic local flavor.

AREAS AND SHOPPING CENTERS

Eleele Shopping Center. Kauai's West Side has a scattering of stores, including those at this no-frills strip mall, Eleele Shopping Center. It has a bank and health clinic, and is a good place to rub elbows with local folk at Times Big Save grocery store. Or grab a quick bite to eat at the casual Grinds Cafe or Subway. ⊠ *4469 Waialo Rd., Eleele* ☎ *808/245–7238* ⊕ *www.eleeleshoppingcenter.com.*

Waimea Canyon Plaza. As the last stop for supplies before heading up to Waimea Canyon, Waimea Canyon Plaza has a Menehune Food Mart with limited groceries, snacks, beverages, fresh and prepared local foods, souvenirs, and island-made gifts for all ages There's also a snack shop. ⊠ *8171 Kekaha Rd., at Rte. 50, Kekaha* ☎ *808/337–1335.*

BOOKS

Talk Story Bookstore. Located in a historic building in quiet Hanapepe town, this cozy bookstore becomes a gathering place on busy Friday evenings during the weekly art nights. Local authors sign their books inside while outside there's live music and food trucks for treats. New, used, and out-of-print books are sold here, one of just two bookstores on Kauai. ⊠ *3785 Hanapepe Rd., Hanapepe* ☎ *808/335–6469* ⊕ *www. talkstorybookstore.com.*

CLOTHING

Paradise Sportswear. This is the retail outlet of the folks who invented Kauai's popular "red dirt" shirts, which are dyed and printed with the characteristic local soil. Ask the salesperson at Paradise Sportswear to tell you the charming story behind these shirts. Sizes from infants up to 5X are available. ⊠ *4350 Waialo Rd., Eleele* ☎ *800/717–3478* ⊕ *www.dirtshirt.com.*

FLOWERS

Kalani Tropicals. Kauai-based Kalani Tropicals will take your order online or by phone and ship heliconia, anthuriums, ginger, and other tropicals as cut flowers or fashioned into distinctive arrangements. ☎ *808/823–6547* ⊕ *kalanitropicals.com.*

FOOD SPECIALTIES

Kauai Coffee Visitor Center and Museum. Kauai produces more coffee than any other island in the state. The local product can be purchased from grocery stores or here at the Kauai Coffee Visitor Center and Museum, where a sampling of the nearly two dozen coffees is available. Be sure to try some of the estate-roasted varieties. ⊠ *870 Halawili Rd., off Rte. 50, Kalaheo* ☎ *808/335–0813, 800/545–8605* ⊕ *www.kauaicoffee.com.*

7

SPAS

THE NORTH SHORE

Fodor's Choice
★

Halelea Spa. This superb spa at the St. Regis Princeville Resort is indeed a House of Joy, as its Hawaiian name translates, so long as you are prepared to pay handsomely for services. Opened in 2009, the 11,000-square-foot Halelea Spa transports users to a place of tranquillity. The spa's 12 luxurious treatment rooms afford a subdued indoor setting outmatched only by the professional service. Take advantage of the dedicated couple's room and enjoy a taro butter, hot *pohaku* (stone) massage. Follow that with a few hours sipping tea in the relaxation lounge, sweating in the sauna, and rinsing in an overhead rain shower. There is a qualified wellness consultant, and spa programs are inspired by Native Hawaiian healing rituals. ⊠ *The St. Regis Princeville Resort, 5520 Ka Haku Rd., Princeville* ☎ *877/787–3447, 808/826–9644* ⊕ *www.stregisprinceville.com* ☞ *Massage $175–$275; bespoke in-room massage $340.*

Hanalei Day Spa. As you travel beyond tony Princeville, life slows down. The single-lane bridges may be one reason. Another is the Hanalei Day Spa, an open-air, thatched-roof, Hawaiian-style hut nestled just off the beach on the grounds of Hanalei Colony Resort in Haena. Though this no-frills day spa offers facials, waxing, wraps, scrubs, and the like, its specialty is massage: Ayurveda, Zen Shiatsu, Swedish, four-handed, and even a baby massage (and lesson for Mom, to boot). Owner Darci Frankel teaches yoga, a discipline she started as a young child. ⊠ *Hanalei Colony Resort, Rte. 560, Haena* ✢ *6 miles past Hanalei* ☎ *808/826–6621* ⊕ *www.hanaleidayspa.com* ☞ *Massage $110–$220.*

THE EAST SIDE

Alexander Day Spa & Salon at the Kauai Marriott. This sister spa of Alexander Simson's Beverly Hills spa focuses on body care rather than exercise, so don't expect any fitness equipment or exercise classes, just pampering and beauty treatments. The Alexander Day Spa & Salon at the Kauai Marriott is a sunny, pleasant facility. Massages are available in treatment rooms and on the beach, although the beach locale isn't as private as you might imagine. Wedding-day and custom spa packages can be arranged. ⊠ *Kauai Marriott Resort & Beach Club, 3610 Rice St., Suite 9A, Lihue* ☎ *808/246–4918* ⊕ *www.alexanderspa.com* ☞ *Massage $70–$185.*

Angeline's Muolaulani Wellness Center. It doesn't get more authentic, or rustic, than this. In the mid-1980s Aunty Angeline Locey opened her Anahola home to offer traditional Hawaiian healing practices. Now, her son and granddaughter carry on the tradition. At Angeline's Muolaulani Wellness Center, there's a two-hour treatment ($160) that starts with a steam, followed by a sea-salt-and-clay body scrub and a two-person massage. The real treat, however, is relaxing on Aunty's open-air garden deck. Hot-stone lomi is also available. Aunty's mission is to promote a healthy body image; as such, au naturel is an option here, but if you're nudity-shy, you can wear a sarong. Detailed directions are given when you book a treatment. Cash only and bring your own towel. ⊠ *Kamalomaloo Pl., Anahola* ☎ *808/822–3235* ⊕ *www. angelineslomikauai.com.*

Golden Lotus Studio. This small studio, tucked off the main road in Kapaa, offers a variety of yoga and dance classes daily, including heated power vinyasa yoga and aerial yoga. Various types of massage are available by appointment, including lomilomi, Ayurveda, deep tissue, and Thai style, starting at $95 an hour. Check their website for special events and workshops, offered frequently. ⊠ *4-941A Kuhio Hwy., Kapaa* ☎ *808/823–9810* ⊕ *www.goldenlotuskauai.org.*

> **TRY A LOMI MASSAGE**
>
> Living in ancient Hawaii wasn't sunbathing and lounging at the beach. Growing taro was hard work, as was building canoes, fishing for dinner, and pounding tapa for clothing, sails, and blankets. Enter *lomilomi*—Hawaiian-style massage. It's often described as being more vigorous, more rhythmic, and faster than Swedish massage, and it incorporates more elbow and forearm work. It might even involve chanting, music, and four hands (in other words, two people).

THE SOUTH SHORE

Fodor's Choice ★ **ANARA Spa.** The luxurious ANARA Spa has all the equipment and services you expect from a top resort spa, along with a pleasant, professional staff. Best of all, it has indoor and outdoor areas that capitalize on the tropical locale and balmy weather, further distinguishing it from the Marriott and St. Regis spas. Its 46,500 square feet of space includes the lovely Garden Treatment Village, an open-air courtyard with private thatched-roof huts, each featuring a relaxation area, misters, and open-air shower in a tropical setting. Ancient Hawaiian remedies and local ingredients are featured in many of the treatments, such as a Lokahi Garden facial, and a warm-stone-and-ti-leaf lomilomi massage. The open-air lava-rock showers are wonderful, introducing many guests to the delightful island practice of showering outdoors. The spa, which includes a full-service salon, adjoins the Hyatt's legendary swimming pool. ⊠ *Hyatt Regency Kauai Resort and Spa, 1571 Poipu Rd., Poipu* ☎ *808/240–6440* ⊕ *www.anaraspa. com* ☞ *Massages from $160–$250.*

THE WEST SIDE

Tri Health Ayurveda Spa. The goal at the Tri Health Ayurveda Spa isn't a onetime massage for momentary bliss, although relaxation is a key ingredient. Rather, this spa's focus is a multiweek, multitreatment, intensive program designed to eliminate toxins stored in the body and increase the flow and energy of all systems. Single sessions are available. Treatments are designed around the ancient Ayurvedic tradition of heat to open the pores, oil to deliver nutrients to tissues and nerve endings, and massage (by two therapists working in synchronized movement) to accelerate circulation. Note: because the massage strokes are long and can run the length of the body, there is no draping involved. Call ahead for an appointment. ⊠ *Kilauea* ☎ *808/828–2104* ⊕ *www. trihealthayurvedaspa.com.*

WATER SPORTS AND TOURS

Updated by
Joan Conrow

Ancient Hawaiians were water sports fanatics—they invented surfing, after all—and that propensity hasn't strayed far from today's mind-set. Even if you're not into water sports or sports in general, there's only a slim chance that you'll leave this island without getting out on the ocean, as Kauai's top attraction—Napali Coast—is something not to be missed.

For those who can't pack enough snorkeling, fishing, body boarding, or surfing time into a vacation, Kauai has it all—everything except parasailing, that is, as it's illegal to do it here (though not on Maui, the Big Island, or Oahu). If you need to rent gear for any of these activities, you'll find plenty of places with large selections at reasonable prices. And no matter what part of the island you're staying on, you'll have several options for choice spots to enjoy playing in the water.

One thing to note, and we can't say this enough—the waters off the coast of Kauai have strong currents and can be unpredictable, so always err on the side of caution and know your limits. Follow the tagline repeated by the island's lifeguards—"When in doubt, don't go out."

BOAT TOURS

Deciding to see Napali Coast by boat is an easy decision. Choosing the outfitter to go with is not. There are numerous boat-tour operators to choose from, and, quite frankly, they all do a good job. Before you even start thinking about whom to go out with, answer these three questions: What kind of boat do I prefer? Where am I staying? Do I want to go in the morning or afternoon? Once you settle on these three, you can easily zero in on the tour outfitter.

First, the boat. The most important thing is to match your personality and that of your group with the personality of the boat. If you like thrills and adventure, the rubber, inflatable rafts—often called Zodiacs, which Jacques Cousteau made famous and which the U.S. Coast Guard uses—will entice you. They're fast, likely to leave you drenched and windswept, and quite bouncy. If you prefer a smoother, more leisurely ride, then the large catamarans are the way to go. The next boat choice is size. Both the rafts and catamarans come in small and large. Again—think smaller, more adventurous; larger, more leisurely. ■ TIP➔ **Do not choose a smaller boat because you think there will be fewer people. There might be fewer people, but you'll be jammed together sitting atop strangers.** If you prefer privacy over socializing, go with a larger boat, so you'll have more room to spread out. The smaller boats will also take you along the coast at a higher rate of speed, making photo opportunities a bit more challenging. One advantage to smaller boats, however, is that—depending on ocean conditions—some may slip into a sea cave or two. If that sounds interesting to you, call the outfitter and ask their policy on entering sea caves. Some won't, no matter the conditions, because they consider the caves sacred or because they don't want to cause any environmental damage.

Boats leave from three points around the island (Hanalei, Port Allen, and Waimea), and all head to the same spot: Napali Coast. Here's the inside skinny on which is the best: If you're staying on the North Shore, choose to depart out of the North Shore. If you're staying anywhere else, depart out of the West Side. It's that easy. Sure, the North Shore is closer to Napali Coast; however, you'll pay more for less overall time. The West Side boat operators may spend more time getting to Napali Coast; however, they'll spend about the same amount of time along Napali, plus you'll pay less. Finally, you'll also have to decide whether you want to go on a morning tour, which includes a deli lunch and a stop for snorkeling, or an afternoon tour, which does not always stop to snorkel but does include a sunset over the ocean. The morning tours with snorkeling are more popular with families and those who love dolphins, as the animals enjoy the "waves" created by the front of the catamarans and might just escort you down the coast. The winter months will also be a good chance to spot some whales breaching, though surf is much rougher along Napali. You don't have to be an expert snorkeler or even have any prior experience, but if it is your first time, note that although there will be some snorkeling instruction, there might not be much. Hawaiian spinner dolphins are so plentiful in the mornings that some tour companies guarantee you'll see them, though you won't get in the water and swim with them. The afternoon tours are more popular with nonsnorkelers—obviously—and photographers interested in capturing the setting sunlight on the coast. ■ TIP➔ **No matter which tour you select, book it online whenever possible.** Most companies offer Web specials, usually around $10 to $20 off per person.

CATAMARAN TOURS

Fodor's Choice
★ **Blue Dolphin Charters.** Blue Dolphin operates 65-foot sailing (rarely raised and always motoring) catamarans designed with three decks of spacious seating with great visibility, as well as motorized rafts. ■ TIP➔ **The lower deck is best for shade seekers.** On Tuesday and Friday, a daylong tour of Napali Coast includes a detour across the channel to Niihau

for snorkeling and diving. Morning snorkel tours of Napali include a deli lunch. Sunset sightseeing tours include a Hawaiian-style buffet. North Shore and South Shore rafting tours are also available, as are daily sportfishing charters of four to eight hours for no more than six guests. Blue Dolphin promises dolphin sightings and the best mai tais "off the island." Book online for cheaper deals on every tour offered. ☒ *4353 Waialo Rd., No. 2-6B7B, Eleele* ☎ *808/335–5553, 877/511–1311* ⊕ *www.kauaiboats. com* ☒ *From $104–$176. Two-hour whale-watching/sunset tours, winter only, $72.*

> ### BOAT TOUR CHECKLIST
>
> ■ Swimsuit
> ■ Sunscreen
> ■ Hat
> ■ Sunglasses
> ■ Beach towel
> ■ Light jacket
> ■ Camera (in waterproof bag, just in case)
> ■ Motion sickness meds (take well before departure)
> ■ Change of clothes (post-cruise)

FAMILY **Capt. Andy's Sailing Adventures.** Departing from Port Allen and running two 55-foot sailing catamarans, Capt. Andy's offers five-hour snorkeling and four-hour sunset tours along Napali Coast. Unlike other charters, they have a 24-foot Zodiac raft that uses hydrophones to hear whales and other underwater sounds. The longtime Kauai company also operates a snorkel barbecue sail and dinner sunset sail aboard its *Southern Star* yacht, originally built for private charters. This boat now operates as host for two of Capt. Andy's daily sailing trips for an upgraded feel. For a shorter adventure, they have a two-hour sunset sail, embarking out of Kukuiula Harbor in Poipu along the South Shore—with live Hawaiian music—on Monday, Wednesday, and Saturday. ■ TIP→ If the winds and swells are up on the North Shore, this is usually a good choice—especially if you're prone to seasickness. This is the only tour-boat operator that allows infants on board—but only on the two-hour trip. Note, if you have reservations for the shorter tour, you'll check in at their Kukuiula Harbor office. ☒ *4353 Waiola Rd., Suite 1A-2A, Eleele* ☎ *808/335–6833* ⊕ *www. napali.com* ☒ *From $109, discounts for online booking.*

Captain Sundown. Sundown has one of the few permits to sail from Hanalei Bay and operates the only sailing catamaran there. Captain Bob has been cruising Napali Coast since 1971—six days a week, sometimes twice a day. (And right alongside Captain Bob is his son, Captain Larry.) To say he knows the area is an understatement. Here's the other good thing about this tour: they take only 15 to 17 passengers on the 40-foot boat. The breathtaking views of the waterfall-laced mountains behind Hanalei and Haena start immediately, and then it's around Kee Beach and the magic of Napali Coast unfolds before you. All the while, the captains are trolling for fish, and if they catch any, guests get to reel 'em in. Afternoon sunset sails (summertime only) run three hours and check in around 3 pm—these are BYOB. Cancellations due to rough surf are more frequent in winter. ☒ *5-5134 Kuhio Hwy., Hanalei* ☎ *808/826–5585* ⊕ *www.captainsundown.com* ☒ *From $160–$195.*

Catamaran Kahanu. Hawaiian owned and operated, Catamaran Kahanu has been in business since 1985 and runs a 40-foot power catamaran with 18-passenger seating. It offers seasonal whale-watching, snorkeling, and sunset cruises, ranging from two to five hours, and departs from Port Allen. The five-hour tour includes snorkeling at Nualolo Kai, plus a deli lunch and soft drinks. The four-hour afternoon tour takes in the sunset and includes a hot dinner. The boat is smaller than most and may feel a tad crowded, but the tour feels more personal, with a laid-back, *ohana* (family) style. Guests can witness the ancient cultural practice of coconut weaving or other Hawaiian craft demonstrations on board. There's no alcohol allowed. ⊠ *4353 Waialo Rd., near Port Allen Marina Center, Eleele* ☎ *808/645–6176, 888/213–7711* ⊕ *www.catamarankahanu.com* 🕮 *From $120.*

> ## BEST BOAT TOURS
>
> **Best for snorkeling:** Z-Tourz
>
> **Best for romance:** Capt. Andy's Poipu Sail
>
> **Best for thrill seekers:** Napali Explorer (Zodiac 1)
>
> **Best for mai tais:** Blue Dolphin Charters
>
> **Best for pregnant women:** Capt. Andy's
>
> **Best for charters:** Captain Sundown
>
> **Best for price:** Napali Riders

HoloHolo Charters. Choose between the 50-foot catamaran called *Leila* for a morning snorkel sail to Napali Coast, or the 65-foot *HoloHolo* seven-hour catamaran trip to the "forbidden island" of Niihau. Both boats have large cabins and little outside seating. HoloHolo also offers a seasonal voyage of Napali from Hanalei Bay on its rigid-hull inflatable rafts, specifically for diving and snorkeling. Originators of the Niihau tour, HoloHolo Charters built their 65-foot powered catamaran with a wide beam to reduce side-to-side motion, and twin 425 HP turbo diesel engines specifically for the 17-mile channel crossing to Niihau. It's the only outfitter running daily Niihau tours. The *HoloHolo* also embarks on a daily sunset and sightseeing tour of Napali Coast. *Leila* can hold 37 passengers, while her big brother can take a maximum of 49. Check-in is at Port Allen Marina Center. ⊠ *4353 Waialo Rd., Suite 5A, Eleele* ☎ *808/335–0815, 800/848–6130* ⊕ *www.holoholocharters.com* 🕮 *From $104–$189.*

Kauai Sea Tours. This company operates the *Lucky Lady,* a 60-foot sailing catamaran designed almost identically to that of Blue Dolphin Charters—with all the same benefits—including great views and spacious seating. Snorkeling tours anchor near Makole (based on the captain's discretion). If snorkeling isn't your thing, try the four-hour sunset tour, with beer, wine, mai tais, pupus, and a hot buffet dinner. Seasonal tours of Napali are offered on inflatible rafts. Check in at Port Allen Marina Center. ⊠ *4353 Waialo Rd., Eleele* ☎ *808/826–7254, 800/733–7997* ⊕ *www.kauaiseatours.com* 🕮 *From $112.*

Liko Kauai Cruises. There are many things to like about Liko Kauai Cruises. The 49-foot powered cat will enter sea caves, ocean conditions permitting. Sometimes, even Captain Liko himself—a Native

If you choose to sail by yourself in Kauai, be prepared for strong currents and know your limits.

Hawaiian—still takes the captain's helm. We particularly like the layout of his boat—most of the seating is in the bow, so there's good visibility. A maximum of 32 passengers make each trip, which last five hours and include snorkeling, food, and soft drinks. Trips usually depart out of Kikiaola Harbor in Waimea, a bit closer to Napali Coast than those leaving from Port Allen. ⊠ *4516 Alawai Rd., Waimea (Kauai County)* ☎ *808/338–0333, 888/732–5456* ⊕ *www.liko-kauai.com* ✉ *$140.*

Napali Catamaran. One of the few tour groups departing Hanalei, this company, formerly known as Whitey's, has been around since 1973. Once on board, it takes about five minutes before you're witnessing the magnificence of Napali Coast. Taking a maximum of 16 passengers, its 34-foot powered catamaran is small enough—and with no mast, short enough—to dip into sea caves. Between March and October, they run two four-hour snorkeling tours per day, stopping at the best snorkeling site along Napali—Nualolo Kai. If it weren't for the bench seating bisecting the boat—meaning one group of passengers enjoys unobstructed views of the open ocean instead of Napali either on the way out or back—we'd really be happy. The rate's a bit pricey; the four-hour tour includes a deli-style lunch. ⊠ *Ching Young Village, 5-5190 Kuhio Hwy., Hanalei* ☎ *808/826–6853, 866/255–6853* ⊕ *www. napalicatamaran.com* ✉ *$180.*

BOAT TOUR WEATHER CANCELLATIONS

If it's raining where you're staying, that doesn't mean it's raining over the water, so don't shy away from a boat tour. Besides, it's not the rain that should concern you—it's the wind and waves. Especially from due north and south, wind creates surface chop and makes for rough riding. Larger craft are designed to handle winter's ocean swells, however, so unless monster waves are out there, your tour should depart without a hitch. If the water is too rough, your boat captain may reroute to calmer waters. It's a tough call to make, but your comfort and safety are always the foremost factor. ■TIP→ In winter months, North Shore departures are canceled much more often than those departing the West Side. This is because the waves are often too big for the boats to leave Hanalei Bay. If you want the closest thing to a guarantee of seeing Napali Coast in winter, choose a West Side outfitter. Oh, and even if your tour boat says it cruises the "entire Napali," keep in mind that "ocean conditions permitting" is always implied.

RAFT TOURS

Capt. Andy's Rafting Expeditions. Departing out of Kikiaola Harbor in Kekaha, Capt. Andy's Rafting offers both snorkeling and beach-landing excursions. The Zodiac rafts are on the smaller side—24 feet with a maximum of 14 passengers—and all seating is on the rubber hulls, so hang on. They operate three different rafts, so there's a good chance of availability. Trips include snorkeling at Nualolo Kai (ocean conditions permitting), sightseeing along Napali Coast, a hiking tour through an ancient Hawaiian fishing village, and a buffet lunch on the beach. A shorter snorkeling tour is also offered. You're closer to the water on the Zodiacs, so you'll have great views of humpbacks, spinner dolphins, sea turtles, and other wildlife. ⊠ *Kikiaola Small Boat Harbor, Kaumualii Hwy., Kekaha* ☎ *808/335–6833, 800/535–0830* ⊕ *www.napali.com* ⊠ *From $175.*

Kauai Sea Tours. This company holds a special permit from the state to land at Nualolo Kai along Napali Coast, ocean conditions permitting. Here, you'll enjoy a picnic lunch, as well as an archaeological tour of an ancient Hawaiian fishing village, ocean conditions permitting. Kauai Sea Tours operates four 24-foot inflatable rafts—maximum occupancy 14. These are small enough for checking out the insides of sea caves and the undersides of waterfalls. Four different tours are available, including snorkeling and whale-watching, depending on the season. ⊠ *Port Allen Marina Center, 4353 Waialo Rd., Eleele* ☎ *808/826–7254, 800/733–7997* ⊕ *www.kauaiseatours.com* ⊠ *From $110.*

Fodor's Choice ★ **Napali Explorer.** These tours operate out of Waimea, a tad closer to Napali Coast than most of the other West Side catamaran tours. The company runs two different sizes of inflatable rubber raft: a 48-foot, 36-passenger craft with an onboard toilet, freshwater shower, shade canopy, and seating in the stern (which is surprisingly smooth and comfortable) and bow (which is where the fun is); and a 26-foot, 14-passenger craft for the all-out fun and thrills of a white-knuckle ride in

8

the bow. The smaller vessel stops at Nualolo Kai and ties up onshore for a tour of the ancient fishing village. Charters are available. ✉ *9814 Kaumalii Hwy., Waimea (Kauai County)* ☎ *808/338–9999* ⊕ *www. napaliexplorer.com* ✉ *From $119.*

Napali Riders. This tour-boat outfitter distinguishes itself in two ways. First, it cruises the entire Napali Coast, clear to Kee Beach and back. Second, it has a reasonable price, because it's a no-frills tour—no lunch provided, just beverages and snacks. The company runs morning and afternoon four-hour snorkeling, sightseeing, and whale-watching trips out of Kikiaola Harbor in Waimea on a 30-foot inflatable raft with a 28-passenger maximum—that's fewer than they used to take, but can still be a bit cramped. ✉ *9600 Kaumualii Hwy., Waimea (Kauai County)* ☎ *808/742–6331* ⊕ *www.napaliriders.com* ✉ *$140.*

Z-Tourz. What we like about Z-Tourz is that it's a boat company that makes snorkeling its priority. Its two-hour tours include South Shore's abundant offshore reefs, as well as Napali Coast. If you want to snorkel with Hawaii's tropical reef fish and turtles (pretty much guaranteed), this is your boat. The craft is a 26-foot rigid-hull inflatable (think Zodiac) with a maximum of 16 passengers. These snorkel tours are guided, so someone actually identifies what you're seeing. Rates include lunch and snorkel gear. ✉ *3417 Poipu Rd., Poipu* ☎ *808/742–7422, 888/998–6879* ⊕ *www.kauaiztours.com* ✉ *From $99.*

RIVERBOAT TOURS TO FERN GROTTO

Smith's Motor Boat Services. This 2-mile trip up the lush and lovely Wailua River, the only navigable waterway in Hawaii, culminates at the infamous Fern Grotto, a yawning lava tube that is covered with fishtail ferns. During the boat ride, guitar and ukulele players regale you with Hawaiian melodies and tell the history of the river. It's a kitschy, but fun, bit of Hawaiiana and the river scenery is beautiful. Flat-bottom, 150-passenger riverboats (that rarely fill up) depart from Wailua Marina at the mouth of the Wailua River. ■TIP➜ **It's extremely rare, but occasionally after heavy rains the tour doesn't disembark at the grotto; if you're traveling in winter, ask beforehand.** Round-trip excursions take 1½ hours, including time to walk around the grotto and environs. Tours run at 9:30, 11, 2, and 3:30 daily. ✉ *5971 Kuhio Hwy., Kapaa* ☎ *808/821–6895* ⊕ *www.smithskauai.com* ✉ *$18.*

BODY BOARDING AND BODYSURFING

The most natural form of wave riding is bodysurfing, a popular sport on Kauai because there are many shore breaks around the island. Wave riders of this style stand waist deep in the water, facing shore, and swim madly as a wave picks them up and breaks. It's great fun and requires no special skills and absolutely no equipment other than a swimsuit. The next step up is body boarding, also called boogie boarding. In this case, wave riders lie with their upper body on a foam board about half the length of a traditional surfboard and kick as the wave propels them toward shore. Again, this is easy to pick up, and there are many places around Kauai to practice. The locals wear short-finned flippers to help them catch waves, which is a good idea to enhance safety in the water. It's worth spending a few minutes watching these experts as they spin, twirl, and flip—that's right—while they slip down the face of the wave. Of course, all beach-safety precautions apply, and just because you see wave riders of any kind in the water doesn't mean the water is safe for everyone. Any snorkeling-gear outfitter also rents body boards.

Some of our favorite bodysurfing and body-boarding beaches are **Brennecke, Wailua, Kealia, Kalihiwai,** and **Hanalei.**

DEEP-SEA FISHING

Simply step aboard and cast your line for mahimahi, ahi, ono, and marlin. That's about how quickly the fishing—mostly trolling with lures—begins on Kauai. The water gets deep quickly here, so there's less cruising time to fishing grounds. Of course, your captain may elect to cruise to a hot location where he's had good luck lately.

There are oodles of charter fishermen around; most depart from Nawiliwili Harbor in Lihue, and most use lures instead of live bait. Inquire about each boat's "fish policy," that is, what happens to the fish if any are caught. Some boats keep all; others will give you enough for a meal or two, even doing the cleaning themselves. On shared charters, ask about the maximum passenger count and about the fishing rotation; you'll want to make sure everyone gets a fair shot at reeling in the big one. Another option is to book a private charter. Shared and private charters run four, six, and eight hours in length.

BOATS AND CHARTERS

Captain Don's Sport Fishing & Ocean Adventure. Captain Don is very flexible and treats everyone like family—he'll stop to snorkel or whale-watch if that's what the group (four to six) wants. Saltwater fly-fishermen (bring your own gear) are welcome. He'll even fish for bait and let you keep part of whatever you catch. The *June Louise* is a 34-foot twin diesel. ⊠ *Nawiliwili Small Boat Harbor, 2494 Niumalu Rd., Nawiliwili* ☎ *808/639–3012* ⊕ *www.captaindonsfishing.com* ⬚ *From $140 (shared); from $600 (private).*

Hana Paa. The advantage with Hana Paa is that it takes fewer people (minimum two, maximum four for a nonprivate excursion), but you pay for it. Charters can accommodate up to six people. The company's fish policy is flexible, and the boat is roomy. The *Maka Hou II* is a 38-foot Bertram. ⊠ *Nawiliwili Small Boat Harbor, 2494 Niumalu Rd., Nawiliwili* ☎ *808/823–6031, 866/776–3474* ⊕ *www.fishkauai.com* ⬚ *From $310 (shared); from $600 (private).*

Happy Times Fishing Charters. If you're staying on the West Side, you'll be glad to know that Napali Explorer (of the longtime rafting tour business) runs fishing trips out of Port Allen under the name Happy Times Fishing Charters. It offers shared and exclusive charters of four, six, and eight hours in a 41-foot Concord called *Happy Times.* The shared

8

tours max out at six fishermen, and a portion of the catch is shared with all. The boat is also used for specialty charters—that is, film crews, surveys, burials, and even Niihau fishing. Rates range from $149 to $189 per person. ✉ *Port Allen Small Boat Harbor, Waialo Rd., Eleele* ☎ *949/791–7605* ⊕ *www.napaliexplorertours.com* ✉ *$149–$189 per person.*

Kai Bear. The father of this father-and-son duo has it figured out: he lets the son run the business and do all the work. Or so he says. Fish policy: share the catch. Trips run from a four-hour, shared charter (six fishermen max) up to an eight-hour, keep-all-the-fish-you-want exclusive. What's particularly nice about this company are the boats: the 38-foot Bertram, *Kai Bear*, and the 42-foot Bertram, *Grander*, which just went through a major overhaul. Very roomy. ✉ *Nawiliwili Small Boat Harbor, 2900 Nawiliwili Rd., Nawiliwili* ☎ *808/652–4556* ⊕ *www.kaibear.com* ✉ *From $159.*

> ### THE ROLLING AND REELING OCEAN
>
> As anyone who's been on a boat in Kauai's waters knows, the Pacific Ocean isn't always so pacific. Even lifelong navy men have admitted to feeling queasy on a Napali boat tour. Some people think the bigger the boat the better, but studies show that the lowest incidence of seasickness occurs on the rubber inflatable rafts. It may have something to do with being closer to the water and moving in a natural rhythm with the waves. If you think you're going to get sick, motion sickness tablets are definitely a good idea.

KAYAKING

Kauai is the only Hawaiian island with navigable rivers. As the oldest inhabited island in the chain, Kauai has had more time for wind and water erosion to deepen and widen cracks into streams and streams into rivers. Because this is a small island, the rivers aren't long, and there are no rapids, which makes them generally safe for kayakers of all levels, even beginners, except when rivers are flowing fast from heavy rains.

For more advanced paddlers, there aren't many places in the world more beautiful for sea kayaking than Napali Coast. If this is your draw to Kauai, plan your vacation for the summer months, when the seas are at their calmest. ■ TIP➔ Tour and kayak-rental reservations are recommended at least two weeks in advance during peak summer and holiday seasons. In general, tours and rentals are available year-round, Monday through Saturday. Pack a swimsuit, sunscreen, a hat, bug repellent, water shoes (sport sandals, aqua socks, old tennis shoes), and motion sickness medication if you're planning on sea kayaking.

RIVER KAYAKING

Tour outfitters operate on the Huleia, Wailua, and Hanalei rivers with guided tours that combine hiking to waterfalls, as in the case of the first two, and snorkeling, as in the case of the third. Another option is

Niihau: The Forbidden Isle

Seventeen miles from Kauai, across the Kaulakahi Channel, sits the privately owned island of Niihau. It's known as the Forbidden Isle, because access is limited to the Robinson family, which owns it, and the 200 or so Native Hawaiians who were born there.

Niihau was bought from King Kamehameha in 1864 by a Scottish widow, Eliza Sinclair. Sinclair was introduced to the island after an unusually wet winter; she saw nothing but green pastures and thought it would be an ideal place to raise cattle. The cost was $10,000. It was a real deal, or so Sinclair thought.

Unfortunately, Niihau's usual rainfall is about 12 inches a year, and the land soon returned to its normal, desertlike state. Regardless, Sinclair did not abandon her venture, and today the island is owned by Bruce and Keith Robinson, Eliza Sinclair's great-great-grandsons.

Visits to the island are restricted to custom hunting expeditions and flightseeing tours through Niihau Helicopter. Tours depart from Kaumakani and avoid the western coastline, especially the village of Puuwai. There's a five-passenger minimum for each flight, and reservations are essential. A picnic lunch on a secluded Niihau beach is included, with time for swimming, beachcombing, and snorkeling. The half-day tour is $385 per person.

For more information, contact **Niihau Tours** (☎ *808/335–3500 or 877/441–3500* ⊕ *www.niihau.us*).

renting kayaks and heading out on your own. Each has its advantages and disadvantages, but it boils down as follows:

If you want to swim at the base of a remote 100-foot waterfall, sign up for a five-hour kayak (4-mile round-trip) and hiking (2-mile round-trip) tour of the **Wailua River.** It includes a dramatic waterfall that is best accessed with the aid of a guide, so you don't get lost. ■TIP➔ Remember—it's dangerous to swim under waterfalls no matter how good a water massage may sound. Rocks and logs are known to plunge down, especially after heavy rains.

If you want to kayak on your own, choose the **Hanalei River.** It's most scenic from the kayak itself—there are no trails to hike to hidden waterfalls. And better yet, a rental company is right on the river—no hauling kayaks on top of your car.

If you're not sure of your kayaking abilities, head to the **Huleia River;** 3½-hour tours include easy paddling upriver, a nature walk through a rain forest with a cascading waterfall, a rope swing for playing Tarzan and Jane, and a ride back downriver—into the wind—on a motorized, double-hull canoe.

As for the kayaks themselves, most companies use the two-person sit-on-top style that is quite buoyant—no Eskimo rolls required. The only possible danger comes in the form of communication. The kayaks seat two people, which means you'll share the work (good) with a guide, or your spouse, child, parent, or friend (the potential danger part). On the river, the two-person kayaks are known as "divorce boats." Counseling is not included in the tour price.

SEA KAYAKING

In its second year and second issue, *National Geographic Adventure* ranked kayaking Napali Coast second on its list of America's Best 100 Adventures, right behind rafting the Colorado River through the Grand Canyon. That pretty much says it all. It's the adventure of a lifetime in one day, involving eight hours of paddling. Although it's good to have some kayaking experience, feel comfortable on the water, and be reasonably fit, it doesn't require the preparation, stamina, or fortitude of, say, climbing Mt. Everest. Tours run May through September, ocean conditions permitting. In the winter months sea-kayaking tours operate on the South Shore—beautiful, but not as dramatic as Napali.

EQUIPMENT AND TOURS

Kayak Kauai. This company pioneered kayaking on Kauai. It offers guided tours on the Hanalei and Wailua rivers, and along Napali Coast in season. It has consolidated operations, and is now conveniently located in the Wailua Marina. From there, it can launch kayaks right into the Wailua River for its five-hour Secret Falls hike-paddle tour and three-hour paddle to a swimming hole. Kayak Kauai also offers a five-hour paddle tour of Hanalei River and Bay, and 12-hour escorted summer sea kayak tours of Napali Coast. Stand-up paddleboard instruction and sea-kayak whale-watching tours round out its repertoire.

The company will shuttle kayakers as needed, and, for rentals, it provides the hauling gear necessary for your rental car. Snorkel gear, body boards, and stand-up paddleboards also can be rented. ⊠ *Wailua Marina, 3-5971 Kuhio Hwy., Wailua (Kauai County)* ☎ *808/826–9844, 888/596–3853* ⊕ *www.kayakkauai.com* ⌑ *From $60 (river tours) and $240 (sea tours); kayak rentals from $45 per day.*

Kayak Wailua. We can't quite figure out how this family-run business offers pretty much the same Wailua River kayaking tour as everyone else—except for lunch and beverages, which are BYO—for the lowest price, but it does. They say it's because they don't discount and don't offer commissions to activities and concierge desks. Their trips, a 4½-hour kayak, hike, and waterfall swim, are offered four times a day, beginning at 9 am, with the last at 1 pm. With the number of boats going out, large groups can be accommodated. No tours are allowed on Wailua River on Sunday. ⊠ *4565 Haleilio Rd., behind old Coco Palms hotel, Kapaa* ☎ *808/822–3388* ⊕ *www.kayakwailua.com* ⌑ *$50.*

Fodor'sChoice **Napali Kayak.** A couple of longtime guides ventured out on their own
★ to create this company, which focuses solely on a 17-mile sea-kayaking paddle along Napali Coast from April to October. These guys are highly experienced and still highly enthusiastic about their livelihood—so much so that REI Adventures hires them to run their multiday, multisport tours. If you're an experienced kayaker and want to try camping on your own at Kalalau (you'll need permits), Napali

Kayak will provide kayaks outfitted with dry bags, extra paddles, and seat backs, while also offering transportation drop-off and pickup. They also do Napali Coast day tours from Hanalei to Polihale, with a lunch break at Milolii, and rent camping equipment and first-aid kits. ⊠ *5-5075 Kuhio Hwy., next to Postcards Café, Hanalei* ☎ *808/826–6900* ⊕ *www.napalikayak.com* 🖃 *From $225.*

FAMILY **Outfitters Kauai.** This well-established tour outfitter operates year-round river-kayak tours on the Huleia and Wailua rivers, as well as sea-kayaking tours along Napali Coast in summer and the South Shore in winter. Outfitters Kauai's specialty, however, is the Kipu Safari. This all-day adventure starts with kayaking up the Huleia River and includes a rope swing over a swimming hole, a wagon ride through a working cattle ranch, a picnic lunch by a private waterfall, hiking, and two "zips" across the rain-forest canopy (strap on a harness, clip into a cable, and zip over a quarter of a mile). They then offer a one-of-a-kind Waterzip Zipline at their mountain stream-fed blue pool. The day ends with a ride on a motorized double-hull canoe. It's a great tour for the family, because no one ever gets bored. ⊠ *2827-A Poipu Rd., Poipu* ☎ *808/742–9667, 888/742–9887* ⊕ *www.outfitterskauai.com* 🖃 *Kipu Safari $193.*

Wailua Kayak & Canoe. This purveyor of kayak rentals is right on the Wailua River, which means no hauling your kayak on top of your car (a definite plus). Guided waterfall tours are also offered. This outfitter promotes itself as "Native Hawaiian owned and operated." No Wailua River tours are offered on Sunday. ⊠ *162 Wailua Rd., Kapaa* ☎ *808/821–1188* ⊕ *www.wailuariverkayaking.com* 🖃 *$50 for a single, $85 for a double; guided tours from $70.*

HAWAII STATE SPORT: CANOE PADDLING

In summer, it's not unusual to see Hawaii's state sport in action: outrigger canoe racing. These are the same styles of canoes ancient Hawaiians paddled in races that pitted one chief's warriors against another's. Summer is regatta season, and the half dozen or more canoe clubs around the island gather to race in ¼-mile, ½-mile, and longer races. You can catch the hundreds of paddlers lining the beaches and cheering on their clubs, oftentimes in Hanalei, Kalapaki, and Waimea Bay, as well as the Wailua River.

KITEBOARDING

Several years ago, the latest wave-riding craze to hit the Islands was kiteboarding, and the sport is still going strong. As the name implies, there's a kite and a board involved. The board you strap on your feet; the kite is attached to a harness around your waist. Steering is accomplished with a rod that's attached to the harness and the kite. Depending on conditions and the desires of the kiteboarder, the kite is played out some 30 to 100 feet in the air. The result is a cross between waterskiing—without the boat—and windsurfing. Speeds are fast and aerobatic maneuvers are involved. Unfortunately, neither lessons nor rental gear is available for the sport on Kauai (Maui is a better bet), so if you aren't a

SCUBA Q&A

Q: Do I have to be certified to go scuba diving?

A: No. You can try Discover Scuba, which allows you to dive up to 40 feet after an introductory lesson in a pool. Most dive outfitters on Kauai offer this introductory program.

Q: Can I dive if I have asthma?

A: Only if your doctor signs a medical release—the original of which you must present to your dive outfitter.

Q: Can I get certified on Kauai?

A: Yes. Start to finish, it'll take three days. Or, you can complete your classroom and confined-water training at home and just do your check-out dives on Kauai.

Q: How old do you have to be to learn how to dive?

A: Most certifying agencies require that you be at least 12 years old (with PADI it's 10) when you start your scuba-diving course. You will normally receive a junior certification, which can be upgraded to a full certification when you are 15 years old.

Q: Can I wear contact lenses or glasses while diving?

A: You can either wear contact lenses with a regular mask or opt for a prescription mask—just let your dive outfitter know in advance.

Q: What if I forget my certification card?

A: Let your dive outfitter know immediately; with advance notice, they can usually dig up your certification information online.

seasoned kiteboarder already, you'll have to be content with watching the pros—who can put on a pretty spectacular show. The most popular year-round spots for kiteboarding are **Kapaa Beach Park, Anini Beach Park,** and **Mahaulepu Beach.** ■TIP→ Many visitors come to Kauai dreaming of parasailing. If that's you, make a stop at Maui or the Big Island. There's no parasailing or commercial jet skiing on Kauai.

SCUBA DIVING

The majority of scuba diving on Kauai occurs on the South Shore. Boat and shore dives are available, although boat sites surpass the shore sites for a couple of reasons. First, they're deeper and exhibit the complete symbiotic relationship of a reef system, and second, the visibility is better a little farther offshore.

The dive operators on Kauai offer a full range of services, including certification dives, referral dives, boat dives, shore dives, night dives, and drift dives. ■TIP→ As for certification, we recommend completing your confined-water training and classroom testing before arriving on the island. That way, you'll spend less time training and more time diving.

BEST SPOTS

The best and safest scuba-diving sites are accessed by boat on the South Shore of the island, right off the shores of Poipu. The captain selects the actual site based on ocean conditions of the day. Beginners may prefer shore dives, which are best at **Koloa Landing** on the South Shore year-round and **Makua (Tunnels) Beach** on the North Shore in the calm summer months. Keep in mind, though, that you'll have to haul your gear a ways down the beach.

For the advanced diver, the island of Niihau—across an open ocean channel in deep and crystal clear waters—beckons and rewards, usually with some big fish. Seasport Divers, Fathom Five, and Bubbles Below venture the 17 miles across the channel in summer when the crossing is smoothest. Divers can expect deep dives, walls, and strong currents at Niihau, where conditions can change rapidly. To make the long journey worthwhile, three dives and Nitrox are included.

EQUIPMENT, LESSONS, AND TOURS

Bubbles Below. Marine ecology is the emphasis here aboard the 36-foot, eight-passenger *Kai Manu*. This longtime Kauai company discovered some pristine dive sites on the West Side of the island where white-tip reef sharks are common—and other divers are not. Thanks to the addition of a 32-foot powered catamaran—the six-passenger *Dive Rocket*—the group also runs Niihau, Napali, and North Shore dives year-round (depending on ocean conditions, of course). They're still known for their south side trips and lead dives at the East Side walls as well, so they truly do circumnavigate the island. A bonus on these tours is the wide variety of food served between dives. Open-water certification dives, check-out dives, and intro shore dives are available upon request. ✉ *Port Allen Small Boat Harbor, 4353 Waialo Rd., Eleele* ☎ *808/332–7333* ⊕ *www.bubblesbelowkauai.com* 🖥 *$135 for two-tank boat dive; $90 for rider/snorkeler; Niihau charter $345.*

Kauai Down Under Dive Team. This company offers boat dives, but specializes in shore diving, typically at Koloa Landing (year-round) and Tunnels (summers). They're not only geared toward beginning divers—for whom they provide a thorough and gentle certification program as well as the Discover Scuba program—but also offer night dives and scooter (think James Bond) dives. Their main emphasis is a detailed review of marine biology, such as pointing out rare dragon eel and harlequin shrimp tucked away in pockets of coral. ■**TIP→** Hands down, we recommend Kauai Down Under for beginners, certification (all levels), and refresher dives. One reason is that their instructor-to-student ratio never exceeds 1:4—that's true of all their dive groups. All dive gear included. ✉ *Sheraton Kauai Resort, 2440 Hoonani Rd., Koloa* ☎ *877/538–3483, 808/742–9534* ⊕ *www.kauaidownunderscuba.com* 🖥 *From $79 for a one-tank certified dive; $450 for certification.*

Fodor's Choice **Ocean Quest Watersports/Fathom Five.** This operator offers it all: boat ★ dives, shore dives, night dives, certification dives. They pretty much do what everyone else does with a few twists. First, they offer a three-tank premium charter for those really serious about diving. Second, they operate a Nitrox continuous-flow mixing system, so you can decide the mix rate. Third, they add on a twilight dive to the standard, one-tank night dive, making the outing worth the effort. Fourth, their shore diving isn't an afterthought. Finally, we think their dive masters are pretty darn good, too. They even dive Niihau in the summer aboard their 35-foot *Force*. In summer, book well in advance. ⊠ *3450 Poipu Rd., Koloa* ☎ *808/742–6991, 800/972–3078* ⊕ *www.fathomfive.com* ✉ *From $130 for boat dives; from $75 for shore dives; $40 for gear rental, if needed.*

Seasport Divers. Rated highly by readers of *Scuba Diving* magazine, Seasport Divers' 48-foot *Anela Kai* tops the chart for dive-boat luxury. But owner Marvin Otsuji didn't stop with that. A second boat—a 32-foot catamaran—is outfitted for diving, but we like it as an all-around charter. The company does brisk business, which means it won't cancel at the last minute because of a lack of reservations, like some other companies, although they may book up to 18 people per boat. ■ TIP→ There are slightly more challenging trips in the morning; mellower dive sites are in the afternoon. The company runs a good-size dive shop for purchases and rentals, as well as a classroom for certification. Night dives are offered, and Niihau trips are available in summer. There's also an outlet in Kapaa. ⊠ *2827 Poipu Rd., look for yellow submarine in parking lot, Poipu* ☎ *808/742–9303, 808/823–9222* ⊕ *www.seasportdivers. com* ✉ *From $135, includes gear; $95 one-tank shore dive.*

SNORKELING

Generally speaking, the calmest water and best snorkeling can be found on Kauai's North Shore in summer and South Shore in winter. The East Side, known as the windward side, has year-round, prevalent northeast trade winds that make snorkeling unpredictable, although there are some good pockets. The best snorkeling on the West Side is accessible only by boat.

A word on feeding fish: don't. As Captain Ted with HoloHolo Charters says, fish have survived and populated reefs for much longer than we have been donning goggles and staring at them. They will continue to do so without our intervention. Besides, fish food messes up the reef and—one thing always leads to another—can eliminate a once-pristine reef environment. As for gear, if you're snorkeling with one of the Napali boat-tour outfitters, they'll provide it; however, depending on the company, it might not be the latest or greatest. If you have your own, bring it. On the other hand, if you're going out with SeaFun or Z-Tourz *(see Boat Tours)*, the gear is top-notch. If you need to rent, hit one of the "snorkel-and-surf" shops such as Snorkel Bob's in Koloa and Kapaa, Nukumoi in Poipu, or Seasport in Poipu and Kapaa, or shop Wal-Mart or Kmart if you want to drag it home. Typically, though, rental gear will be better quality than that found at Wal-Mart or Kmart. ■ TIP→ If you wear glasses, you can rent prescription masks at the rental shops—just don't expect them to match your prescription exactly.

Kauaʻi's calmest water and best snorkeling is on the North Shore in summer and South Shore in winter. Many of the best dive spots are on the South Shore.

BEST SPOTS

Just because we say these are good places to snorkel doesn't mean that the exact moment you arrive, the fish will flock—they are wild, after all.

Beach House (Lawai Beach). Don't pack the beach umbrella, beach mats, or cooler for snorkeling at Beach House. Just bring your snorkeling gear. The beach—named after its neighbor the Beach House restaurant—is on the road to Spouting Horn. It's a small slip of sand during low tide and a rocky shoreline during high tide; however, it's right by the road's edge, and its rocky coastline and somewhat rocky bottom make it great for snorkeling. Enter and exit in the sand channel (not over the rocky reef) that lines up with the Lawai Beach Resort's center atrium. Stay within the rocky points anchoring each end of the beach. The current runs east to west. ⊠ *5017 Lawai Rd., makai side of Lawai Rd., park on road in front of Lawai Beach Resort, Koloa.*

Kee Beach. Although it can get quite crowded, Kee Beach is quite often a good snorkeling destination if the water conditions are right. Just be sure to come during the off-hours, say early in the morning or later in the afternoon, or you will have difficulty finding a parking spot. ■ TIP➡ **Snorkeling here in winter can be hazardous. Summer is the best and safest time, although you should never swim beyond the reef.** During peak times, a parking lot is available back down the road away from the beach. ⊕ *At end of Rte. 560, Haena.*

Lydgate Beach Park. Lydgate Beach Park is typically the safest place to snorkel on Kauaʻi, though not the most exciting. With its lava-rock wall creating a protected swimming pool, it's a good spot for beginners,

TIPS FOR SAFE SNORKELING

Mike Hopkins with SeaFun Kauai, a guided walk-in snorkeling tour operator, suggests these tips for safe snorkeling:

■ Snorkel with a buddy and stay together.

■ Choose a location where lifeguards are present.

■ Ask the lifeguard about conditions.

■ Plan your entry and exit points.

■ Swim into the current on entering and then ride the current back to your exit point.

■ Look up periodically to gauge your location with a reference point on land.

■ When in doubt, try a guided tour.

young and old. The fish are so tame here it's almost like swimming in a saltwater aquarium. There is also a lifeguard, a playground for children, plenty of parking, and full-service restrooms with showers. ⊠ *4470 Nalu Rd.* ✛ *Just south of Wailua River, turn makai off Rte. 56 onto Lehu Dr. and left onto Nalu Rd., Kapaa.*

Fodor'sChoice
★

Niihau. With little river runoff and hardly any boat traffic, the waters off the island of Niihau are some of the clearest in all Hawaii, and that's good for snorkeling and excellent for scuba diving. Like Nualolo Kai, the only way to snorkel here is to sign on with one of the tour boats venturing across a sometimes rough open-ocean channel: Blue Dolphin Charters and HoloHolo.

Nualolo Kai. Nualolo Kai was once an ancient Hawaiian fishpond and is now home to the best snorkeling along Napali Coast (and perhaps on all of Kauai). The only way to access it is by boat, including kayak. Though many boats stop offshore, only a few Napali snorkeling-tour operators are permitted to come ashore. We recommend Napali Explorer and Kauai Sea Tours.

Poipu Beach Park. You'll generally find good year-round snorkeling at Poipu Beach Park, except during summer's south swells (which are not nearly as frequent as winter's north swells). The best snorkeling fronts the Marriott Waiohai Beach Club. Stay inside the crescent created by the sandbar and rocky point, and within sight of the lifeguard tower. The current runs east to west. ⊠ *Hoone Rd.* ✛ *From Poipu Rd., turn right onto Hoone Rd.*

Tunnels (Makua). The search for Tunnels (Makua) is as tricky as the snorkeling. Park at Haena Beach Park and walk east—away from Napali Coast—until you see a sand channel entrance in the water, almost at the point. Once you get here, the reward is fantastic. The name of this beach comes from the many underwater lava tubes, which always attract marine life. The shore is mostly beach rock interrupted by three sand channels. You'll want to enter and exit at one of these channels (or risk stepping on a sea urchin or scraping your stomach on the reef). Follow the sand channel to a drop-off; the snorkeling along here is always full of nice surprises. Expect a current running east to west. Snorkeling here in winter can be hazardous; summer is the best and safest time for snorkeling. ⊠ *Haena Beach Park ✦ Near end of Rte. 560, across from lava-tube sea caves, after stream crossing.*

TOURS

FAMILY
Fodor's Choice
★

SeaFun Kauai. This guided snorkeling tour, for beginners and intermediates alike, is led by a marine expert, so there's instruction plus the guide actually gets into the water with you and identifies marine life. You're guaranteed to spot tons of critters you'd never see on your own. This is a land-based operation and the only one of its kind on Kauai. (Don't think those snorkeling cruises are guided snorkeling tours—they rarely are. A member of the boat's crew serves as lifeguard, not a marine life *guide.*) A half-day tour includes all your snorkeling gear—and a wet suit to keep you warm—and stops at one or two snorkeling locations, chosen based on ocean conditions. They will pick up customers at some of the resorts, depending on locale and destination. ⊠ *1702 Haleukana St., Lihue* ☎ *808/245–6400, 800/452–1113* ⊕ *www.alohakauaitours. com* ⌐ *$80.*

STAND-UP PADDLING

Unlike kiteboarding, this is an increasingly popular sport that even a novice can pick up—*and* have fun doing. Technically, it's not really a new sport but a reinvigorated one from the 1950s. Beginners start with a heftier surfboard and a longer-than-normal canoe paddle. And, just as the name implies, stand-up paddlers stand on their surfboards and paddle out from the beach—no timing a wave and doing a push-up to stand. The perfect place to learn is a river (think **Hanalei** or **Wailua**) or a calm lagoon (try **Anini** or **Kalapaki**). But this sport isn't just for beginners. Tried-and-true surfers turn to it when the waves are not quite right for their preferred sport, because it gives them another reason to be on the water. Stand-up paddlers catch waves earlier and ride them longer than longboard surfers. In the past couple of years, professional stand-up paddling competitions have popped up, and surf shops and instructors have adapted to its quick rise in popularity.

EQUIPMENT AND LESSONS

Not all surf instructors teach stand-up paddling, but more and more are, like Blue Seas Surf School and Titus Kinimaka Hawaiian School of Surfing *(see Surfing).*

Back Door Surf Co. Along with its sister store across the street—Hanalei Surf Shop—Back Door Surf Co. provides just about all the rentals necessary for a fun day at Hanalei Bay, along with clothing and new boards. ⊠ *Ching Young Village, 5-5190 Kuhio Hwy., Hanalei* ☎ *808/826–9000* ⊕ *www.hanaleisurf.com/backdoor.htm.*

Hawaiian Surfing Adventures. This Hanalei location has a wide variety of stand-up boards and paddles for rent, with a few options depending on your schedule. Check in at the storefront and then head down to the

Winter brings big surf to Kauai's North Shore. You can see some of the sport's biggest celebrities catching waves at Haena and Hanalei Bay.

beach, where your gear will be waiting. Lessons are also available on the scenic Hanalei River or in Hanalei Bay, and include 30 minutes of ocean safety, paddling, and wave-reading instruction and an hour in the water to practice with the board. This Native Hawaiian–owned company also offers surfboard and kayak rentals and surfing lessons. ✉ *5134 Kuhio Hwy., Hanalei* ☎ *808/482–0749* ⊕ *www.hawaiiansurfingadventures. com* ✉ *Paddleboard rental from $30; surfboard rentals from $20; lessons from $65–$150.*

Kauai Beach Boys. This outfitter is right on the beach at Kalapaki, so there's no hauling your gear on your car. Classes are also held at Poipu Beach, at the Marriott Waiohai. In addition to stand-up paddle lessons, they offer sailing and surfing lessons, too. ✉ *3610 Rice St., Lihue* ☎ *808/246–6333, 808/742–4442* ⊕ *www.kauaibeachboys.com* ✉ *$79 for 1½-hr surfing lesson.*

SURFING

Good ol' stand-up surfing is alive and well on Kauai, especially in winter's high-surf season on the North Shore. If you're new to the sport, we highly recommend taking a lesson. Not only will this ensure you're up and riding waves in no time, but instructors will provide the right board for your experience and size, help you time a wave, and give you a push to get your momentum going. ■ TIP→ You don't need to be in top physical shape to take a lesson. Because your instructor helps push you into the wave, you won't wear yourself out paddling. If you're

QUESTIONS FOR A SURF INSTRUCTOR

Thinking about taking surf lessons? These are a few good questions to ask your potential surf instructor:

■ Are you legally permitted to operate on the beach?

■ What equipment do you provide? (If you're a beginner, you'll want to hear about their soft-top beginner boards. You'll also want to know if they'll provide rash guards and aqua socks.)

■ Who will be my instructor? (It's not always the name on the company logo. Ask about your instructor's qualifications.)

■ How do you select the location? (Ideally, you'll be assured that they

pick the location because of its gentle waves, sandy beach bottom, and good year-round conditions.)

■ What if the waves are too big? (Under the best circumstances, they'll select another location or reschedule for another day.)

■ How many students do you take at a time? (Don't book if it's more than four students per instructor. You'll definitely want some personal attention.)

■ Are you CPR- and lifeguard-certified? (It's good to know your instructor will be able to help if you get into trouble.)

experienced and want to hit the waves on your own, most surf shops rent boards for all levels, from beginners to advanced.

BEST SPOTS

Perennial-favorite beginning surf spots include **Poipu Beach** (the area fronting the Marriott Waiohai Beach Club), **Hanalei Bay,** and the stream end of **Kalapaki Beach.** More advanced surfers move down the beach in Hanalei to an area fronting a grove of pine trees known as **Pine Trees,** or paddle out past the pier. When the trade winds die, the north ends of **Wailua** and **Kealia** beaches are teeming with surfers. Breaks off **Poipu** and **Beach House/Lawai Beach** attract intermediates year-round. During high surf, the break on the cliff side of **Kalihiwai** is for experts only. Advanced riders will head to Polihale to face the heavy West Side waves when conditions are right.

EQUIPMENT AND LESSONS

FAMILY **Blue Seas Surf School.** Surfer and instructor Charlie Smith specializes in beginners (especially children), and though he operates primarily at Poipu Beach, lessons are offered elsewhere on the island. His soft-top longboards are very stable, making it easier to stand up. He specializes in one-on-one or family lessons, so personal interaction is a priority. He has also added stand-up paddling to his operation. Transportation is provided, if needed. ⊠ *1959 Hoone Rd., Koloa* ☎ *808/634–6979* ⊕ *www.blueseassurfingschool.com* ⊠ *From $75 for a 1½-hr lesson.*

Humpback whales arrive at Kauai in November and stick around until early April. You can see these majestic creatures breach and spout from shore, or take a boat tour.

Hanalei Surf Company. You can rent boards here and shop for rash guards, wet suits, and some hip surf-inspired apparel. ⊠ *Hanalei Center, 5-5161 Kuhio Hwy., Hanalei* ☎ *808/826–9000* ⊕ *www.hanaleisurf.com.*

Nukumoi Surf Co. Owned by the same folks who own Brennecke's restaurant, this shop offers board (surfing, body, and stand-up paddle) rentals, as well as snorkel and beach-gear rental, along with casual clothing. Their primary surf spot is the beach fronting the Sheraton. ⊠ *2100 Hoone Rd., across from Poipu Beach Park, Koloa* ☎ *808/742–8019* ⊕ *www.nukumoi.com* ⊠ *$75 for groups for 2 hrs; $250 for private sessions.*

Progressive Expressions. This full-service shop has a choice of rental boards and a whole lotta shopping for clothes, swimsuits, and casual beach wear. ⊠ *5428 Koloa Rd., Koloa* ☎ *808/742–6041* ⊕ *www. progressiveexpressions.com.*

Tamba Surf Company. This is Kauai's homegrown surf shop, and your best bet for surfboard and snorkel gear rentals on the East Side. Tamba is a big name in local surf apparel. ⊠ *4-1543 Kuhio Hwy., Kapaa* ☎ *808/823–6942* ⊕ *www.tamba.com.*

Titus Kinimaka Hawaiian School of Surfing. Famed as a pioneer of big-wave surfing, this Hawaiian believes in giving back to his sport. Beginning, intermediate, and advanced lessons are available at Hanalei. If you want to learn to surf from a living legend, this is the man. Advanced surfers can also take a tow-in lesson with a Jet Ski. ■TIP→ He employs other instructors, so if you want Titus, be sure to ask for him. (And good luck,

WHAT'S THAT WHALE DOING?

Although humpbacks spend more than 90% of their lives underwater, they can be very active above water while they're in Hawaii. Here are a few maneuvers you may see:

■ Blow: the expulsion of air that looks like a geyser of water.

■ Spy hop: the raising of just the whale's head out of the water, as if to take a look around.

■ Tail slap: the repetitive slap of the tail, or fluke, on the surface of the water.

■ Pec slap: the repetitive slap of one or both fins on the surface of the water.

■ Fluke up dive: the waving of the tail above water as the whale slowly rolls underwater to dive.

■ Breach: the launching of the entire whale's body out of the water.

because if the waves are going off, he'll be surfing, not teaching.) Customers are able to use the board for a while after the lesson is complete. ✉ *Quicksilver, 5-5088 Kuhio Hwy., Hanalei* ☎ *808/652–1116* ⊕ *www. hawaiianschoolofsurfing.com* ✉ *$65, 90-min group; $250 Jet Ski surf; $65, 90-min group stand-up paddle.*

WHALE-WATCHING

Every winter North Pacific humpback whales swim some 3,000 miles over 30 days, give or take a few, from Alaska to Hawaii. Whales arrive as early as November and sometimes stay through April, though they seem to be most populous in February and March. They come to Hawaii to breed, calve, and nurse their young.

TOURS

Of course, nothing beats seeing a whale up close. During the season, any boat on the water is looking for whales; they're hard to avoid, whether the tour is labeled "whale-watching" or not. Consider the whales a benefit to any boating event that may interest you. If whales are definitely your thing, though, you can narrow down your tour-boat decision by asking a few whale-related questions, like whether there's a hydrophone on board, how long the captain has been running tours in Hawaii, and if anyone on the crew is a marine biologist or trained naturalist.

Several boat operators will add two-hour afternoon whale-watching tours during the season that run on the South Shore (not Napali). Operators include **Blue Dolphin, Catamaran Kahanu, HoloHolo,** and **Napali Explorer** *(see Boat Tours).* Trying one of these excursions is a good option for those who have no interest in snorkeling or sightseeing along Napali Coast, although keep in mind, the longer you're on the water, the more likely you'll be to see the humpbacks.

One of the more unique ways to (possibly) see some whales is atop a kayak. For such an encounter, try **Outfitters Kauai**'s South Shore kayak trip *(see Kayaking Tours)*. There are a few lookout spots around the island with good land-based viewing: Kilauea Lighthouse on the North Shore, the Kapaa Scenic Overlook just north of Kapaa town on the East Side, and the cliffs to the east of Keoniloa (Shipwreck) Beach on the South Shore.

GOLF, HIKING, AND OUTDOOR ACTIVITIES

Updated by Charles Roessler

Kaui's outdoor recreation options extend well beyond the sand and surf, with plenty of activities to keep you busy on the ground and even in the air. You can hike the island's many trails, or consider taking your vacation into flight with a treetop zip line. You can have a backcountry adventure in a four-wheel drive, or relax in an inner tube floating down the cane-field irrigation canals.

Before booking tours, check with your concierge to find out what the forecast is for water and weather conditions. ■**TIP→ Don't rely on the Weather Channel for accurate weather reports, as they're often reporting Oahu weather.** If you happen to arrive during a North Shore lull in the surf, you'll want to plan to be on the ocean in a kayak or snorkeling on the reef. If it's raining, ATV tours are the activity of choice.

For the golfer in the family, Kauai's spectacular courses are rated among the most scenic, as well as the most technical. Princeville Golf Course has garnered accolades from numerous national publications, and Poipu Bay Golf Course hosted the prestigious season-end PGA Grand Slam of Golf for 13 years, although Tiger (he won a record five-straight tournaments) and company, unfortunately, now head to Bermuda for this tourney.

One of the most popular Kauai experiences is to see the island from the air. In an hour or so, you can see waterfalls, craters, and other places that are inaccessible even by hiking trails (some say that 70% or more of the island is inaccessible). The majority of flights depart from the Lihue airport and follow a clockwise pattern around the island. ■**TIP→ If you plan to take an aerial tour, it's a good idea to fly when you first arrive, rather than saving it for the end of your trip. It will help you visualize what's where on the island, and it may help you decide what you want to see from a closer vantage point during your stay.** Be prepared to relive your flight in dreams for the rest of your life. The most popular flight is 60 minutes long.

AERIAL TOURS

If you only drive around Kauai in your rental car, you will not see *all* of Kauai. There is truly only one way to see it all, and that's by air. Helicopter tours are the favorite way to get a bird's-eye view of Kauai—they fly at lower altitudes, hover above waterfalls, and wiggle their way into areas that a fixed-wing aircraft cannot. That said, if you've already tried the helitour, how about flying in the open cockpit of a biplane—à la the Red Baron?

Air Tour Kauai. This company, which is operated by the same group that runs Skydive Kauai, can hold up to six people in its Cessna 207 plane. The flights take off from the less crowded Port Allen Airport and will last 65 to 70 minutes. ⊠ *Port Allen Airport, 3441 Kuiloko Rd., Hanapepe* ☎ *808/639–3446* ⊕ *www.airtourkauai.com* ☛ *$109 per person.*

Blue Hawaiian Helicopters. This multi-island operator flies the latest in helicopter technology, the Eco-Star, costing $1.8 million. It has 23% more interior space for its six passengers, has unparalleled viewing, and offers a few extra safety features. As the name implies, the helicopter is also a bit more environmentally friendly, with a 50% noise-reduction rate. Even though flights run a tad shorter than others (50 to 55 minutes instead of the 55 to 65 minutes that other companies tout), they feel complete. A DVD of your tour is available for an additional $25. ⊠ *3651 Ahukini Rd., Heliport 8, Lihue* ☎ *808/245–5800, 800/745–2583* ⊕ *www.bluehawaiian.com* ☛ *$239.*

Fodor's Choice
★
Jack Harter Helicopters. Jack Harter was the first company to offer helicopter tours on Kauai. The company flies the six-passenger ASTAR helicopter with floor-to-ceiling windows, and the four-person Hughes 500, which is flown with no doors. The doorless ride can get windy, but it's the best bet for taking reflection-free photos. Pilots provide information on the Garden Island's history and geography through two-way intercoms. The company flies out of Lihue. Tours are 60 to 65 minutes and 90 to 95 minutes. Receive a $30 discount when you book through their website. ⊠ *4231 Ahukini Rd.* ☎ *808/245–3774, 888/245–2001* ⊕ *www.helicopters-kauai.com* ☛ *From $289.*

Safari Helicopters. This company flies the "Super" ASTAR helicopter, which offers floor-to-ceiling windows on its doors, four roof windows, and Bose X-Generation headphones. Two-way microphones allow passengers to converse with the pilot. There's a 60-minute waterfall tour and a 90-minute "eco-tour," which adds a landing in Olokele Canyon. Passengers are often met by Keith Robinson of *the* Robinson family, who provides a brief tour of the Kauai Wildlife Refuge, with endangered, endemic plants. A DVD is available for $21. ⊠ *3225 Akahi St., Lihue* ☎ *808/246–0136, 800/326–3356* ⊕ *www.safarihelicopters.com* ☛ *From $189; eco-tour is $274.*

Sunshine Helicopter Tours. If the name of this company sounds familiar, it may be because its pilots fly on all the main Hawaiian Islands except Oahu. On Kauai, Sunshine Helicopters departs out of two different locations: Lihue and Princeville. They fly the six-passenger FX STAR from Lihue and super roomy six-passenger WhisperSTAR birds from

9

Princeville. ■TIP➔ Discounts can be substantial by booking online and taking advantage of the "early-bird" seating during off hours. ⊠ *3416 Rice St., Suite 203, Lihue* ☎ *808/240–2577, 866/501–7738* ⊕ *www. sunshinehelicopters.com* ✉ *From $205, Princeville $249.*

Tropical Biplanes. This company flies both a bright-red Waco biplane, built in 2002 and based on a 1936 design, and a Cessna 182 Skylane. The biplane can carry two passengers, the Cessna holds three. ■TIP➔ If a couple takes two seats in the Cessna, they will not sell the third seat, to keep it a personal experience. An open cockpit and staggered wing design mean there's nothing between you and the sights. You'll see the sights at an altitude of 1,500 feet at about 85 mph. ⊠ *Lihue Airport Commuter Terminal, 3901 Mokulele Loop, Lihue* ☎ *808/246–9123, 888/280–9123* ⊕ *www.tropicalbiplanes.com* ✉ *$490 per couple for biplane tours; $169 per person for Cessna tours.*

ATV TOURS

Although all the beaches on the island are public, much of the interior land—once sugar and pineapple plantations—is privately owned. This is really a shame, because the valleys and mountains that make up the vast interior of the island easily rival the beaches in sheer beauty. The good news is some tour operators have agreements with landowners that make exploration possible, albeit a bit bumpy, and unless you have back troubles, that's half the fun. ■TIP➔ If it looks like rain, book an ATV tour ASAP. That's the thing about these tours: the muddier, the better.

Fodor's Choice
★

Kauai ATV Tours. This is *the* thing to do when it rains on Kauai. Consider it an extreme mud bath. Kauai ATV in Koloa is the originator of the island's all-terrain-vehicle tours. The three-hour Koloa tour takes you through a private sugar plantation and historic cane-haul tunnel. The four-hour waterfall tour visits secluded waterfalls and includes a picnic lunch. This popular option includes a hike to secret WWII bunkers and a swim in a freshwater pool at the base of the falls—to rinse off all that mud. You must be 16 or older to operate your own ATV, but Kauai ATV also offers its four-passenger "Ohana Bug" and two-passenger "Mud Bugs" to accommodate families with kids ages five and older. ⊠ *3477A Weliweli Rd., Koloa* ☎ *808/742–2734, 877/707–7088* ⊕ *www.kauaiatv. com* ✉ *From $113.*

Kipu Ranch Adventures. This 3,000-acre property extends from the Huleia River to the top of Mt. Haupu. *Jurassic Park* and *Indiana Jones* were filmed here, and you'll see the locations for them on the three-hour Ranch Tour. The four-hour Waterfall Tour includes a visit to two waterfalls and a picnic lunch. Once a sugar plantation, Kipu Ranch today is a working cattle ranch, so you'll be in the company of bovines as well as pheasants, wild boars, and peacocks. If you're not an experienced ATV driver, they also offer guide-driven tour options. ⊠ *235 Kipu Rd., off Hwy. 50, Lihue* ☎ *808/246–9288* ⊕ *www.kiputours.com* ✉ *From $90.*

BIKING

Kauai is a labyrinth of cane-haul roads, which are fun for exploring on two wheels. The challenge is finding roads where biking is allowed and then not getting lost in the maze. Maybe that explains why Kauai is not a hub for the sport—yet. Still, there are some epic rides for those who are interested—both the adrenaline-rush and the mellower beach-cruiser kind. If you want to grind out some mileage, you could take the main highway that skirts the coastal area, but be careful: there are only a few designated bike lanes, and the terrain is hilly. You may find that keeping your eyes on the road rather than the scenery is your biggest challenge. "Cruisers" should head to Kapaa. A new section of Ke Ala Hele Makalae, a pedestrian and bicycle trail that runs along the East Side of Kauai, was completed in the summer of 2013, extending the multiuse path to about 8 miles. You can rent bikes (with helmets) from the activities desks of certain hotels, but these are not the best quality. You're better off renting from Coconut Coasters or Kauai Cycle in Kapaa, Outfitters Kauai in Poipu, or Pedal 'n' Paddle in Hanalei. Ask for the "Go Green Kauai" map for a full description of Kauai biking options.

Ke Ala Hele Makalae (*coastal path*). This county beach park path follows the coastline on Kauai's East Side and is perfect for cruisers. Eventually, the path will run some 20 miles, but an existing 6½-mile-long stretch offers scenic views, picnic pavilions, and restroom facilities along the way—all in compliance with the Americans with Disabilities Act. The path runs from Lydgate Beach Park to secluded Kuna Bay (aka Donkey Beach). An easy way to access the longest completed section of the path is from Kealia Beach. Park here and head north into rural lands with spectacular coastline vistas, or head south into Kapaa for a more immersive experience. ⊠ *Kealia Beach, Kapaa* ✛ *Trailhead: 1 mile north of Kapaa; park at north end of Kealia Beach* ⊕ *www.kauaipath.org/ kauaicoastalpath.*

Moalepe Trail. This trail is perfect for intermediate to advanced trail-bike riders. The first 2 miles of this 5-mile double-track road wind steeply through pastureland. The real challenge begins when you reach the steep and rutted switchbacks, which during a rainy spell can be hazardous. Moalepe intersects the Kuilau Trail, which you can follow to its end at the Keahua Arboretum stream. ⊠ *Wailua (Kauai County)* ✛ *From Kuhio Hwy. in Kapaa drive mauka (toward mountains) on Kuamoo Rd. for 3 miles and turn right on Kamalu Rd., which dead-ends at Olohena Rd. Turn left and follow until road veers sharply to right.*

Powerline Trail. Advanced riders are challenged by this trail. It's actually an abandoned electric-company service road that splits the island. It's 13 miles long; the first 5 miles go from 620 feet in elevation to almost 2,000. The remaining 8 miles descend gradually over a variety of terrain, some technical. You'll have to carry your bike through some sections, but the views will stay with you forever. ■TIP➔ **When it's wet—in summer or winter—this trail is a mess. Check with a knowledgeable bike shop for trail conditions first and be prepared to improvise.** ⊠ *Powerline Rd., Kilauea* ✛ *The trailhead is mauka (upland), just past*

9

Bikers who prefer a leisurely cruise can pedal along the Ke Ala Hele Makalae trail, an 8-mile, multiuse path in Kapaa.

the stream crossing at Keahua Arboretum, or at the end of Powerline Road in Princeville, past Princeville Ranch Stables.

Spalding Monument Loop. For the novice rider, this loop offers a good workout and a summit ocean view that is not overly strenuous to reach. If you pick up a bike at Coconut Coasters or Kauai Cycle in Kapaa, you can ride a mile up Ke Ala Hele Makalae to reach the head of the loop, and even make a snack stop at the corner food truck without a detour. From near the end of Kealia Beach, ride up a gradual incline 2 miles through horse pastures to Spalding Monument, named for a former plantation owner, although there is no longer any signage. Palms circle the lava-rock wall, where you can picnic while enjoying a 180-degree ocean view. Behind you is the glorious mountain backdrop of Kalalea. The adventurous can follow the very rocky road north toward Kalalea for 2 more miles. Turn right at the highway, and it's another 2 miles south to a parking lot for Donkey Beach on the ocean side. The lot is not far from mile marker 12 and sits on the top of a hill. Follow the path down to the beach and turn right on Ke Ala Hele Makalae, following what was once an old cane-haul road that heads right back into Kapaa town. ⊠ *The loop begins at the end of Kealia Beach, past mile marker 10 on the mauka (mountain) side of the road, Kealia.*

Wailua Forest Management Road. For the novice mountain biker, this is an easy ride, and it's also easy to find. From Route 56 in Wailua, turn *mauka* (toward the mountains) on Kuamoo Road and continue 6 miles to the picnic area known as Keahua Arboretum; park here. The pot-holed four-wheel-drive road includes some stream crossings—△ **stay away during heavy rains, because the streams flood**—and continues for 2 miles to a T-stop, where you should turn right. Stay on the road for about 3 miles until you reach a gate; this is the spot where the gates in the movie *Jurassic Park* were filmed, though it looks nothing like the movie. Go around the gate and down the road for another mile to a confluence of streams at the base of Mt. Waialeale. Be sure to bring your camera. ⊠ *Kuamoo Rd., Kapaa.*

Waimea Canyon Road. For those wanting a very challenging road workout, climb this road, also known as Route 550. After a 3,000-foot climb, the road tops out at mile 12, adjacent to Waimea Canyon, which will pop in and out of view on your right as you ascend. From here it continues several miles (mostly level) past the Kokee Museum and ends at the Kalalau Lookout. It's paved the entire way, uphill 100%, and curvy. ⚠ There's not much of a shoulder on either road—sometimes none—so be extra cautious. The road gets busier as the day wears on, so you may want to consider a sunrise ride. A slightly more moderate uphill climb is Kokee Road, Route 552, from Kekaha, which intersects with Route 550. Bikes aren't allowed on the hiking trails in and around Waimea Canyon and Kokee State Park, but there are miles of wonderful four-wheel-drive roads perfect for mountain biking. Check at Kokee Museum for a map and conditions. ⊠ *Off Rte. 50, near grocery store, Waimea (Kauai County).*

EQUIPMENT AND TOURS

Kauai Cycle. This reliable, full-service bike shop rents, sells, and repairs bikes. Cruisers, mountain bikes (front and full suspension), and road bikes are available, with directions to trails. The Ke Ala Hele Makalae coastal path is right out the back door. ⊠ *4-934 Kuhio Hwy., across from Taco Bell, Kapaa* ☎ *808/821–2115* ⊕ *www.kauaicycle.com* 🚲 *Rentals from $20 per day and $110 per week.*

Outfitters Kauai. Hybrid "comfort" and mountain bikes (both full suspension and hardtails) as well as road bikes are available at this shop in Poipu. You can ride right out the door to tour Poipu, or get information on how to do a self-guided tour of Kokee State Park and Waimea Canyon. The company also leads sunrise and evening coasting tours (under the name **Bicycle Downhill**) from Waimea Canyon past the island's West Side beaches. Stand-up paddle tours are also available. ⊠ *2827-A Poipu Rd., near turnoff to Spouting Horn, Poipu* ☎ *808/742–9667, 888/742–9887* ⊕ *www.outfitterskauai.com* 🚲 *Rentals from $15; tours $104.*

Pedal 'n' Paddle. This company rents old-fashioned, single-speed beach cruisers and hybrid road bikes. In the heart of Hanalei, this is a great way to cruise the town; the more adventuresome cyclist can head to the end of the road. Be careful, though, because there are no bike lanes on the twisting-and-turning road to Kee Beach. ⊠ *Ching Young Village, 5-5190 Kuhio Hwy., Hanalei* ☎ *808/826–9069* ⊕ *www.pedalnpaddle.com* 🚲 *Rentals from $15 per day and $60 per week.*

GOLF

For golfers, the Garden Isle might as well be known as the Robert Trent Jones Jr. Isle. Four of the island's eight courses, including Poipu Bay—onetime home of the PGA Grand Slam of Golf—are the work of Jones, who maintains a home at Princeville. Combine these four courses with those from Jack Nicklaus, Robin Nelson, and local legend Toyo Shirai, and you'll see that golf sets Kauai apart from the other Islands as much as the Pacific Ocean does. ■ TIP➜ Afternoon tee times at most courses can save you big bucks.

Kauai Lagoons Golf Club. The Kiele Moana Nine (ocean) course now features a half mile of oceanfront golf, the longest stretch of continuous ocean holes in Hawaii. Jack Nicklaus returned to do the initial design work and then saw it to completion. The Kiele Moana Nine is coupled with the Kiele Mauka (toward the mountain) Nine to offer players 18 championship-style holes of golf. The 5th hole is particularly striking as it requires a drive over a valley populated by mango and guava trees. Marriott guests curently play for less. ⊠ *3351 Hoolaulea Way, Lihue* ☎ *808/241–6000, 800/634–6400* ⊕ *www.kauailagoonsgolf.com* 🏌 *From $205; after noon $135* 🏌 *18 holes, 7156 yards, par 72.*

Kauai Mini Golf. The only miniature-golf course on the island, Kauai Mini Golf is also a small botanical garden. The 18-hole course was designed to be challenging, beautiful, and family-friendly. Replacing the typical clown's nose and spinning wheels are some water features and tropical tunnels. Surrounding each hole is plant life that walks players through different eras of Hawaiian history. A gift shop with local products and a concessions counter make it a fun activity for any time of day. ⊠ *5-273 Kuhio Hwy., Kilauea* ☎ *808/828–2118* ⊕ *www. kauaiminigolf.com* 🏌 *$18.*

Kiahuna Plantation Golf Course. A meandering creek, lava outcrops, and thickets of trees give Kiahuna its character. Robert Trent Jones Jr. was given a smallish piece of land just inland at Poipu, and defends par with smaller targets, awkward stances, and optical illusions. In 2003 a group of homeowners bought the club and brought Jones back to renovate the course (it was originally built in 1983), adding tees and revamping bunkers. The pro here boasts his course has the best putting greens on the island. This is the only course on Kauai with a complete set of junior's tee boxes. ⊠ *2545 Kiahuna Plantation Dr., Koloa* ☎ *808/742–9595* ⊕ *www.kiahunagolf.com* 🏌 *$110* 🏌 *18 holes, 5878 yards, par 70.*

Poipu Bay Golf Course. Poipu Bay has been called the Pebble Beach of Hawaii, and the comparison is apt. Like Pebble Beach, Poipu is a links course built on headlands, not true links land. There's wildlife galore. It's not unusual for golfers to see monk seals sunning on the beach below, sea turtles bobbing outside the shore break, and humpback whales leaping offshore. From 1994 to 2006, the course (designed by Robert Trent Jones Jr.) hosted the annual PGA Grand Slam of Golf. Tiger Woods was a frequent winner here. Call ahead to take advantage of varying prices for tee times. ⊠ *2250 Ainako St., Koloa* ☎ *808/742–8711* ⊕ *www.poipubaygolf. com* 🏌 *$180–$250* 🏌 *18 holes, 6127 yards, par 72.*

The Makai course at Princeville Makai Golf Club has consistently been ranked a top course in the United States.

Princeville Makai Golf Club. The 27-hole Princeville Makai Golf Club was named for its five ocean-hugging front holes. Designed by golf-course architect Robert Trent Jones Jr. in 1971, the 18-hole championship Makai Course underwent extensive renovations from 2008 to 2010, including new turf throughout, reshaped greens and bunkers, refurbished cart paths and comfort stations, and an extensive practice facility. Since the renovation the Makai Course has consistently been ranked a top golf course in the United States. The club offers free rounds for juniors (15 and under) when accompanied by one paying adult. Check the website for varying rates as well as other nongolf activities at the facility. ⊠ *4080 Lei O Papa Rd., Princeville* ⊕ *www.makaigolf. com* ⊡ *$275* ⅂ *18 holes, 7223 yards, par 72; Woods Course: 9 holes, 3445 yards, par 36.*

Wailua Municipal Golf Course. Considered by many to be one of Hawaii's best golf courses, this seaside course provides an affordable game with minimal water hazards, but it is challenging enough to have been chosen to host three USGA Amateur Public Links Championships. It was first built as a nine-holer in the 1930s. The second nine holes were added in 1961. Course designer Toyo Shirai created a course that is fun but not punishing. The trade winds blow steadily on the East Side of the island and provide a game with challenges. An ocean view and affordability make this one of the most popular courses on the island. Tee times are accepted up to seven days in advance and can be paid in cash, traveler's checks, and some credit cards. ⊠ *3-5350 Kuhio Hwy., Lihue* ☎ *808/241–6666* ⊕ *www.kauai.gov/default.aspx?tabid=66* ⊡ *$48 weekdays, $60 weekends; cart rental $20* ⅂ *18 holes, 6585 yards, par 72.*

HIKING

The best way to experience the aina—the land—on Kauai is to step off the beach and hike into the remote interior. You'll find waterfalls so tall you'll strain your neck looking, pools of crystal clear water for swimming, tropical forests teeming with plant life, and ocean vistas that will make you wish you could stay forever.

■TIP→ **For your safety wear sturdy shoes—preferably water-resistant ones.** All hiking trails on Kauai are free, so far. There's a development plan in the works that could turn the Waimea Canyon and Kokee state parks into admission-charging destinations. Whatever it may be, it will be worth it.

> **LILIKOI ALERT**
>
> If you're hiking in May and June, you'll see *lilikoi*—often referred to as passion fruit—scattered like yellow eggs among the ferns. It tastes as sweet and floral as it smells—bite the tip of the rind off and you'll see speckled jelly with tiny black seeds; then slurp it right out of the skin. If you miss lilikoi season, scout out delicious lilikoi mustards and jams sold by local grocers. Lilikoi pie is also served at a few Hawaiian eateries.

Hanalei-OkolehaoTrail. *Okolehao* basically translates to "moonshine" in Hawaiian. This trail follows the Hihimanu Ridge, which was established in the days of Prohibition, when this backyard liquor was distilled from the roots of ti plants. The 2-mile hike climbs 1,200 feet and offers a 360-degree view of Hanalei Bay and Waioli Valley. Your ascent begins at the China Ditch off the Hanalei River. Follow the trail through a lightly forested grove and then climb up a steep embankment. From here the trail is well marked. Most of the climb is lined with hala, ti, wild orchid, and eucalyptus. You'll get your first of many ocean views at mile marker 1. ⊠ *Hanalei* ✛ *Follow Ohiki Rd. (north of the Hanalei Bridge) 5 miles to U.S. Fish and Wildlife Service parking area. Directly across street is a small bridge that marks trailhead.*

Ho opii Falls. Tucked among the winding roads and grassy pastures of Kapahi, 3 miles inland from Kapaa town, is an easy hike to two waterfalls. A 10-minute walk will deliver you to the creek. Follow it around to see the first set of falls. The more impressive second falls are a mere 25 minutes away. The swimming hole alone is worth the journey. Just climb the rooted path next to the first falls and turn left on the trail above. Turn left on the very next trail to descend back into the canyon and follow the leafy path that zigzags along the creek—the falls and the swimming hole lie below. ⊠ *Kapaa* ✛ *On the north end of Kapaa, ¼ mile past the last lookout, is a side road called Kawaihau. Follow the road up 3 miles, then turn right on Kapahi Rd. into a residential neighborhood. Kapahi Rd. dead-ends near the trailhead. Look for the yellow gate on your left.*

Fodor's Choice **Kalalau Trail.** Of all the hikes on the island, Kalalau Trail is by far the
★ most famous and in many regards the most strenuous. A moderate hiker can handle the 2-mile trek to Hanakapiai Beach, and for the seasoned outdoorsman, the additional 2 miles up to the falls is manageable. But be prepared to rock-hop along a creek and ford waters that can get

waist high during the rain. Round-trip to Hanakapiai Falls is 8 miles. This steep and often muddy trail is best approached with a walking stick. If there has been any steady rain, wait for drier days for a more enjoyable trek. The narrow trail delivers one startling ocean view after another along a path that is alternately shady and sunny. Wear hiking shoes or sandals, and bring drinking water since the creeks on the trail are not potable. Plenty of food is always encouraged on a strenuous hike such as this one. If you plan to venture the full 11 miles into Kalalau, you need to acquire a camping permit, either online or at the State Building in Lihue, for $20 per person per night. You should

> ### WATERFALL WARNING
>
> The many waterfalls on Kauai can be quite alluring; however, it's important to:
>
> ■ Evaluate water conditions before entering—do not enter a waterfall pool during or after heavy rains.
>
> ■ Never dive into the pool.
>
> ■ Remember that the leptospirosis bacteria may be present in freshwater streams and pools.
>
> ■ Wear water-friendly shoes; the rocks can be quite slippery as you're entering and exiting the pool.

secure a permit well in advance of your trip. ⊹ *Drive north past Hanalei to end of road. Trailhead is directly across from Kee Beach* ⊕ *www.kalalautrail.com* ✉ *$20 per person per night.*

Mahaulepu Heritage Trail. This trail offers the novice hiker an accessible way to appreciate the rugged southern coast of Kauai. A cross-country course wends its way along the water, high above the ocean, through a lava field, and past a sacred *heiau* (stone structure). Walk all the way to Mahaulepu, 2 miles north, for a two-hour round-trip. ⊹ *Drive north on Poipu Rd., turn right at Poipu Bay Golf Course sign. The street name is Ainako, but sign is hard to see. Drive down to beach and park in lot* ⊕ *www.hikemahaulepu.org.*

Sleeping Giant Trail. An easily accessible trail practically in the heart of Kapaa, the moderately strenuous Sleeping Giant Trail—or simply Sleeping Giant—gains 1,000 feet over 2 miles. We prefer an early-morning—say, sunrise—hike, with sparkling blue-water vistas, up the east-side trailhead. At the top you can see a grassy grove with a picnic table. It is a local favorite, with many East Siders meeting here to exercise. ⊠ *Haleilio Rd., off Rte. 56, Wailua (Kauai County).*

Waimea Canyon and Kokee State Parks. This park contains a 50-mile network of hiking trails of varying difficulty that take you through acres of native forests, across the highest-elevation swamp in the world, to the river at the base of the canyon, and onto pinnacles of land sticking their necks out over Napali Coast. All hikers should register at Kokee Natural History Museum, where you can find trail maps, current trail information, and specific directions.

The **Kukui Trail** descends 2½ miles and 2,200 feet into Waimea Canyon to the edge of the Waimea River—it's a steep climb. The **Awaawapuhi Trail,** with 1,600 feet of elevation gains and losses over 3¼ miles, feels more gentle than the Kukui Trail, but it offers its own

9

LEPTOSPIROSIS

Leptospirosis is a bacterial disease that is transmitted from animals to humans. It can survive for long periods of time in freshwater and mud contaminated by the urine of infected animals, such as pigs, rats, and goats.

The bacteria enter the body through the eyes, ears, nose, mouth, and broken skin. To avoid infection, don't drink untreated water from the Kauai's streams; don't wade in waters above the chest or submerge skin with cuts and abrasions in island streams or rivers.

Symptoms are often mild and resemble the flu—fever, diarrhea, chills, nausea, headache, vomiting, and body pains—and may occur 2 to 20 days after exposure. If you think you have these symptoms, see a doctor right away.

huffing-and-puffing sections in its descent along a spiny ridge to a perch overlooking the ocean.

The 3½-mile **Alakai Swamp Trail** is accessed via the **Pihea Trail** or a four-wheel-drive road. There's one strenuous valley section, but otherwise it's a pretty level trail—once you access it. This trail is a bird-watcher's delight and includes a painterly view of Wainiha and Hanalei valleys at the trail's end. The trail traverses the purported highest-elevation swamp in the world via a boardwalk so as not to disturb the fragile plant and wildlife. It is typically the coolest of the hikes due to the tree canopy, elevation, and cloud coverage.

The **Canyon Trail** offers much in its short trek: spectacular vistas of the canyon and the only dependable waterfall in Waimea Canyon. The easy 2-mile hike can be cut in half if you have a four-wheel-drive vehicle. The late-afternoon sun sets the canyon walls ablaze in color. ⊠ *Kokee Natural History Museum, 3600 Kokee Rd., Kekaha* ☎ *808/335–9975 for trail conditions* ⊕ *www.kokee.org.*

EQUIPMENT AND TOURS

Fodor's Choice
★
Kauai Nature Tours. Father and son scientists started this hiking tour business. As such, their emphasis is on education and the environment. If you're interested in flora, fauna, volcanology, geology, oceanography, and the like, this is the company for you. They offer daylong hikes along coastal areas, beaches, and in the mountains. ■ TIP→ If you have a desire to see a specific location, just ask. They will do custom hikes to spots they don't normally hit if there is interest. Hikes range from easy to strenuous. Transportation is often provided from your hotel. ⊠ *5162 Lawai Rd., Koloa* ☎ *808/742–8305, 888/233–8365* ⊕ *www. kauainaturetours.com* 🖼 *From $135.*

Princeville Ranch Adventures. This 4-mile hike traverses Princeville Ranch, crossing through a rain forest and to a five-tier waterfall for lunch and swimming. Moderately strenuous hiking is required. ⊠ *Rte. 56, between mile markers 27 and 28, Princeville* ☎ *808/826–7669, 888/955–7669* ⊕ *www.princevilleranch.com* 🖼 *$99.*

HORSEBACK RIDING

Most of the horseback-riding tours on Kauai are primarily walking tours with little trotting and no cantering or galloping, so no experience is required. Zip. Zilch. Nada. If you're interested, most of the stables offer private lessons. The most popular tours are the ones including a picnic lunch by the water. Your only dilemma may be deciding what kind of water you want—waterfalls or ocean. You may want to make your decision based on where you're staying. The "waterfall picnic" tours are on the wetter North Shore, and the "beach picnic" tours take place on the South Side.

CJM Country Stables. Just past the Hyatt in Poipu, CJM Stables offers a three-hour picnic ride with noshing on the beach, as well as their more popular two-hour trail ride without the picnic break. The landscape here is rugged and beautiful, featuring sand dunes and limestone bluffs. CJM can get you as close as anyone to the secluded Mahaulepu Bay. They sponsor seasonal rodeos that are free and open to the public, and participate in other popular community events. ⊠ *Poipu Rd., 1½ miles from Grand Hyatt Kauai, Koloa* ☎ *808/742–6096* ⊕ *www.cjmstables. com* ⊠ *From $110.*

Esprit de Corps. If you ride, this is the company for you. Esprit De Corps Riding Academy now offers private two- and three-hour waterfall picnic rides for advanced riders at Silverfalls Ranch in Kilauea. Group rides at a walk, as well as a 90-minute custom ride are also featured. Lessons with a certified instructor are held in a covered arena for beginner through advanced riders ages six and up, both in English and Western saddles. Weddings on horseback can be arranged (in fact, Dale, the owner, is a wedding officiant and planner). Make sure to call ahead because they are by appointment only. ⊠ *1491 Kualapa Pl., Kapaa* ☎ *808/822–4688* ⊕ *www.kauaihorses.com* ⊠ *From $99.*

Fodor'sChoice ★ **Princeville Ranch Adventures.** A longtime *kamaaina* (resident) family operates Princeville Ranch. They originated the waterfall picnic tour, which runs 3½ hours and includes a short but steep hike down to Kalihiwai Falls, a dramatic three-tier waterfall, for swimming and picnicking. Princeville also has shorter, straight riding tours and private rides. A popular option is the three-hour combination Ride N' Glide tour with three zip lines. ⊠ *Kuhio Hwy., off Kapaka Rd., between mile markers 27 and 28, Princeville* ☎ *808/826–7669* ⊕ *www.princevilleranch.com* ⊠ *Ride only from $99; private tours from $175.*

MOUNTAIN TUBING

For the past 40 years, Hawaii's sugarcane plantations have closed one by one. In the fall of 2009, Gay & Robinson announced the closure of Kauai's last plantation, leaving only one in Maui, the last in the state. The sugarcane irrigation ditches remain, striating these islands like spokes in a wheel. Inspired by the Hawaiian *auwai*, which diverted water from streams to taro fields, these engineering feats harnessed the rain. One ingenious tour company on Kauai has figured out a way to make exploring them an adventure: float inflatable tubes down the route.

9

FAMILY **Kauai Backcountry Adventures.** Both zip-line and tubing tours are offered. Popular with all ages, the tubing adventure can book up two weeks in advance in busy summer months. Here's how it works: you recline in an inner tube and float down fern-lined irrigation ditches that were built more than a century ago—the engineering is impressive—to divert water from Mt. Waialeale to sugar and pineapple fields around the island. They'll even give you a headlamp so you can see as you float through five covered tunnels. The scenery from the island's interior at the base of Mt. Waialeale on Lihue Plantation land is superb. Ages five and up are welcome. The tour takes about three hours and includes a picnic lunch and a swim in a swimming hole. ■TIP→ You'll definitely want to pack water-friendly shoes (or rent some from the outfitter), sunscreen, a hat, bug repellent, and a beach towel. Tours are offered four times daily. ⊠ *3-4131 Kuhio Hwy., across from gas station, Hanamaulu* ☎ *808/245-2506, 888/270-0555* ⊕ *www.kauaibackcountry.com* 🖃 *$110 per person.*

SKYDIVING

If you're a thrill seeker, it doesn't get any better than jumping out of an airplane over an island—oh, the views—and floating peacefully back down to earth tethered to a parachute.

Skydive Kauai. Ten thousand feet over Kauai and falling at a rate of 120 mph is probably as thrilling as it gets while airborne. First, there's the 25-minute plane ride to altitude in a Cessna 182, then the exhilaration of the first step into sky, the sensation of sailing weightless in the air over Kauai, and finally the peaceful buoyancy beneath the canopy of your parachute. A tandem free-fall rates among the most unforgettable experiences of a lifetime. Wed that to the aerial view over Kauai and you've got a winning marriage that you can relive with an HD video memory. ⊠ *Port Allen Airport, 3666 Kuiloko Rd., Hanapepe* ☎ *808/335-5859* ⊕ *www.skydivekauai.com* 🖃 *$263.*

TENNIS

If you're interested in booking some court time on Kauai, there are public tennis courts in Waimea, Kekaha, Hanapepe, Koloa, Kalaheo, Puhi, Lihue, Wailua Homesteads, Wailua Houselots, and Kapaa New Park.

Many hotels and resorts have tennis courts on property; even if you're not staying there, you can still rent court time. Rates range from $10 to $20 per person per hour. On the South Shore, try the **Grand Hyatt Kauai** (808/742-1234) and Poipu Kai Tennis. On the North Shore try the **Hanalei Bay Resort** (808/826-6522 Ext. 8225) or **Princeville Racquet Club** (808/826-1863).

For specific directions or more information, call the **County of Kauai Parks and Recreation Office** (808/241-4463).

On the North Shore, adventure seekers will find a nine-zip-line course run by Princeville Ranch Adventures.

ZIP-LINE TOURS

The latest adventure on Kauai is "zipping," or "zip-lining." Regardless of what you call it, chances are you'll scream like a rock star while trying it. Strap on a harness, clip onto a cable running from one side of a river or valley to the other, and zip across. The step off is the scariest part. ■TIP➔ Pack knee-length shorts or pants, athletic shoes, and courage for this adventure.

Fodor's Choice
★
Just Live. When Nichol Baier and Julie Lester started Just Live in 2003, their market was exclusively school-age children, but soon they added visitor tours. Experiential education through adventure is how they describe it. Whatever you call it, sailing 70 feet above the ground for three-plus hours will take your vacation to another level. This is the only treetop zip line on Kauai where your feet never touch ground once you're in the air: seven zips and four canopy bridges make the Tree Top Tour their most popular one. For the heroic at heart, there's the Zipline Eco Adventure, which includes three zip lines, two canopy bridges, a climbing wall, a 100-foot rappelling tower, and a "Monster Swing." If you're short on time—or courage—you can opt for the Wikiwiki Zipline Tour, which includes three zip lines and two canopy bridges in about two hours. They now have a shop with outdoor gear specifically for the island's activities, although their primary focus remains community programming. Enjoy knowing that money spent here serves Kauai's children. ✉ *3416 Rice St., Nawiliwili, Anchor Cove, Lihue* ☎ *808/482–1295* ⊕ *www.zipkauai.com* 🎫 *From $79.*

Outfitters Kauai. This company offers a half-day, multisport adventure of zip-lining, suspension-bridge crossings, and aerial walkways with hiking in between. Their most popular tour (Zipline Trek Nui Nui Loa) features an 1,800-foot tandem zip—that's right, you don't have to go it alone. Plus, a unique WaterZip cools things off if you work up a sweat. A shorter version of this adventure—the Zipline Lele Eono—is also offered. Outfitters Kauai also includes zip-lining as part of its Kipu Safari tour. ⊠ *2827-A Poipu Rd., Poipu* ☎ *808/742–9667, 888/742–9887* ⊕ *www.outfitterskauai.com* ⌨ *From $116 to $186.*

Princeville Ranch Adventures. The North Shore's answer to zip-lining is a nine-zip-line course with a bit of hiking, and suspension-bridge crossing thrown in for a half-day adventure. The 4½-hour Zip N' Dip tour includes a picnic and swimming at a waterfall pool, while the Zip Express whizzes you through the entire course in three hours. Both excursions conclude with a 1,200-foot tandem zip across a valley. Guides are energetic and fun. This is as close as it gets to flying; just watch out for the albatross. ⊠ *Rte. 56, between mile markers 27 and 28, Princeville* ☎ *808/826–7669, 888/955–7669* ⊕ *www.princevilleranch.com* ⌨ *From $125.*

UNDERSTANDING KAUAI

HAWAIIAN VOCABULARY

HAWAIIAN VOCABULARY

Although an understanding of Hawaiian is by no means required on a trip to the Aloha State, a *malihini*, or newcomer, will find plenty of opportunities to pick up a few of the local words and phrases. Traditional names and expressions are widely used in the Islands. You're likely to read or hear at least a few words.

With a basic understanding and some uninhibited practice, anyone can have enough command of the local tongue to ask for directions and to order from a restaurant menu. One visitor announced she would not leave until she could pronounce the name of the state fish, the *humuhumunukunukuāpua'a*.

Simplifying the learning process is the fact that the Hawaiian language contains only eight consonants—*H, K, L, M, N, P, W*, and the silent *'okina*, or glottal stop, written '—plus the five vowels. All syllables end in a vowel. Each vowel, with the exception of a few diphthongized double vowels such as *au* (pronounced "ow") or *ai* (pronounced "eye"), is pronounced separately. Thus *'Iolani* is four syllables (ee-oh-la-nee), not three (yo-la-nee). Although some Hawaiian words have only vowels, most contain consonants, but consonants are never doubled.

Pronunciation is simple. Pronounce *A* "ah" as in *father*; *E* "ay" as in *weigh*; *I* "ee" as in *marine*; *O* "oh" as in *no*; *U* "oo" as in *true*.

Consonants mirror their English equivalents, with the exception of *W*. When the letter begins any syllable other than the first one in a word, it is usually pronounced as a *V*. *'Awa*, the Polynesian drink, is pronounced "ava," *'ewa* is pronounced "eva."

Almost all long Hawaiian words are combinations of shorter words; they are not difficult to pronounce if you segment them. *Kalaniana'ole*, the highway running east from Honolulu, is easily understood as *Kalani ana 'ole*. Apply the standard pronunciation rules—the stress falls on the next-to-last syllable of most two- or three-syllable Hawaiian words—and Kalaniana'ole Highway is as easy to say as Main Street.

Now about that fish. Try *humu-humu nuku-nuku āpu a'a*.

The other unusual element in Hawaiian language is the *kahakō*, or macron, written as a short line (ˉ) placed over a vowel. The kahakō puts emphasis on a syllable that would normally not be stressed. The most familiar example is probably *Waikīkī*. With no macrons, the stress would fall on the middle syllable; with only one macron, on the last syllable, the stress would fall on the first and last syllables. Some words become plural with the addition of a macron, often on a syllable that would have been stressed anyway. No Hawaiian word becomes plural with the addition of an *S*, since that letter does not exist in the language.

The Hawaiian diacritical marks are not printed in this guide.

Pidgin

You may hear pidgin, the unofficial language of Hawaii. It is a Creole language, with its own grammar, evolved from the mixture of English, Hawaiian, Japanese, Portuguese, and other languages spoken in 19th-century Hawaii.

Glossary

What follows is a glossary of some of the most commonly used Hawaiian words. Hawaiian residents appreciate visitors who at least try to pick up the local language.

'a'ā: rough, crumbling lava, contrasting with *pāhoehoe*, which is smooth.

'ae: yes.

aikane: friend.

āina: land.

akamai: smart, clever, possessing savoir faire.

akua: god.

ala: a road, path, or trail.

ali'i: a Hawaiian chief, a member of the chiefly class.

aloha: love, affection, kindness; also a salutation meaning both greetings and farewell.

'ānuenue: rainbow.

'a'ole: no.

'apōpō: tomorrow.

'auwai: a ditch.

auwē: alas, woe is me!

'ehu: a red-haired Hawaiian.

'ewa: in the direction of 'Ewa plantation, west of Honolulu.

hala: the pandanus tree, whose leaves (*lau hala*) are used to make baskets and plaited mats.

hālau: school.

hale: a house.

hale pule: church, house of worship.

ha mea iki or **ha mea 'ole:** you're welcome.

hana: to work.

haole: ghost. Since the first foreigners were Caucasian, *haole* now means a Caucasian person.

hapa: a part, sometimes a half; often used as a short form of *hapa haole*, to mean a person who is part-Caucasian.

hau'oli: to rejoice. *Hau'oli Makahiki Hou* means Happy New Year. *Hau'oli lā hānau* means Happy Birthday.

heiau: an outdoor stone platform; an ancient Hawaiian place of worship.

holo: to run.

holoholo: to go for a walk, ride, or sail.

holokū: a long Hawaiian dress, somewhat fitted, with a yoke and a train. Influenced by European fashion, it was worn at court, and at least one local translates the word as "expensive mu'umu'u."

holomū: a post–World War II cross between a *holokū* and a mu'umu'u, less fitted than the former but less voluminous than the latter, and having no train.

honi: to kiss; a kiss. A phrase that some tourists may find useful, quoted from a popular hula, is *Honi Ka'ua Wikiwiki:* Kiss me quick!

honu: turtle.

ho'omalimali: flattery, a deceptive "line," bunk, baloney, hooey.

huhū: angry.

hui: a group, club, or assembly. A church may refer to its congregation as a *hui* and a social club may be called a *hui*.

hukilau: a seine; a communal fishing party in which everyone helps to drive the fish into a huge net, pull it in, and divide the catch.

hula: the dance of Hawai'i.

iki: little.

ipo: sweetheart.

ka: the. This is the definite article for most singular words; for plural nouns, the definite article is usually *nā*. Since there is no S in Hawaiian, the article may be your only clue that a noun is plural.

kahuna: a priest, doctor, or other trained person of old Hawai'i, endowed with special professional skills that often included prophecy or other supernatural powers; the plural form is *kāhuna*.

kai: the sea, saltwater.

kalo: the taro plant from whose root *poi* (paste) is made.

kamā'aina: literally, a child of the soil; it refers to people who were born in the Islands or have lived there for a long time.

kanaka: originally a man or humanity, it is now used to denote a male Hawaiian or part-Hawaiian, but is occasionally taken as a slur when used by non-Hawaiians. *Kanaka maoli*, originally a full-blooded Hawaiian person, is used by some native Hawaiian rights activists to embrace part-Hawaiians as well.

kāne: a man, a husband. If you see this word on a door, it's the men's room. If you see *kane* on a door, it's probably a misspelling; that is the Hawaiian name for the skin fungus tinea.

kapa: also called by its Tahitian name, *tapa*, a cloth made of beaten bark dyed and stamped with a repeat design.

kapakahi: crooked, cockeyed, uneven. You've got your hat on *kapakahi*.

kapu: keep out, prohibited. This is the Hawaiian version of the more widely known Tongan word *tabu* (taboo).

kapuna: grandparent; elder.

kēia lā: today.

keiki: a child; *keikikāne* is a boy, *keiki-wahine* a girl.

kona: the leeward side of the Islands, the direction (south) from which the *kona* wind and *kona* rain come.

kula: upland.

kuleana: a homestead or small plot of ground on which a family has been installed for some generations without necessarily owning it. By extension, *kuleana* is used to denote any area or department in which one has a special interest or prerogative. You'll hear it used this way: If you want to hire a surfboard, see Moki; that's his *kuleana*.

lā: sun.

lamalama: to fish with a torch.

lānai: a porch, a balcony, an outdoor living room. Almost every house in Hawai'i has one. Don't confuse this two-syllable word with the three-syllable name of the island, Lāna'i.

lani: heaven, the sky.

lau hala: the leaf of the *hala,* or pandanus tree, widely used in handicrafts.

lei: a garland of flowers.

limu: sun.

lolo: stupid.

luna: a plantation overseer or foreman.

mahalo: thank you.

makai: toward the ocean.

malihini: a newcomer to the Islands.

mana: the spiritual power that the Hawaiian believed inhabited all things and creatures.

manō: shark.

manuwahi: free, gratis.

mauka: toward the mountains.

mauna: mountain.

mele: a Hawaiian song or chant, often of epic proportions.

Mele Kalikimaka: Merry Christmas (a transliteration from the English phrase).

Menehune: a Hawaiian pixie. The *Mene-hune* were a legendary race of little people who accomplished prodigious work, such as building fishponds and temples in the course of a single night.

moana: the ocean.

mu'umu'u: the voluminous dress in which the missionaries enveloped Hawaiian women. Now made in brightly printed cottons and silks, it is an indispensable garment. Culturally sensitive locals have embraced the Hawaiian spelling but often shorten the spoken word to "mu'u." Most English dictionaries include the spelling "muumuu."

nani: beautiful.

nui: big.

ohana: family.

'ono: delicious.

pāhoehoe: smooth, unbroken, satiny lava.

Pākē: Chinese. This *Pākē* carver makes beautiful things.

palapala: document, printed matter.

pali: a cliff, precipice.

pānini: prickly pear cactus.

paniolo: a Hawaiian cowboy, a rough transliteration of *español*, the language of the Islands' earliest cowboys.

pau: finished, done.

pilikia: trouble. The Hawaiian word is much more widely used here than its English equivalent.

puka: a hole.

pupule: crazy, like the celebrated Princess Pupule. This word has replaced its English equivalent in local usage.

pu'u: volcanic cinder cone.

waha: mouth.

wahine: a female, a woman, a wife, and a sign on the ladies' room door; the plural form is *wāhine*.

wai: freshwater, as opposed to saltwater, which is *kai*.

wailele: waterfall.

wikiwiki: to hurry, hurry up (since this is a reduplication of *wiki*, quick, neither W is pronounced as a V).

TRAVEL SMART
KAUAI

GETTING HERE AND AROUND

▌ AIR TRAVEL

Flying time is about 10 hours from New York, 8 hours from Chicago, and 5 hours from Los Angeles.

Some of the major airline carriers serving Hawaii fly directly from the U.S. mainland to Kauai, allowing you to bypass connecting flights out of Honolulu. Although Lihue Airport is smaller and more casual than Honolulu International, it can also be quite busy during peak times. Allot extra travel time during morning and afternoon rush-hour traffic periods to avoid stressing over missing a flight.

Plan to arrive at the airport approximately 60 minutes before departure for interisland flights and slightly longer than that for flights to the mainland.

Plants and plant products are subject to regulation by the Department of Agriculture, both on entering and leaving Hawaii. Upon leaving the Islands, you'll have to have your bags x-rayed and tagged at one of the airport's agricultural inspection stations before you proceed to check-in. Pineapples and coconuts with the packer's agricultural inspection stamp pass freely; papayas must be treated, inspected, and stamped. All other fruits are banned for export to the U.S. mainland. Flowers pass—except for gardenias, rose leaves, jade vine, and mauna loa. Also banned are insects, snails, soil, cotton, cacti, sugarcane, and all berry plants.

You'll have to leave dogs and other pets at home. A 120-day quarantine is imposed to keep out rabies, which is nonexistent in Hawaii. If specific pre- and postarrival requirements are met, animals may qualify for a 30-day or 5-day-or-less quarantine.

Air Travel Resources in Hawaii State of Hawaii Airports Division Offices. ☎ 808/836–6413 ⊕ www.hawaii.gov/dot/airports.

AIRPORTS

Honolulu International Airport (HNL) is the main stopover for most domestic and international flights. From Honolulu, there are interisland flights to Kauai departing regularly from early morning until evening. In addition, some carriers offer nonstop service directly from the U.S. mainland to Lihue Airport (LIH).

HONOLULU/OAHU AIRPORT

Hawaii's major airport is Honolulu International, on Oahu, 20 minutes (9 miles) west of Waikiki. To travel interisland from Honolulu on Hawaiian Air you will depart from the connected interisland terminal. For other airlines you will leave from the commuter-airline terminal, located in a separate structure adjacent to the main terminal building. A free bus service, the Wiki Wiki Shuttle, operates between terminals.

Information Honolulu International Airport (HNL). ☎ 808/836–6413 ⊕ www.hawaii.gov/dot/airports.

KAUAI

On Kauai, visitors fly into Lihue Airport, on the East Side of the island. Visitor information booths are outside each baggage-claim area. Visitors will also find news- and lei stands, an HMS Host restaurant, and a Travel Traders gift shop at the airport.

Information Lihue Airport (LIH). ☎ 808/274–3800 ⊕ www.hawaii.gov/dot/airports.

GROUND TRANSPORTATION

Marriott Kauai and Kauai Beach Resort provide airport shuttles to and from the Lihue Airport. In addition, travelers who've booked a tour with Kauai Island Tours, Roberts Hawaii, or Polynesian Adventure Tours will be picked up at the airport.

SpeediShuttle offers transportation between the airport and hotels, resorts, and timeshare complexes on the island. There is an online reservation and fare quote system for information and bookings. Or, you can hire a taxi or limousine. Cabs are available curbside at baggage claim. Cab fares to locations around the island are estimated as follows: Poipu $35–$41, Wailua–Waipouli $17–$20, Lihue–Kukui Grove $10, Princeville–Haena $72–$95. There are two limousine companies that service Lihue Airport: Any Time Shuttle and Kauai North Shore Limo.

Contacts Any Time Shuttle. ☎ 808/927–1120. **Kauai North Shore Limo.** ☎ 808/634–7260 ⊕ kauainorthshorelimo.com. **SpeediShuttle.** ☎ 877/242–5777 ⊕ www.speedishuttle.com.

FLIGHTS

Alaska Airlines has a daily Seattle–Lihue flight. US Airways flies into Lihue from San Francisco and Denver and also has flights into Oahu, Maui, and the Big Island. American Airlines offers a daily, nonstop Los Angeles–Kauai flight, in addition to its service into Honolulu, Maui, and the Big Island. Delta has a Los Angeles–Lihue flight and also serves Oahu (Honolulu) and Maui. United Airlines provides direct service to Lihue Airport from Denver, Los Angeles, and San Francisco. The carrier also flies into Honolulu, Maui, and the Big Island.

Airline Contacts American Airlines. ☎ 800/433–7300 ⊕ www.aa.com. **US Airways.** ☎ 800/428–4322 ⊕ www.usairways.com. **Delta Airlines.** ☎ 800/221–1212 ⊕ www.delta.com. **Hawaiian Airlines.** ☎ 800/367–5320 ⊕ www.hawaiianair.com. **United Airlines.** ☎ 800/864–8331 ⊕ www.united.com.

INTERISLAND FLIGHTS

Interisland flight travel has become expensive in recent years, so be ready to pay should you wish to visit neighboring islands. Hawaiian Airlines services Kauai. In addition to offering a discount for booking online, all have free frequent-flier programs that will entitle you to rewards and upgrades the more you fly. Be sure to compare prices offered by all the interisland carriers. If you are somewhat flexible with your days and times

for island-hopping, you should have no problem getting a round-trip ticket.

Interisland Carriers Hawaiian Airlines. ☎ 800/367–5320 ⊕ www.hawaiianair.com.

▌BUS TRAVEL

On Kauai, the County Transportation Agency operates the Kauai Bus, which provides service between Hanalei and Kekaha. It also provides limited service to the airport and to Koloa and Poipu. The fare is $2 for adults, and frequent-rider passes are available.

Information Kauai Bus. ☎ 808/246–8110 ⊕ www.kauai.com/kauai-bus.

▌CAR TRAVEL

The best way to experience all of Kauai's stunning beauty is to get in a car and explore. The 15-mile stretch of Napali Coast, with its breathtaking, verdant-green sheer cliffs, is the only part of the island that's not accessible by car. Otherwise, one main road can get you from Barking Sands Beach on the West Side to Haena on the North Shore.

Asking for directions will almost always produce a helpful explanation from the locals, but you should be prepared for an island term or two. Instead of using compass directions, remember that Hawaii residents refer to places as being either *mauka* (toward the mountains) or *makai* (toward the ocean) from one another. Hawaii has a strict seat-belt law. All those riding in the vehicle must wear a seat belt. The fine for not wearing a seat belt is $112. There is also a law forbidding the use of handheld devices while driving. Jaywalking is also common in the Islands, so please pay careful attention to the roads. It also is considered rude to honk your horn, so be patient if someone is turning or proceeding through an intersection.

While driving on Kauai, you will come across several one-lane bridges. If you are the first to approach a bridge, the car on the other side will wait while you cross. If a car on the other side is closer to the bridge, then you should wait while the driver crosses. If you're enjoying the island's dramatic views, pull over to the shoulder so you don't block traffic.

GASOLINE

You can count on having to pay more at the pump for gasoline on Kauai than on the U.S. mainland. There are no gas stations past Princeville on the North Shore, and no stations past Waimea on the West Side, so if you're running low, fuel up before heading out to the end of the road.

PARKING

On Kauai there are no parking meters, parking garages, parking tags, or paid parking. If there's room on the side of the road, you can park there. A good rule of thumb is if there are other cars parked in that area, it's safe to do the same.

ROAD CONDITIONS

Kauai has a relatively well-maintained highway running south from Lihue to Barking Sands Beach; a spur at Waimea takes you along Waimea Canyon Drive to Kokee State Park. A northern route also winds its way from Lihue to the end of the road at Haena, the beginning of the rugged and roadless Napali Coast. Opt for a four-wheel-drive vehicle if dirt-road exploration holds any appeal.

ROADSIDE EMERGENCIES

If you find yourself in an emergency or accident while driving on Kauai, pull over if you can. If you have a cell phone with you, call the roadside assistance number on your rental-car contract or AAA Help. If you find that your car has been broken into or stolen, report it immediately to your rental-car company and an agent can assist you. If it's an emergency and someone is hurt, call 911 immediately and stay there until medical personnel arrive.

Emergency Services AAA Help.
☏ *800/222-4357.*

CAR RENTAL

Should you plan to do any sightseeing on Kauai, it is best to rent a car. Even if all you want to do is relax at your resort, you may want to hop in the car to check out one of the island's popular restaurants.

While on Kauai, you can rent anything from an econobox to a Ferrari. Rates are usually better if you reserve through a rental agency's website. It's wise to make reservations far in advance and make sure that a confirmed reservation guarantees you a car, especially if you're visiting during peak seasons or for major conventions or sporting events. Rates begin at about $25 to $35 a day for an economy car with air-conditioning, automatic transmission, and unlimited mileage, depending on your pickup location. This does not include the airport concession fee, general excise tax, rental-vehicle surcharge, or vehicle license fee. When you reserve a car, ask about cancellation penalties. Many rental companies in Hawaii offer coupons for discounts at various attractions that could save you money later on in your trip.

In Hawaii you must be 21 years of age to rent a car, and you must have a valid driver's license and a major credit card. Those under 25 will pay a daily surcharge of $15–$25. Request car seats and extras such as GPS when you book. Hawaii's Child Restraint Law requires that all children three years and younger be in an approved child safety seat in the backseat of a vehicle. Children ages four to seven must be seated in a rear booster seat or child restraint such as a lap and shoulder belt. Car seats and boosters range from $5 to $8 per day.

Your unexpired driver's license is valid for rental for up to 90 days.

Since the road circling the island is usually two lanes, allow plenty of time to return your vehicle so that you can make your flight. Traffic can be bad during morning and afternoon rush hour. Give yourself about two hours before departure time to return your vehicle.

LOCAL DO'S AND TABOOS

GREETINGS

Hawaii is a very friendly place, and this is reflected in the day-to-day encounters with friends, family, and even business associates. Women often hug and kiss one another on the cheek, and men shake hands and sometimes combine that with a friendly hug. When a man and a woman are greeting each other and are good friends, it is not unusual for them to hug and kiss on the cheek. Children are taught to call any elders "auntie" or "uncle," even if they aren't related. It's a way to show respect and can result in a local Hawaiian child having dozens of aunties or uncles. It's also reflective of the strong sense of *ohana* (family) that exists in the Islands.

When you walk off a long flight, perhaps a bit groggy and stiff, nothing quite compares with a Hawaiian lei greeting. The casual ceremony ranks as one of the fastest ways to make the transition from the worries of home to the joys of your vacation. Though the tradition has created an expectation that everyone receives this floral garland when he or she steps off the plane, the State of Hawaii cannot greet each of its nearly 7 million annual visitors.

If you've booked a vacation with a wholesaler or tour company, a lei greeting might be included in your package, so check before you leave. If not, it's easy to arrange a lei greeting for yourself or your companions before you arrive into Lihue Airport. Kamaaina Leis, Flowers & Greeters has been providing lei greetings for visitors to the Islands since 1983. To be really wowed by the experience, request a lei of plumeria, some of the most divine-smelling blossoms on the planet. A plumeria or dendrobium orchid lei is considered standard and costs approximately $25 per person.

Kamaaina Leis, Flowers & Greeters.
☎ *808/836–3246* ⊕ *www.alohaleigreetings.com.*

LANGUAGE

Hawaii was admitted to the Union in 1959, so residents can be sensitive when visitors refer to their own hometowns as "back in the States." Remember, when in Hawaii, refer to the contiguous 48 states as "the mainland" and not as "the United States." When you do, you won't appear to be such a *malahini* (newcomer).

English is the primary language on the Islands. Making the effort to learn some Hawaiian words can be rewarding, however. Despite the length of many Hawaiian words, the Hawaiian alphabet is actually one of the world's shortest, with only 12 letters: the five vowels, *a, e, i, o, u,* and seven consonants, *h, k, l, m, n, p, w.* Hawaiian words you're most likely to encounter during your visit to the Islands are *aloha, mahalo* (thank you), *keiki* (child), *haole* (Caucasian or foreigner, often a derogatory term), *mauka* (toward the mountains), *makai* (toward the ocean), and *pau* (finished, all done). Hawaiian history includes waves of immigrants, each bringing its own language. To communicate with each other, they developed a sort of slang known as "pidgin." If you listen closely, you'll know what is being said by the inflections and by the extensive use of body language. For example, when you know what you want to say but don't know how to say it, just say, "You know, da kine." For an informative and somewhat hilarious view of things Hawaiian, check out Jerry Hopkins's series of books titled *Pidgin to the Max* and *Fax to the Max,* available at most local bookstores in the Hawaiiana sections.

ESSENTIALS

▮ COMMUNICATIONS

INTERNET

Most of the major hotels and resorts offer high-speed access in rooms and/or lobbies. You should check with your hotel in advance to confirm that access is wireless; if not, ask whether in-room cables are provided. If you're staying at a small inn or B&B without Internet access, ask the proprietor for the nearest café or coffee shop with wireless access.

▮ HEALTH

In addition to being the Aloha State, Hawaii is known as the Health State. The life expectancy here is 79 years, the longest in the nation. Balmy weather makes it easy to remain active year-round, and the low-stress aloha attitude certainly contributes to general well-being. When you are visiting the Islands, however, there are a few health issues to keep in mind.

The Hawaii State Department of Health recommends that you drink 16 ounces of water per hour to avoid dehydration when hiking or spending time in the sun. Use sunblock, wear UV-reflective sunglasses, and protect your head with a visor or hat for shade. If you're not acclimated to warm, humid weather, you should allow plenty of time for rest stops and refreshments. When visiting freshwater streams, be aware of the tropical disease leptospirosis, which is spread by animal urine and carried into streams and mud. Symptoms include fever, headache, nausea, and red eyes and may not appear immediately. If left untreated, it can cause liver and kidney damage, respiratory failure, internal bleeding, and even death. To avoid this, don't swim or wade in freshwater streams or ponds if you have open sores, and don't drink from any freshwater streams or ponds, especially after heavy rains.

On the Islands, fog is a rare occurrence, but there can often be "vog," an airborne haze of gases released from volcanic vents on the Big Island. During certain weather conditions such as "Kona Winds," the vog can settle over the Islands and wreak havoc with respiratory and other health conditions, especially asthma or emphysema. If susceptible, stay indoors and get emergency assistance if needed.

The Islands have their share of bugs and insects that enjoy the tropical climate as much as visitors do. Most are harmless but annoying. When planning to spend time outdoors in hiking areas, wear long-sleeved clothing and pants and use mosquito repellent containing DEET. In very damp places you may encounter the dreaded local centipede. On the Islands they usually come in one of three colors: brown, blue, or bright orange. They range from the size of a worm to an 8-inch cigar. Their sting is very painful, and the reaction is similar to bee- and wasp-sting reactions. If stung, immediately run very hot water over the wound for 20 minutes or so. When camping, shake out your sleeping bag before climbing in, and check your shoes in the morning, as the centipedes like cozy places. If planning on hiking or traveling in remote areas, always carry a first-aid kit and appropriate medications for sting reactions.

▮ HOURS OF OPERATION

Even people in paradise have to work. Generally, local business hours are weekdays 8–5. Banks are usually open Monday–Thursday 8:30–4 and until 6 on Friday. Some banks have Saturday-morning hours.

Many self-serve gas stations stay open around the clock, with full-service stations usually open from around 7 am until 9 pm. The larger U.S. post offices are open weekdays 8:30 am–4:30 pm and Saturday 8:30–noon. Check operating hours for smaller post offices.

Most museums generally open their doors between 9 am and 10 am and stay open until 5 pm Tuesday–Saturday. Many museums operate with afternoon hours only on Sunday and close on Monday. Visitor-attraction hours vary throughout the state, but most sights are open daily, with the exception of major holidays such as Christmas. Check local publications upon arrival for attraction hours and schedules if visiting over holiday periods. The local dailies carry a listing of local cultural events for those time periods.

Stores in resort areas sometimes open as early as 8, with shopping-center opening hours varying from 9:30 to 10 on weekdays and Saturday, a bit later on Sunday. Bigger malls stay open until 9 weekdays and Saturday and close at 5 on Sunday. Boutiques in resort areas may stay open as late as 11.

▌ MONEY

Prices ⇨ *throughout this guide* are given for adults. Substantially reduced fees are almost always available for children, students, and senior citizens.

CREDIT CARDS

It's a good idea to inform your credit-card company before you travel. Otherwise, the credit-card company might put a hold on your card owing to unusual activity—not a good thing halfway through your trip. Record all your credit-card numbers—as well as the phone numbers to call if your cards are lost or stolen—in a safe place, so you're prepared should something go wrong. Both MasterCard and Visa have general numbers you can call (collect if you're abroad) if your card is lost, but you're better off calling the number of your issuing bank, since MasterCard and Visa usually just transfer you to your bank; your bank's number is usually printed on your card.

Reporting Lost Cards American Express. ☎ *800/528–4800* ⊕ *www.americanexpress. com.* **Diners Club.** ☎ *800/234–6377* ⊕ *www. dinersclub.com.* **Discover.** ☎ *800/347–2683* ⊕ *www.discovercard.com.* **MasterCard.** ☎ *800/622–7747* ⊕ *www.mastercard.com.* **Visa.** ☎ *800/847–2911* ⊕ *www.visa.com.*

▌ PACKING

Hawaii is casual: sandals, bathing suits, and comfortable, informal clothing are the norm. In summer, synthetic slacks and shirts, although easy to care for, can be uncomfortably warm.

One of the most important things to tuck into your suitcase is sunscreen, though it is readily available at most stores.

As for clothing in the Hawaiian Islands, there's a saying that when a man wears a suit during the day, he's either going for a loan or he's a lawyer trying a case. Only a few upscale restaurants require a jacket for dinner. The aloha shirt is accepted dress in Hawaii for business and most social occasions. Shorts are acceptable daytime attire, along with a T-shirt or polo shirt. There's no need to buy expensive sandals on the mainland—here you can get flip-flops for a couple of dollars and off-brand sandals for $20. Golfers should remember that many courses have dress codes requiring a collared shirt; call courses you're interested in for details. If you're not prepared, you can pick up appropriate clothing at resort pro shops. If you're visiting in winter, bring a sweater or light- to medium-weight jacket. A polar fleece pullover is ideal and makes a great impromptu travel pillow.

▌ SAFETY

Hawaii is generally a safe tourist destination, but it's still wise to follow the same common-sense safety precautions you would normally follow in your own hometown.

Be wary of those hawking "too good to be true" prices on everything from car rentals to attractions. Many of these offers are just a lure to get you in the door for time-share presentations. When handed a flier, read the fine print before you make your decision to participate.

Safety Transportation Security Administration. ⊕ *www.tsa.gov.*

▌TAXES

There's a 4.16% state sales tax on all purchases, including food. As of July 2010, a hotel room tax plus the state sales tax add approximately 14% to your hotel bill. A $3-per-day road tax is also assessed on each rental vehicle.

▌TIME

Hawaii is on Hawaiian standard time, five hours behind New York and two hours behind Los Angeles for the winter months.

While the U.S. mainland uses daylight saving time from March until November, Hawaii does not, so add an extra hour of time difference between the Islands and U.S. mainland destinations during that part of the year. You may also find that things generally move more slowly here. That has nothing to do with your watch—it's just the laid-back way called Hawaiian time.

▌TIPPING

Tip cabdrivers 15% of the fare. Standard tips for restaurants and bar tabs run from 15% to 20% of the bill, depending on the standard of service. Bellhops at hotels usually receive $1 per bag, more if you have bulky items such as bicycles and surfboards. Tip the hotel room maid $1 per night, paid daily. Tip doormen $1 for assistance with taxis; tips for concierges vary depending on the service. For example, tip more for "hard-to-get" event tickets or dining reservations.

FODORS.COM CONNECTION

Before your trip, be sure to check out what other travelers are saying in Travel Ratings and Talk Forums on www.fodors.com.

For single-day guided activities like a boat trip to Napali, a zip-lining tour, or surf lessons, you should tip each guide at least $10–$20 if you feel he or she enhanced your experience. Oftentimes, the tour company takes the bulk of your booking price, and the locals who are sharing their alohas with you are depending on your tips.

▌TOURS

Globus has two Hawaii itineraries that include Kauai, one of which is an escorted cruise on Norwegian Cruise Lines' *Pride of America* that includes two days on the Garden Island. Tauck Travel offers an 11-night *Best of Hawaii* tour that includes two nights on Kauai with leisure time for either relaxation or exploration.

EscortedHawaiiTours.com, owned and operated by Atlas Cruises & Tours, sells more than a dozen Hawaii trips ranging from 7 to 12 nights operated by various guided-tour companies including Globus and Tauck. Several of these trips include two to three nights on Kauai.

Recommended Companies Atlas Cruises & Tours. ☎ *800/942–3301* ⊕ *www. atlastravelweb.com.* **Globus.** ☎ *866/755–8581* ⊕ *www.globusjourneys.com.* **Tauck Travel.** ☎ *800/788–7885* ⊕ *www.tauck.com.*

SPECIAL-INTEREST TOURS
BIRD-WATCHING
Hawaii has more than 150 species of birds that live in the Hawaiian Islands. Field Guides has a three-island (Oahu, Kauai, and the Big Island), 10-day guided bird-watching trip for 14 birding enthusiasts that focuses on endemic land birds and specialty seabirds. While on Kauai, birders will visit Kokee State Park, Alakai Wilderness Preserve, and Kilauea Point. The trip

costs about $4,950 per person and includes accommodations, meals, ground transportation, interisland air, an eight-hour pelagic boat trip, and guided bird-watching excursions. Travelers must purchase their own airfare to and from their gateway city. Field Guides has been offering worldwide birding tours since 1984.

Victor Emanuel Nature Tours, the largest company in the world specializing in birding tours, has two nine-day trips that include Kauai. The guide for both tours is Bob Sundstrom, a skilled birder with a special interest in birdsong who has been leading birding tours in Hawaii and other destinations since 1989. *Spring Hawaii* is the theme of the late February/early March birding trip, when seabird diversity on the island is at its peak. Birders will see the *koloa* (Hawaiian duck), one of Hawaii's most endangered wetland birds, as well as Laysan albatrosses, red- and white-tailed tropic birds, red-footed boobies, wedge-tailed shearwaters, great frigate birds, brown boobies, and possibly even red-billed tropic birds. Participants in the *Fall Hawaii* birding trip will visit Oahu, Kauai, and the Big Island in October. Birders will see Kauai honeycreepers and Hawaiian short-eared owls at Kokee State Park and Alakai Swamp and seabirds at the National Wildlife Refuges at Kilauea and Hanalei. Both the *Spring Hawaii* and *Fall Hawaii* tours cost about $4,295 per person. Both trips include accommodations, meals, interisland air, ground transportation, and guided excursions. Travelers must purchase their own airline ticket to and from their gateway city. Tours begin in Honolulu and end up in Hilo.

Contacts Field Guides. ☎ *800/728–4953* ⊕ *www.fieldguides.com.* **Victor Emanuel Nature Tours.** ☎ *800/328–8368* ⊕ *www.ventbird.com.*

CULTURE

RoadScholar (formerly Elderhostel), a nonprofit educational travel organization, offers several guided tours for older adults that focus on Hawaiian culture. With all the tours listed, travelers must purchase their own airline tickets to Hawaii. We've chosen a few of our favorite tours here, but more information on tour subjects can be found on the organization's website.

Best of Kauai's Natural and Cultural Wonders is a six-night tour presented in association with the Kauai Historical Consortium. You'll visit Hanalei, Kilauea Point National Wildlife Refuge, Grove Farm Homestead Museum, Kauai Museum, and Kokee Natural History Museum. You'll learn *lauhala* weaving and other traditional arts and crafts and discover why the island truly is like no other. The cost of this tour starts at $1,725 per person and includes accommodations, meals, ground transportation, admission fees, as well as tipping charges and a travel assistance plan.

The Best of Hawaii and Kauai is a 10-night tour, split up by five nights on the Big Island of Hawaii and five nights on Kauai. Exploring the natural beauty of these two islands, you'll visit Volcanoes National Park and the Hamakua Coast on Hawaii, then explore the Kilauea Point National Wildlife Refuge and the National Tropical Botanical Gardens on Kauai, learning about these two islands' diverse birdlife, marine life, forests, volcanoes, and more. Prices start at $2,748 per person and include accommodations, meals, ground transportation, admission fees, and interisland air travel between Kauai and the Big Island.

Contact Road Scholar. ☎ *800/454–5768* ⊕ *www.roadscholar.org.*

ECOTOURS

Want to spend a week in Kauai hiking, snorkeling, surfing, and paddling? Kayak Kauai has a seven-day *Discovery Tour* where you will explore Kauai's peaks and canyons, rivers and coastlines, and discover lagoons with crystal clear water and breathtaking waterfalls, sacred trails, and miles of ivory-white sand beaches. Tours are offered every month and include accommodations, airport shuttles, van support during the week, communal gear, linens, all meals, guides, day tours, and activities. *Discovery Tour* is rated moderate but can be challenging at times, and participants should be in good physical condition. With a group of four or more, it is priced at $1,750 per person. Travelers must purchase their own airline tickets between their gateway cities and Kauai.

Contact Kayak Kauai. ☎ *808/826–9844, 808/826–9844* ⊕ *www.kayakkauai.com.*

HIKING

Hiking the Garden Island is the theme of a weeklong trip to Kauai sponsored by Sierra Club Outings. In addition to day-long hikes of 5 to 9 miles through many of the rain forests in Kokee State Park, participants will have opportunities for snorkeling and swimming at secluded beaches, as well as bird-watching. Hikers also will help in the maintenance of some of the trails. Accommodations are in shared cabins and, as with all Sierra Club Outings, participants are expected to help prepare some of the meals using only local, fresh ingredients. The trip costs about $1,695 per person and includes accommodations, meals, and ground transportation.

Hawaii Three Island Hiker is a seven-night hiking tour to Kauai, Maui, and the Big Island. Included in the per-person price of about $3,900 are accommodations, meals, interisland air between the Islands, shuttle transportation, support vehicle, professional guides, a T-shirt, and a water bottle. Hikers will spend three nights on Kauai exploring Napali Coast, including hikes to Hanakapiai Falls and the Nulolo Cliffs/Awaawapuhi Loop. Another highlight of the adventure is a cruise and snorkel trip along the North Shore. The trip is rated moderately easy to moderate. The World Outdoors has been organizing and leading adventure trips around the world for 20 years.

Timberline Adventures has a seven-night *Islands Classic* tour that includes Kauai and the Big Island. Participants will hike more than 25 miles total as they explore the rugged southern coastline on the Shipwreck Beach trail, the lush rain forests of Kokee State Park, majestic Waimea Canyon, the incredible waterfalls and cliffs along Napali Coast, and even the quiet Sleeping Giant. Then it's island-hopping across the chain to the Big Island of Hawaii where participants explore Volcanoes National Park. Included in the per-person price of about $3,095 are accommodations on the West Side, North Shore, and Big Island, and meals and ground transportation.

Travelers must purchase their own tickets to and from their gateway city.

Contacts Sierra Club Outings. ☎ *415/977–5500* ⊕ *www.sierraclub.org/outings.* **Timberline Adventures.** ☎ *800/417–2453* ⊕ *www.timbertours.com.* **The World Outdoors.** ☎ *800/488–8483* ⊕ *www.theworldoutdoors.com.*

LUXURY

For the ultimate luxurious vacation adventure experience, you'll want to book one of the Pure Kauai vacations. Included in all these high-end arrangements are private accommodations at elegant estates and villas, along with a personal concierge. Most anything can be arranged, from gourmet meals prepared by world-class chefs to outdoor activities, as well as massage and spa treatments. The company can create customized vacations with itineraries of any length and theme. Vacationers must purchase their own airfare between Kauai and their gateway city.

Contact Pure Kauai. ☎ *866/457–7873, 808/828–6570* ⊕ *www.purekauai.com.*

▌ TRIP INSURANCE

Comprehensive trip insurance is valuable if you're booking a very expensive or complicated trip (particularly to an isolated region) or if you're booking far in advance. Comprehensive policies typically cover trip cancellation and interruption, letting you cancel or cut your trip short because of illness, or, in some cases, acts of terrorism in your destination. Such policies might also cover evacuation and medical care. Some also cover you for trip delays because of bad weather or mechanical problems as well as for lost or delayed luggage.

Another type of coverage to consider is financial default—that is, when your trip is disrupted because a tour operator, airline, or cruise line goes out of business. Generally you must buy this when you book your trip or shortly thereafter, and it's available to you only if your operator isn't on a list of excluded companies.

Always read the fine print of your policy to make sure that you're covered for the risks that most concern you. Compare several policies to be sure you're getting the best price and range of coverage available.

Insurance Comparison Information
Insure My Trip. ☎ *800/487–4722* ⊕ *www. insuremytrip.com.* **Square Mouth.** ☎ *800/240–0369* ⊕ *www.squaremouth.com.*

Comprehensive Insurers AIG Travel Guard. ☎ *800/826–4919* ⊕ *www.travelguard.com.* **Allianz Global Assistance.** ☎ *800/284–8300* ⊕ *www.allianztravelinsurance.com.* **CSA Travel Protection.** ☎ *800/873–9855, 800/711–1197* ⊕ *www.csatravelprotection.com.* **Travel Insured International.** ☎ *800/243–3174* ⊕ *www.travelinsured.com.* **Travelex Insurance.** ☎ *800/819-9004, 888/457–4602* ⊕ *www.travelexinsurance.com.*

▌ VISITOR INFORMATION

Before you go, contact the Kauai Visitors Bureau for a free travel planner that has information on accommodations, transportation, sports and activities, dining, arts and entertainment, and culture. You can also take a virtual tour of the island that includes great photos and helpful planning information.

The Hawaii Tourism Authority's Travel Smart Hawaii site offers tips on everything from packing to flying. Also visit

the Hawaii State Vacation Planner for all information on the destination, including camping.

ONLINE TRAVEL TOOLS

The Hawaii Department of Land and Natural Resources has information on hiking, fishing, and camping permits and licenses; online brochures on hiking safety and mountain and ocean preservation; and details on volunteer programs. The Kauai Visitors Bureau has Kauai-specific information on everything from activities to lodging options and organizes it by geographic regions on the island.

Contacts Title Hawaii Department of Land and Natural Resources. ✉ *Kalanimoku Building, 1151 Punchbowl St., Honolulu* ☎ *808/587–0400* ⊕ *http://dlnr.hawaii.gov.* **Hawaii Tourism Authority.** ✉ *1801 Kalakaua Avenue, 1st Floor, Honolulu* ☎ *808/ 973–2255* ⊕ *www. hawaiitourismauthority.org.*

ALL ABOUT KAUAI

Resources Hawaii Beach Safety. ⊕ *hawaiibeachsafety.com.* **Hawaii Department of Land and Natural Resources.** ⊕ *www.state.hi.us/dlnr.* **Kauai Vacation Explorer.** ⊕ *www.kauaiexplorer.com.* **Kauai Visitors Bureau.** ⊕ *www.gohawaii.com/kauai.*

INDEX

PHOTO CREDITS

Front cover: MNStudio | Dreamstime.com [Description: Napali Coast, Kauai, Hawaii]. Back cover, from left to right: Mark52/Shutterstock; (center and right), Kauai Visitors Bureau. Spine: Panachai Cherdchucheep/Shutterstock. 1, Steveheap | Dreamstime.com. 2, Danwatt417 | Dreamstime.com. Chapter 1: Experience Kauai: 8-9, Mfron | Dreamstime.com. 16 (left), Jerryway | Dreamstime.com. 16 (top), Hawaii Tourism Authority (HTA) / Tor Johnson. 16 (bottom center), Kamchatka | Dreamstime.com. 16 (bottom right), Starwood Hotels & Resorts. 17 (top), Ron Niebrugge / Alamy. 17 (right), YinYang/iStockphoto. 17 (bottom), Louis01 | Dreamstime.com. 36, Polynesian Cultural Center. 37 (top), Hawaii Tourism Authority (HTA) / Kirk Lee Aeder. 37 (bottom), iStockphoto. 38, Linda Ching/ HVCB. 39 (top), Hawaii Tourism Authority (HTA) / Dana Edmunds. 39 (bottom), Sri Maiava Rusden/HVCB. 40, HVCB. 41 (top), Hawaii Tourism Authority (HTA) / Sri Maiava Rusden Island. 41 (bottom), jhorrocks / iStockphoto. Chapter 2: Exploring Kauai: 43, Nstanev | Dreamstime.com. 44, Sergiyn | Dreamstime.com. 45 (top), Deedeedixon | Dreamstime.com. 45 (bottom), Joel Carillet/iStockphoto. 46, Kikuko Nakayama/Flickr, [CC BY-SA 2.0]. 47, Hawaii Tourism Authority (HTA) / Ron Garnett. 51, Nainoac | Dreamstime.com. 55, Joel Carillet/iStockphoto. 63, Roger Fletcher/ Alamy. 73, Ron Dahlquist/Kauai Visitors Bureau. Chapter 3: Beaches: 75, Hawaii Tourism Authority (HTA) / Tor Johnson. 76, Hawaii Tourism Authority (HTA) / Tor Johnson. 80, Junko Kubota/iStockphoto. 84, MNStudio | Dreamstime.com. 87, Raycan | Dreamstime.com. 91, Hawaii Tourism Authority (HTA) / Tor Johnson. Chapter 4: Where to Eat: 93, Hawaii Visitors & Convention Bureau. 94, John Sigler/ iStockphoto. 106, muhawi001/Flickr. Chapter 5: Where to Stay: 113, Courtesy of Hyatt Corporation. 114, Princeville Resort. Chapter 6: Nightlife and Performing Arts: 127, Brad Hagan/Flickr, [CC BY 2.0] 128, Hawaii Tourism Authority (HTA) / Tor Johnson. 133, Lara Farhadi/Flickr, [CC BY 2.0]. Chapter 7: Shops & Spas: 135, Dana Edmunds. 136, Hawaii Tourism Authority (HTA) / Tor Johnson. 141, Brian Raisbeck/iStockphoto. Chapter 8: Water Sports & Tours: 147, YinYang/iStockphoto. 148, Hawaii Tourism Authority (HTA) / Dana Edmunds. 152, Americanspirit | Dreamstime.com. 163, YinYang/iStockphoto. 166, jarvis gray/Shutterstock. 168, Douglas Peebles/ eStock Photo. Chapter 9: Golf, Hiking & Outdoor Activities: 171, Jim Kruger/iStockphoto. 172, Hawaii Tourism Authority (HTA) / Tor Johnson. 176, Hawaii Tourism Authority (HTA) / Tor Johnson. 179, Courtesy of St. Regis Princeville. 185, Princeville Ranch Adventures. About Our Writers: All photos are courtesy of the writers.

ABOUT OUR WRITERS

Charles E. Roessler is a long-time Kauai resident who was an editor for the *Japan Times* and the *Buffalo News* after teaching English and journalism for 10 years. He contributes to the *New York Times* as a stringer/freelancer and loves Kauai, especially playing tennis and swimming at Anini Beach. Charles updated the Experience, Exploring, and Golf, Hiking, and Outdoor Activities sections of this guide.

Joan Conrow is a Kauai-based independent journalist and blogger who has written about Hawaii politics, culture, environment, and lifestyles for many regional and national publications. She helped write the original Fodor's guide to Kauai and updated the Shops and Spas, Where to Eat, Where to Stay, Water Sports and Tours, Beaches, and Entertainment and Nightlife sections of this guide.

4/27   LIH - 1:00PM   UA 1152
        SANF - 11:11PM   915
        Chicago - 6:00 AM   8/18 AM
            CLE
4/28